Ex Libris

Daily
Guideposts, 1978

For Shirley,
who cares

Daily Guideposts, 1978

by FRED BAUER

Guideposts

Carmel, New York, 10512

Acknowledgments

Many people have contributed to this book and I would like to express my deep gratitude to Linda Gramatky Smith, Eleanor Sass and Terri Urciolo for their editorial assistance; to Arthur Gordon for his wise counsel and invaluable suggestions; to Sal Lazzarotti for designing the book; to Tu Bich for book layout; and to the countless friends who have helped and continue to help open my ears and eyes to new spiritual truths.

F.B.

Foreword

Without growth, living things die.

For plant life, water and sunlight and soil are the ingredients needed to sustain life. For people, food and water are the requirements. But the Bible tells us that man does not live by bread alone. (Matthew 4:4) That is because he is a spiritual being and requires spiritual nourishment as well as physical.

If this book has a theme, it is growth—growth of body, mind and spirit. If it has an underlying premise, it is that our Heavenly Father is for us, loves us, wants us happy and healthy, and that He will help us achieve lives of fulfillment if we study His word, seek His wisdom, accept His authority and follow His guidance.

Henry Wadsworth Longfellow lived for 75 years, and his writing career reportedly was productive to the end. Once, a person asked the white-haired poet for the secret of his physical and mental robustness.

"You see that apple tree," Longfellow said, pointing to one nearby. "It is very old, but I never saw prettier blossoms on it than those. The tree grows a little new wood each year, and I suppose it is out of that new wood that those new blossoms come. Like the apple tree, I try to grow a little new wood each year."

Christians need to do the same. Otherwise, we risk the danger of spiritual lethargy and decay.

Last year, DAILY GUIDEPOSTS was offered to magazine subscribers for the first time and, judging from the response, there are great numbers in our audience interested in daily spiritual growth. Because of the many requests for more material in the same vein, the editors of *Guideposts* asked me to prepare another book for 1978. This I have done with the same goal as before: to present illuminating and inspiring stories, poems and prayers that have direct and practical application to your daily life.

My hope is that this book will help you grow new spiritual wood and, as a result, blossom in love and service to God and others. My prayer is that these words from my pen and these meditations from my heart are acceptable in the sight of God, my strength and my Redeemer.

May God bless you richly this year and throughout all the years of your life.

FRED BAUER

JANUARY 1978

S	M	T	W	T	F	S
1	2	3	4	5	6	7
8	9	10	11	12	13	14
15	16	17	18	19	20	21
22	23	24	25	26	27	28
29	30	31				

"God loveth a cheerful giver" (II Corinthians 9:7) and the blessings He dispenses on the generous are many and varied. In this first month of the year, practice the Christ-like virtue of giving at every opportunity. Discover how difficult it is to outgive God.

JANUARY 1978

1 One song leads to another,
One friend to another friend,
So I'll travel along
With a friend and a song.
                    Wilfred Gibson

Janus, the Roman god, from whom we take the word January, was known as "the deity of good beginnings." The temple of Janus in Rome, built on an east-west line (where the day begins and ends,) featured the famous two-faced statue, the young countenance of Janus looking east and the old one looking west.

On this first day of the Christian year, (Pope Gregory XIII is responsible for revising the calendar we have been using since 1582), it is wise to emulate Janus and do a double take in both directions, forward and backward. Look behind as a way of seeing the distance we have come. Though that may not be as far as we might have wished, there are in all our cases blessings to enumerate and appreciate. Then look ahead. Make plans, select goals, dream big. In Proverbs (29:18) we are told that where there is no vision the people perish. Take sight on some worthy undertaking today. Ask God to guide you in the days and months ahead. Then set out on your adventure with faith and enthusiasm. May you have Godspeed.

Keep me forward looking, Lord,
To the future, unexplored.

2 "Consider the ravens: for they neither sow nor reap; which neither have storehouse nor barn; and God feedeth them: how much more are ye better than the fowls?"
Luke 12:24

A new white quilt covered the ground this morning, and as I admired its downy beauty from my dining-room window, I saw several small birds huddled in the bushes below—their feathers all fluffed up like shivering men huddled in overcoats. It was then that I noticed the squirrels had emptied the feeder. Putting on my boots, I went outside and replenished the holder with sunflower seeds and cleared a spot for grain. Soon the yard and surrounding trees were alive with sound, a chattering convention—juncoes, doves, sparrows, bluejays and cardinals on the ground, downies and nuthatches on the suet log, and finches, titmice, chickadees and Carolina wrens at the feeder. I had seen their need and responded.

Sometimes, though, I am the bird in the bush, the one with needs. I am cold and feeling alone, and wondering if anyone sees or hears or cares. When that happens, I try to remember that Jesus told His disciples He would send them a Comforter in the form of His Holy Spirit (John 14:16) and that He would neither leave them nor forsake them (Hebrews 13:5). As believers, you and I have these promises to fortify us when things grow desperate, when we don't know which way to turn, when our troubles multiply without solution, when we are ready to give up, to throw in the towel, to call it quits. Your Heavenly Father knows your needs and He will supply them. Place your trust in Him.

Thank You, Holy Spirit, for being ever present, ever near.

3 "Let the words of my mouth, and the meditation of my heart be acceptable in thy sight, O Lord, my strength and my redeemer." **Psalm 19:14**

A year ago on this date in my hometown of Princeton, New

4

Jersey, the 200th anniversary of the famous Revolutionary War battle was re-enacted. Several hundred men—some attired in the flamboyant redcoats worn by the British and some in the ragtag uniforms of General George Washington's Continentals—did mock battle. Muskets fired, cannons roared, bayonets flashed, drums rolled, horses reared, and thousands of spectators had a better idea of what took place on that pivotal battlefield after the smoke had cleared and the troops of King George had been vanquished.

But what is fascinating to me is how Washington used the elements of surprise to gain victory, just as he did a week earlier on Christmas night, 1776, when he crossed the Delaware River and routed the startled Hessians at Trenton. On January 2, 1777, Washington again moved during the night, outflanked his opponents and launched a surprise attack in the morning. His maneuver, a classic study in military strategy, proved to be a crucial Revolutionary War triumph.

The element of surprise can work for everyone every day. It is a particularly effective tool in dealing with human relations problems—volatile tempers, ruffled feathers, offended egos and all manner of verbal pyrotechnics.

The Bible tells us that a soft answer can turn away wrath (Proverbs 15:1) and three verses later that "a wholesome tongue is a tree of life." If you come under attack today, try the element of surprise in your response. Measure your words, speak slowly, softly. Like Washington, you will not only surprise your adversary but will probably win the day, too.

Lord, teach me to swallow my pride and control my tongue.

"For now we see through a glass, darkly; but then face to face; now I know in part; but then shall I know even as also I am known." **I Corinthians 13:12**

Once a young couple lost their only child, a beautiful three-year old daughter, as the result of a freak accident. Unable to justify this tragedy with their concept of a loving God, they went to their minister for help. "Why?" they asked.

"It was God's will," the minister told them.

The couple couldn't accept that answer and sought out the assistant pastor. He quoted yards of Scripture, trying to give them comfort, but his many words fell on deaf ears.

Finally, they turned to a frail old woman in the church. She had little formal education, but she knew her Bible well. Surely, she could give them a spiritual answer. After hearing the details of the child's death, the old woman didn't utter a single word. Instead, she tenderly wrapped her arms around the heartbroken couple's shoulders, and together they cried the hurt away.

Sometimes when answers aren't easy, our best statement is silent caring.

School us in comforting the afflicted, Lord, so that we can minister Your healing.

5

"A man's true wealth is the good he does in this world." Bendixline

"We'll put you on the road to riches," the advertisement for a new business franchise promised, and for all I know, the company would indeed; but whenever I see such catch phrases I have to smile. The appeal is general enough to draw in most all of us. Doesn't everyone want to get on the road to riches? Of course. The only thing better than being on the road is to have arrived at one's destination—wealthy, powerful, famous.

What most of these ads fail to detail is the price one must pay, the tolls one is charged to travel this turnpike to Treasureland. The time, the initial financial investment, the risk, the training, the sacrifices. Some willingly pay them and make the trip without losing their souls.

But some people who go atripping on this highway get very confused, disoriented, lost. There is a revealing story in the Bible of a young man who traveled the road to riches but found it unsatisfying. "Good Master, what shall I do to inherit eternal life?" he asked Jesus. (Luke 18:18, 22-23) Christ told him, "Sell all that thou hast, and distribute unto the poor." The rich young ruler went away very sad, because he knew he couldn't get off that road.

Help us to get our priorities straight, Lord, while there is still time.

6 (Epiphany)
" . . . Freely ye have received, freely give."
Matthew 10:8

In some countries around the world, today is the equivalent of our Christmas. Epiphany, which means "a manifestation" in Greek, commemorates three times in the life of Christ when His divinity was affirmed. The first was the visit of the gift-bearing Wise Men. The second was at His baptism in the Jordan River when the Holy Spirit descended on Him in the form of a dove and a voice hailed him as the Son of God. And the third was at the wedding feast in Cana where He turned water into wine, the first of His miracles. All three events are said to have happened on the same calendar date.

But of the three manifestations, the first, the coming of the Magi, is the reason for today's celebration; and in the tradition of the Three Kings, the custom of giving gifts will be repeated again today as it has been for many centuries.

Nothing is really more symbolic of Christ's life than giving. God gave His only Son, and Christ gave His life. Such love deserves a gift in return—our lives in His service.

> *Were the whole realm of nature mine,*
> *That were a present far too small;*
> *Love so amazing, so divine.*
> *Demands my soul, my life, my all.*
> *Isaac Watts hymn*

7 In the sweet by and by,
We shall meet on that beautiful shore.
S. F. Bennett hymn

People who have suffered clinical death—that is, being pronounced dead but later regaining consciousness—report amazingly similar experiences. Research conducted by Dr. Raymond A. Moody, Jr., in his books LIFE AFTER LIFE and REFLECTIONS ON LIFE AFTER LIFE (Mockingbird Books)shows that in case after case people were aware of what was going on all about them even though all of their life signs were gone. They also reported being pulled through a dark tunnel, of having "out of body" vantage points, of meeting friends and relatives who had died before them, of seeing a Being of Light (thought to be God by many). Afterwards, most said that they had come back to life reluctantly because "life beyond this life" seemed so peaceful. Because of their experiences, the consensus was that they no longer feared death.

What did Dr. Moody conclude from his interviews with over 300 persons who had known clinical death? "I have come to accept as a matter of faith," he has stated, "that there is a life after death."

Some will argue that his research is hardly proof positive of an afterlife, but for many it is additional evidence that Christ meant what He said to the thief on the cross: "Today shalt thou be with me in paradise." (Luke 23:43)

You have promised eternal life, Lord, and we are
strenghthened by that promise.

8 I believe in the Sun
even when it is not shining.
I believe in Love
even when I feel it not.
I believe in God
even when He is silent.
Anonymous

I once read the quotation above on a plaque in a barbershop.

8

The barber told me that it had meant a lot to him, and that many others had thanked him for posting it. For me the message communicates a deep truth: there are many things in this world that we accept "by faith."

We know that the sun is not gone, just because it has disappeared behind a cloud. And I know that I love my wife and that she loves me even on those days when I don't feel very loving or lovable. And Christians know that God exists even when they wait on Him to answer their prayers. All around us we see living testimony to the fact that He loves us. Live one day at a time, trusting that He is there, caring for you, concerned about you and sustaining you every moment of the day.

Thank You, Lord, for being a part of my life, whether seen or unseen.

 "Live your life so you won't be ashamed to sell your parrot to the town gossip."
Will Rogers

A woman from the South writes, "I need your prayers. I have been labeled something I am not because of vicious gossip. Pray that I can find a way to combat this untruth." .

Abraham Lincoln came under heavy attack while he was President and was reviled by many leaders of the day. In response to all the things he was called, Lincoln posed this question: "How many legs does a lamb have if you call its tail a leg?" His answer was "Four, because calling a tail a leg doesn't make it one."

When you are maligned—and everyone is at one time or another—your best defense is the life you live. If you are honest, fair, just, those who know you will speak on your behalf. What others say won't matter. Don't let others damage your self-esteem if their charges are without foundation. Ask for God's grace to strengthen you and go forward with your head held high.

Remind me, Lord, that the Golden Rule also applies to gossip.

10 "Forbearing one another, and forgiving one another, . . . as Christ forgave you, so also do ye." Colossians 3:13

Recently I was talking with Colleen Townsend Evans, the former actress who has become one of my favorite inspirational authors. Our discussion centered on a chapter in her book START LOVING: THE MIRACLE OF FORGIVING (Doubleday), which touches on the problem of dealing with people who are unforgiving.

Colleen was reminded of an estranged marriage that resulted when the husband left home because of his infatuation with another woman. The spurned wife was inconsolable; she claimed she could not go on unless her husband returned. Her prayers were ceaseless: *Please, God, send him back to me.* In time the man did return, full of remorse, begging forgiveness. But then, Colleen recalls, the wife did a strange thing. She refused to forgive him for his offense, and though they were reunited in the same house, their estrangement continued— until the woman (with Colleen's help) was able to see how destructive her actions were. Only then was she able to wash the slate clean and begin her marriage anew.

Have you been soul-wounded by someone recently? Has your heart hardened against him or her? Are you full of hate? Humanly, it is very difficult to forgive, but with divine assistance you are more than able to overcome any mental block. Ask God to intervene and change feelings of hurt and hate to feelings of love and compassion. He performs such miracles daily.

Melt my heart with Your love, Father, when I am slow to forgive.

 11 If we upon earth are amazed at His grace
What will it be when we see Him?
If here, tho' but dimly, His beauty we trace.
What will it be when we see him?
Ada R. Habershon hymn

Every couple of years I go to the eye doctor to get my eyes

examined, and the last time I was there the optician reminded me of a forgotten fact: we don't really see with our eyes. The image comes through the cornea and bounces onto the retina at the back of the eyeball. From there, electric impulses take the image to the part of the brain where it can then be "seen." People can have healthy-looking eyes, big and beautiful, but not be able to see if the receiving part of their brain is damaged.

In a spiritual sense, God gives His children a special way of looking at things that other people don't have. He supplies His followers with a keener vision, a deeper understanding. Today, ask God to help you see beyond the physical plane. Perhaps there is some need a friend or loved one has, a need that is hidden by brave words or disguised actions. Reach out in love to heal their hurts. "Eye hath not seen, nor ear heard the things which God hath prepared for them that love him." (I Corinthians 2:9)

Let me see other people with Your eyes, Lord, full of love and compassion and wisdom.

**Once I was blind
but now I can see;
The light of the world is Jesus.**
P. P. Bliss

Once I read of a man whose plane crashed in a vast snow-covered forest. Miraculously he lived, but while he was trying to find help a blizzard struck. Blinded by snow, he wandered the whole night in circles and eventually froze to death—only a short distance from a rescue station.

Had he been an experienced woodsman he might have survived by following the example of animals and burrowing under fallen pine boughs and other foliage. He also might have tried to mark his trail to record where he had been. Smart hikers mark their progress through a wood with blazes, usually cuts on trees; then if they want to backtrack they won't get lost and walk in circles.

Many people spend their lives walking in circles, lost and unable to extricate themselves from their narrow, boxlike existences. In the Bible we read about many lost, sinful, confused men and women who were redeemed by God's saving grace. If you feel trapped by circumstances and are covering the same ground year after year, maybe you need to ask God to help you find your bearings. He has redirected many a lost, woebegone pilgrim, and He can help you. He can make your life productive, creative, fulfilling—all the things you've dreamed of. Talk to Him about your dreams, the deep desires and goals of your soul. Listen to the counsel He gives. Then follow the blazes He sets before you.

> *Guide me, O Thou great Jehovah,*
> *Pilgrim thro' this barren land.*
> *William Williams*

13

You, Lord, are the music of my soul.
You, Lord, took my broken life and made it whole.
F. B.

Once a writing assignment took me to San Juan, Puerto Rico. There, one night after dinner, I sat with several other diners for a long time listening to a native of the island playing calypso music on a crude steel drum. Using mallets, the young man produced some toe-tapping sounds from his makeshift instrument.

Thinking about that experience drives home an important point to me. Some people have the wherewithal to surround themselves with the finest instruments—grand pianos, handmade violins, exquisite harps—but don't have the skill or talent or discipline to get music from them. But a young man beating on the bottom of a steel container was able to make a whole roomful of people happy with his joyous music.

The secret is to make most of life's gifts. Don't complain to God about what He hasn't supplied you. Thank Him today for His many gifts, especially for life itself. Because when you are alive, really alive in every sense of the word, there are no limits placed on what you can accomplish. It's up to you.

Impress upon us, O Holy Spirit, that we were created in God's image and as such have unlimited potential.

"Thou hast made us for Thyself and our hearts are restless until they rest in Thee."

St. Augustine

Leo Tolstoi's popular novel ANNA KARENINA tells the tragic story of a woman who abandons her husband and children for an adulterous affair with another man, Aleksei. When he tires of her and goes off to war, Anna throws herself beneath the wheels of a train and is killed. The story written a hundred years ago remains alive and read today because it deals with a timeless subject—the search by humankind for three elusive abstracts: freedom, love and happiness.

All of us share the search with Anna, not that we all throw away one life for another, but most have been tempted to take some drastic action when hopelessness wraps our soul like a python. Where is freedom—unfettered, unlimited, unconditional? Where is love—deep, constant, abiding? Where is happiness—daily, ecstatic, full? The answer, according to the Bible, is in Christ. In Colossians (2:9,10) we read: "For in Him dwelleth all the fullness of the Godhead bodily. And we are complete in Him . . . " You are complete when you come to know Christ as your Savior. His indwelling Spirit is your key to love and freedom and happiness.

Thank You, God, for the joy and peace that You have brought into our lives.

Oh, what a happy soul am I,
Although I cannot see.
I am resolved that in this world
Contented will I be.

How many blessing I enjoy
That other people don't;
To weep and sigh because I'm blind,
I cannot and I won't.

Fanny Crosby

Famous hymnwriter Fanny Crosby lost her eyesight a few weeks after she was born and lived the rest of her 95 years totally blind. How did she cope with her handicap? In a word: victoriously. The poem above, written when she was still a young girl, testifies to the faith she embraced all her days. Not only did she live triumphantly, but also her inspired hymns helped untold millions to articulate the belief they held but could not express.

You and I may not be able to write like Fanny Crosby, but we can live like her no matter what the size or severity of our crosses. Christ told His followers to "learn of me and ye shall find rest unto your souls. For my yoke is easy, and my burden is light." (Matthew 11:29,30) If you take the Lord at His word, you can live the rest of your days in peace. That doesn't mean you won't have any problems, but you'll have the same vision of Heaven that helped Fanny Crosby to see truth better than most sighted people.

Lord, give me eyes which see beyond life's debilitating problems to its magnificent possibilities!

 "Love never faileth." I Corinthians 13:8

If one were to judge from the popular magazines of the land, he might conclude that money and sex are the principle marriage problems today. Not so, according to one source. In a recent survey, women rated "low self-esteem" as the top item on a list of marital problems.

What can husbands do to help wives with long-standing feelings of low self-esteem? I'd say they might start by being a friend. It is amazing how much better we sometimes treat people outside our immediate families than we do those within. We are often gentler with work associates, neighbors and fellow church members than we are with our own mates.

Be a friend who supports, cares, fully accepts, appreciates and expresses his love. St. Paul said it best. "Love suffers long and is kind; love envieth not, . . . is not puffed up . . . seeketh not her own, is not easily provoked, thinketh no evil . . . rejoiceth in the truth; beareth all things, believeth all things; hopeth all things, endureth all things." (I Corinthians 13: 4-7) Mates who use this verse as a standard and a guide are on the right track to a good relationship.

Lord, show us how to be more loving.

 "Fear not, for I am with thee."

Isaiah 41:10

While I was working with Bill Glass on his book FREE AT LAST (Word Books) about his organization's exciting prison ministry, the former all-pro football player with Detroit and Cleveland told me he believed there is only one way for committed Christians to live their lives—"with abandon, by going all out, by shooting the tube." That last expression fascinated me, and I asked Bill its origin. This is what he told me:

"One day I asked a surfer in Hawaii what was the single, most exhilarating thing about riding a surfboard.

" 'That's easy,' he responded, 'shooting the tube.' The young man explained that one does that when he rides his board through the curl of a wave as it begins to cup over him. 'It's dangerous,' the surfer admitted, 'but fantastic. Like being in a crystal cathedral.' "

Someone once wrote that man was not made for safe harbors, and I believe that to be true. If we are to learn, to advance, to grow, we must be willing to launch out into the dark unknown. Christians have an advantage in uncharted waters because they have a guide to protect them from rocky shoals and high seas. God will see you through every trial, and in the end bring you safely to port. He promises it in the Book of Life.

When I am tempted to play life safe, Lord, remind me that You didn't.

18

"It is one of the most beautiful compensations of life that no man can sincerely try to help another without helping himself."

Ralph Waldo Emerson

There is an old story a minister-friend of mine used to tell about the evangelist who asked a congregation, "How many want to go to Heaven?"

Everyone raised his or her hand except old Jake, whose poor eyesight was only exceeded by his poor hearing. "What about you, Jake?" the preacher asked incredulously. "Don't you want to go to Heaven?"

"Oh, yes, of course," answered Jake belatedly. "I want to go *sometime*. I thought you were getting up a load to leave right now."

Life is dear to all healthy-minded people and leaving it prematurely is never desirable, whether one has the assurance of Heaven or not. A widow-friend, well into her eighties, once asked me why I thought God didn't take her home.

"You must still have some purpose here," I suggested. Then we talked about some of the people her life still touched, and she agreed she might be a Christian witness to them. Today, look for ways to be a blessing to others and you will glorify your Heavenly Father who gave you life and will sustain it until your tasks on earth are finished.

Lord, help us focus on the here and now, not the then and there.

19

Weary souls fore'er rejoice,
While they hear that sweetest voice,
Whisper softly, "Wand'rer come!
Follow me, I'll guide thee home."

Marcus Morris Wells

Recently, a state supreme court ruled that a spectrogram (or voice print) could not be used as evidence against the defendant in a certain trial. The majority opinion of the court stated that voice-print recordings were not as scientifically acceptable as fingerprints. In other words, there are times when one voice is difficult to distinguish from another.

Probably every person who has attempted to live the spiritual life has experienced the phenomenon of hearing mixed voices when he or she has sought divine guidance. When a decision is particularly difficult, the question may arise: Am I hearing God's directions, the devil's, or my own wishes? The Bible tells us one particularly illuminating story about a young man named Samuel who schooled under the aging priest, Eli. One night Samuel was awakened three times by a voice and each time he went to Eli, who finally perceived that the Lord was calling his apprentice. The priest told the young man what to do and the next time God called, Samuel answered, "Speak; for thy servant heareth." (I Samuel 3:10)

Like sheep who know the voice of their shepherd, people who are in regular communication with their Heavenly Father can recognize His voice without trouble. And when He calls they answer like Samuel: "Speak; for thy servant heareth."

Teach me to know Your voice, O Holy Spirit, and to walk in the light it provides.

 "When a man points a finger at someone else, he should remember that four of his fingers are pointing at himself."

Louis Nizer

Roy Clark, the much-loved country and western singer, was once told by a well-meaning preacher that he couldn't be both a Christian and a professional entertainer. In fact, the minister went so far as to say unless Roy found another job he couldn't join his church.

Because Roy loved to sing and believed his talent God-given, he refused to give up his career, which is fortunate. Today he not only brings joy to millions with his music, but he is also a strong witness for his faith.

Christians need to be careful making judgments about who can serve Christ, where they can serve Him or in what capacity.

First of all, unless a line of work is dishonest or immoral, we are on thin ice when we castigate another's vocation as being inferior or unworthy. Each of us has different gifts, different ministries. Don't be a hypocrite, Christ said. Before you try to remove the mote (speck) from your brother's eye, first remove the beam (board, log) from your own. (Matthew 7:5)

Remind us, Lord, that we are called to serve, not to judge.

 "The difficulties in life are intended to make us better, not bitter." **Anonymous**

I once overheard a conversation between my wife and another young woman—a recent mother—that surprised me. The young mother had had a very difficult time, laboring long and hard before she finally gave birth to a healthy son. "But," she said, cuddling the baby to her, "all that difficulty is a dim memory now."

Apparently, this is a common statement by mothers following childbirth because I have heard since from other women that the hard work of giving birth isn't prominent in their thinking. "A minor footnote compared to the immense joy of my child," one told me.

Sometimes when we are in a dark spiritual or physical dungeon, it seems as if the night will never pass. We toil in vain, trying to eliminate problems. We question the strength of our faith, the devotion of loved ones, the constancy of God's love.

Yet in the ripeness of time, when a problem has run its course, we suddenly find ourselves out of our tunnel and into sunshine so bright and air so clean and invigorating that we can hardly remember the pain which held our minds and souls captive. If you are presently going through an ordeal which you think will never end, ask God to help you with your burden. Jesus said, "Come unto me, all ye that labour and are heavy laden, and I will give you rest." (Matthew 11:28) Whatever your concern, He will not leave you comfortless.

Teach me to walk with You, Lord, one day at a time.

"If we could read the secret history of our enemies, we should find in each person's life, sorrow and suffering enough to disarm all hostility."

Henry Wadsworth Longfellow

Major league baseball manager Alvin Dark once had some interesting things to say about subordinating oneself to authority while he was having difficulty with his boss, the fiery and tempestuous Charles O. Finley, owner of the Oakland Athletics. (It should be noted here for those who don't follow baseball that though Mr. Dark is no longer in Mr. Finley's employ, he lasted longer than many Oakland managers.)

When asked by reporters how he managed to withstand Mr. Finley's criticism and interference, Mr. Dark answered that his Christian faith helped him immensely. How so, his inquisitors wanted to know. Whereupon Mr. Dark pointed them to the Scriptures, particularly I Peter 2:13-18 which advises Christians to "be subject to your masters."

Does that mean we are to obey blindly all authority whether it be cruel, inhuman, unfair or unjust? To understand the passage from I Peter one should be reminded that many Christians were slaves in a Rome-dominated empire at that time. The writer of the letter was calling for patience in the face of suffering because it was Christ-like. Such a posture, it was suggested, was a good witness for one's faith; and furthermore, evil masters would be brought to justice.

But what about today? Must we always accept authority even if it is dishonest or unjust? No, of course not. Many Christians in Nazi Germany struggled with the question and rebelled. Still, the key is Christ-likeness. And one of His wisest injunctions is apropos: "If it be possible, as much as lieth in you, live peaceably with all men." (Romans 12:18)

Lord, help me show others the love and tolerance that You show me.

23

A man's reach should exceed his grasp
Or what's a heaven for?

Robert Browning

Five hundred years ago, Sir Thomas More (1478-1535) was born. An English statesman, poet, lawyer and humanist, his famous struggle with King Henry VIII over church-versus-state supremacy has been well recorded in history; and the movie "A Man for All Seasons" added to the general public's knowledge of this indomitable Christian martyr. (More was executed for his defiance of the King and 300 years later was recognized a saint of the Church.)

What is not as well known is that Sir Thomas wrote a book entitled UTOPIA (taken from a Greek word which means "no place") about an idealized and idyllic land where men lived in perfect peace, perfect harmony and perfect health.

Today when we hear the word "utopia" used, it is most often in the context of some questionable social improvement scheme. Which raises the question: Are Christians utopian dreamers? The answer is: of course. Except that their dreams are based on more than cotton-candy wishes. Christians are committed to striving for a more just, more humane, more loving world, because Christ requires His followers to do so. He showed us by example how we should move and act, especially in our treatment of others. Though we will never measure up to His model, we should never lose sight of the goal, utopian or not.

Today, O Holy Spirit, inspire me to climb mountains that would be insurmountable without Your power.

24

"Let us not love in word, neither in tongue; but in deed and in truth."   **I John 3:18**

At a college basketball game recently, a collision occurred between two opposing players, and they went sprawling to the floor, out of bounds near where I was sitting. I watched somewhat amused when the player who accidentally committed the foul offered a hand to help lift his opponent from the floor. The player brushed aside the extended hand, refusing the symbolic apology, and got to his feet on his own.

Too often, I'm afraid, we build needless interpersonal barriers because our pride gets in the way. Healing broken relationships is the proper role of a committed Christian rather than perpetuating old grudges and feelings of resentment. Don't pass up an opportunity to resolve a dispute in your life today. Better still, don't take offense at some minor, possibly unintentional, slight. The world already has too many people bent on turning molehills into mountains.

Give me the insight to see my own faults, Father, and the grace to forgive others for theirs.

25

"... for behold, the kingdom of God is within you."   **Luke 17:21**

Doris, I'll call her, is a physically healthy, attractive, middle-aged woman whom I've known for a long time. She has a loving husband, who is moderately successful in his line of work, and three bright children. On the surface, one would assume Doris to be a very happy person, but she has been in and out of mental hospitals most of her adult life. Recently I had a private conversation with her, and she told me some things about her self-image that translated into one simple message: *I don't like myself.*

What would you tell someone who believes they are worthless, a failure, a flop? In Doris' case, she professes a strong Christian faith and she does try to live like a person who is a follower of Christ. What she told me, though she doesn't understand, contradicts the Gospel. Why? Because if you and I were created in God's image, there is nothing inferior about us. As someone said, "God doesn't make junk."

The starting point for you and me is to realize that God loves us, is for us and wants the best for us. Furthermore, He will protect and help us live creative, fulfilling lives if we place ourselves in His hands and trust Him. But we can never accomplish the work He has for us if we, like Doris, keep telling ourselves that we're useless.

If you say such a thing often enough, your subconscious will turn it into fact. Today, *right now*, repeat this thought out loud. "I am a child of God, a special person in His sight, and with that knowledge I'll go about my work confidently and enthusiastically, knowing He will bless my efforts." If you believe that, you'll be anything but a failure.

God, thank You for loving me first.

 "Reflect upon your present blessings, of which every man has many; not on your past misfortunes, of which all men have some."

Charles Dickens

One winter, while visiting friends in the Midwest, I looked out the window of their home and saw several cedar waxwings gathered at a birdfeeder. "Look, cedar waxwings!" I exclaimed. My hosts were unimpressed. "We have them all the time. There are plenty of berries around, and they stay here all winter." Familiarity with these regular callers made my friends take them for granted, while their rarity made them special to me.

Familiarity, it has been said, breeds contempt. It is also an obstruction to vision and often prevents us from appreciating much of life's beauty. Someone once told me that if you really want to know a mountain trail you should hike it many times a year, observing the changes it undergoes from season to season. It is the same with friends. You must walk with them in sunshine and rain to really know them.

Take special pains today to look deeply at the people, places and things around you which you may take for granted. Consider the blessings that are yours, everyday blessings like work, loved ones, friends, shelter, food and birds, even the common ones whose uncommon beauty and inspiring song often go unnoticed. Then, thank God for His unceasing goodness to you.

Remind me that beauty is in the eye of the beholder, Lord, whenever I begin to dwell on the grotesque or ugly.

27 "For God so loved the world, that he gave his only begotten Son, that whosoever believeth in him should not perish, but have everlasting life."

John 3:16

Though I've not seen it, I am told that the altar of Christ Church, Yokohama, Japan, is adorned with a beautiful wooden crucifix. It was handcarved by Nobumichi Inouye, a Japanese architect of unusual talent. But what is even more fascinating is the story behind the crucifix. While researching the project, Nobumichi became so moved by the life of Christ that he became a believer.

Have you ever asked yourself why Christianity continues to touch and change the hearts of men and women almost 2,000 years after Christ's birth? Some would have us believe that He was just another great spiritual leader—a Socrates or a Gandhi—but none has had the following of the humble Galilean carpenter. There is a reason, of course, and if you count yourself among His children, you know why. Like Nobumichi Inouye, you have discovered that the Nazarene, the humble-born son of Mary, was also the Son of God.

Thank You, Lord, for showing me the way, the truth and the life.

28 We should never be discouraged
Take it to the Lord in prayer . . .
In His arms He'll take and shield thee,
Thou wilt find a solace there.
Joseph Scriven,
from "What a Friend We Have in Jesus"

Each Monday morning at 9:45, I meet with others on the staff of *Guideposts* for Prayer Fellowship, a time when we raise to God concerns of our own as well as those of readers who write to us about their needs. (Thousands of people around the country join us in the spirit of prayer at this time and we invite you to do likewise.)

This week I read a letter from a woman in the Southwest whose concern had been a seemingly incorrigible son. Many months ago she told us that her son had gotten into trouble with the law. He faced a tough, no-nonsense type of judge whom the mother feared "would throw the book at Tom". She asked that we pray that the man would be merciful and fair. This we did.

"You cannot believe the warmth and the love this judge showed our son," she wrote. "It was a total turnaround from previous conferences. I know it was the result of prayer."

The letter went on to relate that the son had received a suspended sentence, had been placed on probation and had since gotten a job which he is performing well.

Prayer is often the court of last resort when it, in fact, should be the first. That's because it is the Supreme Court, and its Chief Justice is capable of miraculous things. He can ease the hearts of troubled mothers, give busy judges compassion and wisdom, and redirect the lives of wayward people, young and old. If you are facing a problem which seems overwhelming, perhaps you need to take it to your Heavenly Father for disposal. He has the power to handle any case.

Lord, help me remember that I don't have to go it alone.

"A good name is better than precious ointment . . . "   **Ecclesiastes 7:1**

One day not long ago I had a pleasant conversation in New York with Bishop Fulton J. Sheen. Eighty-two years old at last count, he's still as dyamic as when I first saw him on TV in the 1950's when he was doing his "Life is Worth Living" program. Well, he's still writing and speaking about his faith, optimistically telling all that when you're in the service of the Lord life is indeed worth living.

One of my favorite stories of Bishop Sheen's is about a Louisiana doctor who spent his entire life caring for the poor in the community. He worked in a small second-floor office above a general store and his shingle below stated simply "Dr. Updike—Upstairs."

When the man died after a life of faithful service, the townspeople sought a way to honor him. Expense was no object. Yet nothing seemed appropriate. Finally, one of his appreciative patients had a solution. Taking the nameplate from the physician's old office site, the former patient took it to the doctor's grave and all who passed got the message: "Dr. Updike—Upstairs"

Lord, inspire us daily to live lives of service and love.

30

When I walk through death's dark valley,
   I was broken with woe,
All my friends seemed to forsake me,
   and I knew not where to go.
Then I heard the Saviour calling,
   midst the darkness and the din,
And He whispered "I'll be with you,
   I'll be with you to the end."
                              Lee Fisher

Several years ago, my friend George Beverly Shea introduced me to those great lines above and to their author, Lee Fisher, a talented minister-writer with the Billy Graham organization. The verse is from a hymn, "He's the Christ of Every Crisis." I sent the poem to Bev some time after his dear wife, Erma, had passed away. "Does Lee's hymn overstate God's sustaining power?" I asked Bev.

"No," he answered, "the longer I live, the truer God's promises become."

We are called to walk some difficult roads in life, ones that test us to the limit. But it is all bearable, if we put our hand in His. There is, as Lee Fisher wrote, a Christ in every crisis.

I know the road won't always be smooth, Lord, but I'll manage if You travel with me.

31   "Be of good cheer, I have overcome the world."   John 16:33

A top executive who had lost his job of 30 years came home considering suicide. He couldn't bring himself to tell his wife of the humiliation nor could he bear the thought of his friends knowing. He went into the bedroom where he kept his gun and took it in his hands. He could end it in a minute, he thought, but something stopped him. *Maybe tomorrow when his wife went shopping. . . .*

That night he slept fitfully and in the morning at breakfast he was a nervous wreck. Then while he was reading the paper, the phone rang. It was a friend of a friend who had heard the unemployment news. He was considering starting a new business and needed a partner. It was the chance of a lifetime.

The fired executive went into the bedroom, threw the gun in the wastebasket and fell on his knees in prayer.

Victory is never final, Churchill pointed out, and defeat is seldom fatal. When you stumble or fall, when you lose something important, when you commit a serious error or fail miserably, be careful of judging yourself too harshly. Self-condemnation only compounds your depression. Sleep on the problem; pray about it. The next day you'll be more capable of assessing the situation.

"What a difference a day makes," goes the popular song. And it is true that 24 hours can make a monumental difference in our attitudes and outlooks. In fact, sometimes just eight hours sleep can give us a new lease on life.

Thank You, Father, for Your healing gift of sleep. Help me get enough rest to serve You fully.

FEBRUARY 1978

S	M	T	W	T	F	S
			1	2	3	4
5	6	7	8	9	10	11
12	13	14	15	16	17	18
19	20	21	22	23	24	25
26	27	28				

Each is given different gifts, we are told in I Corinthians 12:4, and God did not create you without special talents. This month, concentrate on serving Him in whatever way He directs, and do it with your whole heart. You're sure to gain new spiritual insights if you do.

FEBRUARY 1978

1
There is no storm He cannot master,
No stormy sea He cannot still,
No hole resulting from disaster
That God Almighty cannot fill.   F. B.

One stormy evening a girl of about eight stopped playing with her dolls to console a little brother who had become frightened by the loud thunder. "Come here," she said soothingly, and the two of them sat on her bed. "What you need to do, David," she coached, "is to remember the Bethlehem manger and imagine that you are covered by the same light that shone down on the baby Jesus. Just pretend that God's light is covering you, protecting you from head to toe."

David quit whimpering, apparently comforted by his sister's suggestion. But just then the day's loudest thunder clapped, and they both jumped high off the bed. "And if that doesn't work," Sis said, grabbing a blanket, "you cover your head like this!"

In many ways, we are all a lot like the girl in the story: able to give others advice for handling their worries and fears. But when we ourselves are the ones with the problem, it is a little more difficult to calmly and objectively assess the situation. Faith is something we learn from practice, not from preaching.

When peace eludes me, Lord, help me hear Your calming voice.

Have thine own way, Lord, have thine own way.
Thou art the Potter, I am the clay.
Mold me and make me after Thy will,
While I am waiting, yielded and still.

Adelaide Pollard

At a school open house one night, I came upon a young woman operating a potter's wheel. Deftly she molded wet brown clay into a symmetrical bowl. When she was finished, I stood admiring what seemed to be a perfectly shaped vessel.

"How did you make it so round?" I asked.

"With gentle pressure on the clay," she answered.

The Bible makes several allusions to the God-potter-man-clay analogy, and with good reason. If we want God's direction and blessing in our lives, we must become pliable like clay, allowing Him to mold us into serving people.

"Doesn't that make us ciphers, automatons, puppets?" someone might ask. The answer is no, because we are left with our individual wills, and none of us are totally yielding to God's instructions. He made us living vessels, and as such we have the choice of being obedient or not. Like the potter, He may apply gentle pressure to the clay, but we can accept or reject His guidance.

Our lives invariably testify to the depth of our Christian commitment. Those who resist His molding and shaping are often self-centered and self-indulgent. But those who are malleable and yielding, open and teachable, receptive to His guidance and wisdom are serving vessels, generously pouring out heavenly blessing wherever they go.

Help me find and accept Your will in my life, Lord.

Only believe, only believe
All things are possible, only believe.

Paul Rader hymn

The other night I saw a college rendition of the delightfully entertaining play "Sweet Charity." In one scene, Charity becomes trapped in an elevator with a man who suffers claustrophobia. He panics when no one comes to his aid immediately. While he is growing more and more anxious, Charity tries to reassure him everything will be all right. "What you have to tell yourself," she counsels, "is that you're the bravest individual in the whole wide world." Then as happens in all musicals, she sings a song on the subject.

The truth of the matter is that in large measure we are what we tell ourselves we are. If you and I are convinced we are weak, sickly, stupid, imprudent with money, poor conversationalists, inept parents, whatever, we tend to fulfill our self image. The mind is one of the most powerful things in the world, and depending on how you use it, it can exert a tremendous positive or negative force.

Jesus knew this, and He appealed to men to turn from their sinful ways and commit their lives to the service of God. How did He suggest men change? By pulling themselves up by their own bootstraps? No, the first step, He said, is believing. Once someone is spiritually reborn, he finds a new power that enables him to accomplish all the things he wanted to do but couldn't by himself. Repeat these words when you face a difficult challenge: "I can do all things through Christ which strengheneth me." (Philippians 4:13)

Lord, today I'm going to take hold of the power You promised and put it to work in my life.

"For the woman said within herself, 'If I may but touch his garment, I shall be whole.' "
Matthew 9:21

Last night I came home from a trip totally exhausted. My wife, Shirley, anticipated my state of mind so she prepared stuffed pork chops, one of my favorites. After a delicious meal, we turned on the stereo, lit some wood in the fireplace and relaxed, talking about recent happenings. To top it off, she gave me a back rub that chased the last bit of tension out of me.

Touch is one of the underrated senses, I believe. It has great therapeutic value, and nothing expresses love and affection in quite the same way. Smiley Blanton, an outstanding psychiatrist and writer (LOVE OR PERISH, THE HEALING POWER OF POETRY and other books) once wrote:

"Love is like gratitude: it's not much good unless you show it, and touch is often the surest way. There is a magic in touch."

If you want to get closer to someone or heal some estrangement, touch may be the key. It is often a more effective ice breaker than words. A handshake, a hug or squeeze, a kiss, a pat on the back, all are good ways of expressing the fact that you care for another person. Use God's wonderful gift of touch today. You could make someone's day brighter.

Help me express love, Lord, when words aren't easy.

5 "Come unto me, all ye that labour and are heavy laden, and I will give you rest."
Matthew 11:28

"He has an Atlas complex," a woman friend said of a colleague of hers who seemed to be caught up in his own importance. "He thinks he's indispensable to the human race."

Atlas, you'll recall, got himself into quite a pickle when he opposed Zeus in war. After Zeus had won the battle—in part because he employed his famous 100-handed monster—Atlas received as punishment the task of holding the world on his shoulders forever.

Of course, the story of Atlas is a myth. But it is no myth that a good many people go through life feeling they have the weight of the world on their shoulders. They are tragic cases, really, bent over by their eternal burdens.

Fortunately, there is good news for them and anyone who believes he must go through life alone, carrying his problems by himself. The good news is that mankind has a Comforter in the Holy Spirit sent, as Christ promised, to help His followers.

If you are loaded down with cares today, problems that are too heavy to carry alone, do as the old song advises: Take your burdens to the Lord, and leave them there.

Teach me to rely on Your strength, Lord, when the load is heavy.

6

" . . . because I live, ye shall live also."

John 14:19

Whether the story is true or not, it has had a long life. According to those who have repeated it, President Woodrow Wilson once got a call in the middle of the night from an acquaintance who informed him that a Wilson appointee had suddenly died. "That is too bad," replied the sleepy President.

"Yes, it is a tragedy," the friend said. Then the real purpose for calling emerged. "Do you think I might take his place?"

There was a pause at the other end of the line before Wilson replied: "It's all right with me, if it's all right with the undertaker."

All of us at one time or another have fantasized about taking someone else's place. Whether it be someone more handsome or beautiful, richer or wiser, or more influential, most of us must plead guilty. It's human nature. But one person with whom we don't wish to change places is a dead one. That's because life is the most prized of all possessions. And eternal life has been the dream of all the Ponce de Leons who ever walked this earth.

If you are interested in a life that has no end, then you need to drink of the water Jesus prescribed for the Samaritan woman, whom He told: "Whosoever drinketh of the water that I shall give him shall never thirst; but the water that I shall give him shall be in him a well of water springing up into everlasting life." (John 4:14)

Most merciful God, we thank You for your promise of a life without end for those who believe.

7 **Though gray be your hair
With little to part
This does not denote
The age of your heart.**
Michael Franklin Ellis

"I may be sixty-five," I heard a man facing retirement say, "but I refuse to be *welked.*" As a writer, I am fascinated by quaint expressions, so I went to my small dictionary to look up the word "welk." No luck. Further investigation in Webster's huge dictionary led me to this definition: "to fade away or dry up." The word, coming from the German, is now obsolete. Paraphrasing Douglas MacArthur's famous quote would make it read: "Old soldiers never die, they just welk."

Everyone over 35 has paid some mind to aging, to fading, to drying up. Is there any secret for avoiding it or slowing down the process? "It's simply a case of mind over matter," goes one old saw. "It doesn't matter if you don't mind."

My thought on the subject of welking, for what it's worth, is that humans have three ages—physical, chronological and mental—and the third is the most important longevity yardstick of all. If you are tuned in to life—still interested, still learning, still enthused about sunrises and sunsets, new births and rebirths, still willing to involve yourself in the lives of others—then you don't need to worry about drying up. You're still vital and growing.

Thank You, God, that it is never too late to improve, to change, to grow.

8 **(Ash Wednesday)
"And he was there in the wilderness forty days, tempted of Satan and was with the wild beasts; and the angels ministered unto him."** **Mark 1:13**

Today marks the beginning of Lent, the season leading up to the most significant holy day on the Christian calendar, Easter. Why do these dates vary from year to year?

Early in the fourth century it was decided to celebrate Easter on the Sunday after the first full moon following the spring equinox, which allows the date to fall between March 22 and April 25. This year Easter is March 26.

Lent originally was a 40-hour fast period from Good Friday till Easter Sunday morning, but in the year 325 this period set aside for self-examination and penitence was extended to 40 days. (The period is actually 46 days because Sundays are not counted.)

Why 40 days? Because Lent is a time for self-denial and fasting for many Christians and the number 40 has great Biblical significance. Moses is presumed to have been without food on Mount Sinai for 40 days, the children of Israel wandered the wilderness on limited rations for 40 years. Elijah fasted 40 days and so did Christ following His baptism.

In some church traditions, the sign of the cross in ashes is placed on the believer's forehead. The minister says, "Remember man that thou art dust and unto dust thou shalt return." (Genesis 3:19)

It is a reminder that we have a finite number of years. Whether you use this Lenten period for self-denial or the addition of some spiritual discipline, it is a good time to take inventory of your faith, to renew your commitment, to restate your dedication.

Light our lives, Lord, so we see ourselves as You see us.

 "You give but little when you give your possessions. It is when you give yourself that you truly give."
Kahlil Gibran

The other night my wife, Shirley, was reading a children's story to my sons Christopher and Daniel which caught my attention. It is called THE GIVING TREE, and it was written by Shel Silverstein.

The tale is about the friendship between a young boy and a tree. Over the years, the tree provides many gifts to its visitor—branches to swing on in his childhood, apples to sell in adolescence, wood to build a house in adulthood. Finally the tree is reduced to a stump, and when his friend—now stooped and aged—comes to visit, the tree is sorrowful because it has nothing left to give.

The old man laughs. "I don't need much any more," he says. "Just a place to sit and rest." And that's what he does at the book's end, sits down on the happy stump and rests.

Sometimes, like the old tree, we don't think we have much to give, but when that is so God doesn't ask for much. Jesus' story of the widow's mite (Luke 21:2-4) is one of the greatest sermons on giving that has ever been preached. Give out of your poverty, the Bible tells us, and you will receive a blessing so great you'll not be able to hold it. Test the principle today and be prepared for an outpouring of God's unfathomable love.

Lord, when I am tempted to complain, remind me that I have been given far more than I have given.

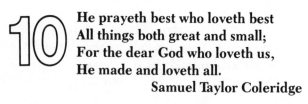

**He prayeth best who loveth best
All things both great and small;
For the dear God who loveth us,
He made and loveth all.**
Samuel Taylor Coleridge

Last night while browsing through a book of poems, I came upon the memorable Coleridge lines above from "The Rime of the Ancient Mariner." The famous ballad about a sailing ship becalmed and its suffering seamen is filled with vivid portraits of a vessel caught in the doldrums: " . . . water, water everywhere/ nor any drop to drink . . . Without a breeze, without a tide/ she steadies with upright keel . . . As idle as a painted ship/upon a painted ocean."

Old sailors who navigated ships near the equator often had tales to tell about doldrums, when their vessels languished from lack of wind. People, too, experience doldrums, times of listlessness or stagnation or inactivity, periods when their lives rest on plateaus of paralysis. Sometimes they are the result of outside forces—illness or unemployment, for example. Sometimes they are self-induced. Whatever, a doldrum can be either a period of great mental anguish and torment or a period of reflection, recouping, restoration and planning.

Perhaps you are in one of those "in-between" phases of your life right now. If so, don't lose hope or become discouraged. There may be a reason for the respite, and it may have positive results. Ask God to help you make the best of your circumstance.

Father, we know that You have a plan for each of us and will reveal it when the time is right.

 "Thou hast touched me, and I have been translated into thy peace."
St. Augustine

The temperature was near zero yesterday, and though I was tempted to hole up, I ventured out for a walk and was invigorated by the cold. It helps get the blood stirring, I guess.

While I was out I remembered a conversation I once had with a writer who had made several trips with polar expedition teams. What impressed me were not his observations about the cold and harshness of the Arctic and Antarctica, however, but rather his descriptions of the austere land's beauty, and of the peace that sweeps over him when he is there.

Though I appreciate a peaceful spot as much as anyone, I'm not about to travel thousands of miles to live in weather 50 degrees below zero to get it. No, I believe you and I can find it much closer to home than that. Where? Right inside each of us. Christ said, "the kingdom of God is within" (Luke 17:21), and we know that where God is, there is perfect peace.

If you are nervous, worn out, worried, exhausted, stop what you are doing for a moment. Close your eyes and picture some beautiful scene—a lake, a waterfall, a meadow, a mountaintop view. Ponder the beauty of that Heavenly creation. Thank God for His goodness to you, for His unending gifts. Then, go forth in the peace He supplies.

Thank You, Lord, for giving us a peace that passes all understanding.

12 (Lincoln's Birthday)
"Read this book (the Bible) for what on reason you can accept and take the rest on faith, and you will live and die a better man."

Abraham Lincoln

"Before I joined a book club, I never got around to buying the books I wanted to read," a friend told me not long ago. "Now I receive many books through the mail—and I still don't get around to reading them."

Some people practically furnish their houses with books, displaying them not only on shelves, but also on tables, mantels, in bedrooms, bathrooms, everywhere. And as a matter of fact, the colorful jackets of books are very decorative and eye-appealing.

However, nothing substantive takes place, nothing illuminative or inspiring, as long as one only looks at a book's cover. Nor will one learn anything by merely holding a volume in hand. Osmosis isn't a principle that works in matters of the mind. No, to learn from a book, one must read it. Study it. Think about the premises and test them against other knowledge.

All of this is particularly true of the Bible. People who think the Bible is an irrelevant, outdated, impractical book have not really read it closely. Because if you and I read it like students, we will discover the Bible is not primarily about people who lived long ago, but about you and me and how we can find meaning in our lives. Get in the practice of using your Bible every day, memorize key verses, apply them, live them, and you will find a treasure no book club can match.

Thank You, Lord, for speaking to us through Your word.

13 "Beware ye of the leaven of the Pharisees, which is hypocrisy. For there is nothing covered, that shall not be revealed; neither hid, that shall not be known."

Luke 12:1,2

38

John Ruskin once wrote that "The essence of lying is in decep-
tion, not in words; a lie may be told by silence, by equivocation,
by the accent on a syllable to a sentence; and all these kinds of
lies are worse and baser by many degrees than a lie plainly
worded."

There is an interesting passage on the subject of honesty in
Matthew (5:33-37) which concludes with Jesus' admonition:
"Let your communications be 'yea, yea; nay, nay . . . ' " In
other words, always tell the truth. Men and women of God
should not have to be reminded of this duty, yet all of us are
guilty, I suppose, of embellishing events, exaggerating our
roles in happenings, taking slight liberties with the facts to
make ourselves look more pious, more noble, more courageous
than might be the case. Though one might say these are minor
infractions, they could well be the seed beds out of which grow
taller and more substantive deceptions. Whatever, Christians
need no other counsel on the matter. In all our dealings, God
requires you and me to tell the truth. Period.

*Father, forgive us when we stray from the facts and cloud
truth with fiction.*

14 (Valentine's Day)
"Ah, how skillful grows the hand
That obeyeth Love's comand!
It is the heart and not the brain
That to the highest doth attain,
And he who followeth Love's behest
Far excelleth all the rest!"
Henry Wadsworth Longfellow

Valentine, an obscure third century priest, was martyred in the
year 270. There is little explanation in history books as to how
he became the lover's saint, other than the possibility that the
Church decided to use his death to compete with the Roman
holiday, Lupercalia. It was a pagan festival which featured a
ritual similar to our old box socials. On the Roman holiday,
girls' names were placed in a box and boys drew them out. As a

result, they were entitled to the young lady's companionship for the holiday.

Old Ben Franklin, the originator of the postal system, probably did more for the popularization of exchanging valentines than anyone. Low postal rates in the 18th century made it possible for young men and women to exchange sentiments by mail, an opportunity particularly appealing to secret admirers or those imbued with Captain John Smith-like shyness when it came to expressing matters of the heart.

Whether you do it by card or verbally, be sure to communicate your feelings on this holiday for lovers. Though we shouldn't need a special reason to tell someone special, "I love you," Valentine's Day gives us one.

Lord, thank You for Your great expression of love to us in the Person of Jesus who came to show us what real love is.

"Count it all joy . . . when you meet various trials, for you know that the testing of your faith produces steadfastness."

James 1:2

Once I toured a large fish hatchery in Ohio. Our guide pointed out the various species being raised in the many pools which spread over several acres.

Most of the waters were still (except at feeding time) but one pool featured running water that flowed rapidly from one end to the other, and the fish—rainbow trout in this case—were required to swim against the current in order to maintain their places. It was explained that trout thrive in cool, running water. Swimming against the current requires more effort, and because of the constant exercise they eat more and grow faster. In other words, the struggle produces growth.

Often we think it would be nice to have a life with no problems, no troubles, no doubts. But problems are a condition of life, and coping with them is the lot of every healthy-minded person. Christians have a leg up on most because they have a personal God to help them. Furthermore, you and I are spiritually strengthened by our trials. When the going gets rough, don't curse God for sending obstacles; ask Him to show you how to use the experience to grow in faith.

Give me more than a fair-weather faith, Lord.

"Your Father knoweth what things ye have need of, before ye ask him."
Matthew 6:8

During the period of heavy snow, frigid weather and heating fuel shortages of a year ago, a friend reported by long distance telephone that he and his family had been marooned in their home for several days.

"How's your food supply?" I asked.

"Holding up," he answered good-naturedly. Then he added: "We're not down to the *licklog* yet."

I hadn't heard that word for a long time. Do you know what a licklog is? It is a grooved log in which the indentations are filled with salt for livestock. When the salt is gone, farmers say animals are down to the licklog.

People get down to the licklog of life sometimes, too. In fact, most of us regardless of age or position or wealth come to times when we are laid low by external circumstances—the loss of a loved one, a business reversal or a serious illness. When we are down, humbled, reduced, then we are in the perfect position to pray. For when we are flat, the first step in rising is getting to one's knees. And when you and I get on our knees—figuratively or literally—we are assured of God's help. He will provide salt for our licklog.

Father, show me how to "let go and let God."

"Greater love hath no man than this, that a man lay down his life for his friends."
John 15:13

Yesterday while reading from Dr. Kenneth Taylor's most helpful and refreshing paraphrase of the Bible, "The Living Bible,"

I noticed a frontispiece taken from William Tyndale's prologue to the first printed English New Testament, published surreptitiously in Germany in 1525. In it Tyndale asks those who follow him with "higher gifts of grace to interpret the sense of the Scripture and the meaning of the Spirit" to amend it. "For we have not received the gifts of God for ourselves only, or for to hide them; but for to bestow them unto the congregation which is the body of Christ."

When I think of the monumental contribution this leader of the Christian Reformation made, I am reminded again of the legacy followers of Christ have been given. Tyndale was strangled and his body burned in 1536 (when he was about 44) because he was considered a heretic by the Church. In truth, he is one of the authentic heroes of our faith, one who was willing to give his life so lay people would have access to the Holy Word.

When you read your Bible today, whether it be King James or Phillips or Revised Standard or the Living Bible version, remember that you are able to do so because of the courage of people like William Tyndale.

Lord, thank You for Your word and the free access
we have to it.

"Every good and perfect gift is from above and cometh down from the Father, with whom is no variableness nor shadow of turning."

James 1:17

"Of course, there is cruelty," black writer Toni Morrison told a Philadelphia audience recently while talking about the history of inhumanity. "Cruelty is a mystery. But if we see the world as one long, brutal game, we bump into another mystery: the mystery of beauty."

All of life seems to boil down to perspective. If one views people as harsh, brutal, self-serving, dishonest and unjust, then there is plenty of evidence to prove such is the case. But if you are wise enough to select the lovely and beautiful around you, to accept life as an unmerited, unearned gift from God, then you will always be ahead of the game, always be one up on negative thinkers. The choice is yours.

Today Father, help me look for the beauty of the earth—and find it.

19

"**Be not high-minded nor trust in uncertain riches, but in the living God, who giveth us richly all things to enjoy.**"

I Timothy 6:17

A half-dozen years ago, Jeb Stuart Magruder was a presidential aide with easy access to people of financial and political power. Today, he is an executive with Young Life, a Colorado-based Christian organization which ministers to the needs of teen-agers across the nation. How did he get from there to here?

In a nutshell, he had a spiritual rebirth and made the discovery of Jesus Christ while he was serving seven months in prison for his part in the Watergate cover-up conspiracy.

"There was always the feeling of trying to succeed for materialistic reasons," Magruder says, reflecting on his Washington days. "Some of the most wealthy people in this country are the saddest. The thing that was missing in my life was faith. . . ."

Jeb Magruder, his wife Gail (who wrote the moving book entitled A GIFT OF LOVE) and their family have been given a revelation some people go a lifetime without receiving: that there is something more to life than a big house, a big car, a big bank account, a big name, a big reputation.

Those who covet such worldly possessions and would be willing to sell their souls for them don't realize that they'd be trading for a pile of ashes. Jesus said to His disciples, "What shall it profit a man, if he shall gain the whole world, and lose his own soul?" (Mark 8:36) If you already have your priorities set and know what is really important in life, you have insight worth more than all the silver and gold in the world.

When our hearts long for wealth or position, Lord, remind us that only You can satisfy.

(Washington's Birthday)
"Finally brethren, whatsoever things are true, whatsoever things are honest . . . think on these things."

Philippians 4:8

Today, America will observe the birth of its first president, George Washington, born February 22, 1732. History tells us he was a man of great faith, a man of great courage, a man of integrity. But more than any virtue, honesty is the one most associated with his name, primarily because of an apocryphal story, the one in which young George admitted guilt when his father asked him who had felled his cherry tree. Spurious or not, the tale has survived for better than 200 years and it has served as a worthy illustration for millions of parents, hoping to impress upon their children the importance of truthtelling.

Though none would admit it, there are those in positions of leadership today who view honesty as an old-fashioned practice, a square word, a relative virtue, "good for others but not for me." Still, nothing is more important in relationships, be they between countries, between opposing political parties, between businessman and customer, between husband and wife, between parent and child, than forthrightness and honesty.

A mason uses a tool to measure the straightness of his work. It is called a level. From it comes the expression "on the level." If you long for the return of the time when a man's word was his bond, then you and I need to practice an honesty that is without qualification or exception. It is more than overdue. The Bible tells us "The night is far spent, the day is at hand: let us therefore cast off the works of darkness, and let us put on the armour of light. Let us walk honestly, as in the day . . . " (Romans 13:12, 13)

Lord, let me be as honest with others as I would have them be with me.

"Lay not up for yourselves treasures upon earth, where moth and rust doth corrupt, and where thieves break through and steal. But lay up for yourselves treasures in heaven, where neither moth nor rust doth corrupt, and where thieves do not break through nor steal."

Matthew 6:19,20

Though some might argue that there are more, literature through the ages speaks of seven deadly sins. What are they? Alphabetically, they include: avarice (or greed), envy, gluttony, lust, pride, sloth and wrath. For the next few days, let us look at each more closely.

1. Greed

Greed is no stranger to any of us, for to some degree we are all infected with the malady that gripped Midas, the legendary king. Despite the fact that he already had great riches, Midas wanted more and he implored the gods to grant him the power to transform all that he touched to gold. His wish was granted, and for a while he was elated. Then, he tried to eat and his food turned to gold, too.

"Rid me of this curse," he begged, and the gods told him he could be free of his golden touch if he would bathe in a certain river. When he did, he was relieved of his problem, as the ground over which the river rolled turned to gold. (That, according to this legend, is why sand is golden.)

Few people are satisfied with their lot. Not even Adam and Eve were content in their paradise. Yet, the wisdom of the ages repeats this truth again and again: *Things* cannot satisfy. What, then, can bring fulfillment and contentment? The Psalmist tells us:

"Happy is that people whose god is the Lord." When our god is materialism and our goal is more earthly riches, we chase an elusive rainbow.

Help me, Lord, to distinguish between the temporal and the eternal.

"... love envieth not ..."
I Corinthians 13:4

2. Envy, another deadly sin.

An addendum to the story of the Prodigal Son (Luke 15:11-32) is as revealing about human nature as the main anecdote. After the wayward son returned, his father threw a celebration party. But an elder son was appalled to learn that the fatted calf had been killed for his younger brother.

"I have served you faithfully for many years," the elder brother said to his father, "but you never gave me a calf so I could have a party with my friends." His father tried to explain, but the son was probably too overcome with jealousy to understand.

Trying to be fair, to divide everything—including love—equally is one of the enigmatic puzzles of parenthood. No matter how hard one tries, children perceive injustice even where there is none and the result can be resentment and hurt feelings.

The word covet is a synonym for envy, and it appears in the tenth commandment: "Thou shalt not covet thy neighbor's house, thou shalt not covet thy neighbor's wife, nor his man servant, nor his maid servant, nor his ox, nor his ass, nor anything that is thy neighbor's." (Exodus 20:17)

One way to guard against envy is to concentrate on all the blessings God has bestowed upon you. Like gifts of the Spirit, the Lord in His infinite wisdom has given each of us different things. Thank Him for what you have and try to make the most of it; otherwise all your life you'll never have enough.

You know my needs, Lord. Help me trust You to meet them.

"For the drunkard and the glutton shall come to poverty."
Proverbs 23:21

3. Gluttony, another deadly sin

A form of extreme self-indulgence, gluttony would, on the face of the word, seem to be solely concerned with food, but there are other applications. Take this letter for example. It comes from a woman in a Midwestern city:

"My husband was once a mild drinker, but today he is an alcoholic who fails to recognize it. He has drinks at lunch, drinks before he comes home at night, drinks before dinner and drinks before he goes to bed. His gluttonous appetite for booze is ruining my life and the lives of our children. Pray that God will make Harold aware of his problem and help him defeat it."

In addition to food and drink, there are other forms of gluttony. One also can be gluttonous about sports, about club-work, about money, about sex. Gluttony connotes immoderation or some phase of one's life that is out of control. It obviously qualifies as a lethal sin, something that can rob life of balance and perspective. The Bible says that your body is the temple of the Holy Spirit. (I Corinthians 6:19) Anything that builds up that temple (such as eating wholesome food or doing exercise, in moderation) must be considered good by God. Anything you do to destroy it is a sin.

Help us defeat damaging habits, Lord, and discipline us to develop worthwhile ones.

"For the flesh lusteth against the Spirit, and the Spirit against the flesh, and these are contrary the one to the other . . . "
Galatians 5:17

4. Lust, another deadly sin

A well-known head of state got himself deeply enmeshed in controversy not long ago when he admitted he was guilty of lust in his heart. Then, he quoted Matthew 5:28 to support his point. The speaker is Jesus Christ: "Whosoever looketh on a woman to lust after her hath committed adultery with her already in his heart."

It is interesting to note that the quotation would seem to limit sexual lusting to the male gender. Observation would lead me to believe, however, that women also are capable of lust. Whatever, the statement makes it clear that lust is no minor spiritual offense.

What I'd like is a good definition of lust. The dictionary uses words such as lasciviousness, intense longing, wanton, craving. I think we can do better.

Lust, I would submit, is a base urge that has nothing to do with love. Neither does it have any interest in a second party's desires or fulfillment. Lust is singular, concerned only with personal gratification as opposed to mutual interest. And therein is its sinful aspect. Lust is selfish, exploitative, depersonalized, inconsiderate of another's rights or wishes.

When you or I engage in such activities, sexual or otherwise, we do battle with the golden rule which admonishes us to do unto others as we would have them do unto us. (Matthew 7:12)

Give us clean hearts and minds, Lord, so that we can look each other in the eye without deceit.

 "Pride goeth before destruction, and an haughty spirit before a fall."
Proverbs 16:18

5. Pride, another deadly sin

One of the best-known stories in Greek mythology concerns the tale of the beautiful youth Narcissus and the nymph Echo. When Narcissus spurns Echo, you'll recall, she causes him to fall in love with his own water-reflected image. Unable to consummate that love, the lad is changed into a flower which bears his name.

Narcissism is the psychological term for neurotic self-love, and self-love is another synonym for pride—as is vanity, egotism and arrogance. Such self-centeredness is the sin of which the Pharisees were guilty. Jesus condemned them for flaunting their righteousness in public, saying, "Therefore when thou doest *thine* alms, do not sound a trumpet before thee, as the hypocrites do in the synagogues and in the streets, that they may have glory of men. Verily I say unto you, They have their reward." (Matthew 6:2)

Humility is the other side of the pride coin, and its price is a subordination of self-love in favor of God's love for others. Not that we should be devoid of self-love. Christ recognized that esteem for ourselves is perfectly normal when He said "Love your neighbors as yourselves."

But the problem is balance. Humility does not come easy for most of us, and we need God's help to keep us from thinking more highly of ourselves than we ought. Take pride in your work, take pride in your mate or children, take pride in your church, but not pride in your righteousness, or possessions, or looks, or position. Such pride will separate you from God and anything which does that is indeed a sin.

Lord, help us have a healthy self-esteem that stops short of destructive pride.

For all sad words of tongue or pen,
The saddest are these: "It might have been!"
John Greenleaf Whittier

6. Sloth, another deadly sin

Nothing in children's literature serves to better illustrate the point that perseverance pays off than Aesop's ancient story of the race between the turtle and the hare. While the tortoise put his shoulder to the wheel and his nose to the grindstone (so to speak), his lackadaisical opponent slept under a tree, sure he could catch up any time he chose. But the erratic rabbit was wrong. While he lolled in the shade, Mr. Tortoise crawled off with the victor's laurels.

Some might blame the rabbit's setback on sloth or laziness. Had he run first and rested later, he most certainly would have been victorious. But the rabbit suffered the fate of others who get their priorities mixed. One of the most regrettable happenings in the lives of men and women is their failure to do their best. "Anything worth doing is worth doing right," is a maxim most of us have heard from our youth, and it is true. No one ever reached his or her true potential by making a half-hearted effort.

Christ told His followers what He believed about lethargic commitment when He said, "Because thou art lukewarm . . . I will spew thee out of my mouth." (Revelation 3:16) Enthusiasm (from a Greek word *entheos* which means full of spirit, full of God) is a hallmark of dedicated Christians and slothfulness is the antithesis of spirituality. If you would be worthy of His high calling, both your words and deeds will reflect your love of God.

Lord, help us to be diligent in our work that we may please You as well as our fellow man.

27

"Let not the sun go down upon your wrath."
Ephesians 4:26

7. Wrath, another deadly sin

Not long ago, I heard about two brothers who got into an argument over the disposition of their mother's estate. The younger of the two vowed never to speak to the other again and he kept his promise for nearly 18 years.

But then he suffered a heart attack and was hospitalized. There, a minister talked to him about eternity and after several conversations the man accepted Christ. Immediately, he took paper and pen and wrote his estranged brother, telling him about finding the Lord and how he now had it in his heart to ask his forgiveness. Furthermore, he invited his brother to come visit him.

It was with great relief that he sent the letter and with anticipation that he awaited a reply. Several days passed. Then, a nurse brought him a letter—his same letter. "Return to sender," was written on the envelope, "Addressee deceased."

The verse above is wise counsel indeed, because the best

solution for dealing with a strained relationship is to attempt a resolution as soon as possible. Don't let long periods pass before you try to heal some rift. It will only be more difficult as time goes by. If you have some broken or bruised relationship in your life, ask God to help you heal it. He can help you find the words to set things straight. Often a solution begins with the simple phrase, "I'm sorry."

When I'm tempted to harbor anger, Lord, soften my heart and mellow my words.

 "The Bible is the one Book to which any thoughtful man may go with any honest question of life or destiny and find the answer of God by honest searching."
John Ruskin

With the temperature hovering around 10 degrees and the wind gusting to maybe 20 miles-per-hour, I imagine the two chill-factors were the equivalent of a 10-degree below zero reading last night. But I had two warming factors working for me—a blazing log fire and a seed catalog which had arrived in the afternoon mail. Leafing through a seed book with all its pictures of gorgeous blossoms and succulent vegetables may seem a fanciful exercise to some, but for me it's a meaningful ritual, one that each year helps me to bridge that frigid hurdle between winter and spring.

Why is a seed catalog so uplifting? I suppose it's because of the promise, the anticipatory pleasures it portends. I perceive the Bible to be a seed catalog, too. A seed catalog of faith. When we're ill or full of doubt or in one of life's gray valleys, we need something to give us hope and reassurance. Scripture is full of promises that will come to fruition if we put its principles to work.

However, my seed catalog like my Bible will do no good unless I act. I'll have to order some seeds, maybe start some flats and raise some hothouse plants. Then, when spring comes, I'll have to put my seeds or plants into the ground to realize a harvest. It's the same with faith. Unless you and I read God's word and plant the seeds of truth He supplies, we can't grow into the people we were born to be.

Lord, we long for roots, deep roots that will make us strong, resolute beings. Help us plant the seeds of love and nurture our growth.

MARCH 1978

S	M	T	W	T	F	S
			1	2	3	4
5	6	7	8	9	10	11
12	13	14	15	16	17	18
19	20	21	22	23	24	25
26	27	28	29	30	31	

"All things work together for good to those who love the Lord." (Romans 8:28) Return to this verse each time that some negative experience occurs this month. Remember, a minus sign needs only God's cross to turn it into a plus.

MARCH 1978

1 "A person who points out what is wrong renders only half a service unless he can point out what is right."

Anonymous

There is a widely used teaching method called "role playing" which is a most effective way of gaining new understanding of another's position. In dealing with marriage problems, for example, professional counsellors have helped husbands gain new insights into their wives' thinking and vice versa when couples are asked to switch roles.

The counsellor will usually take a common family problem, say the handling of money or the disciplining of a child, and ask the couple to discuss the situation from the other partner's point of view, or more precisely, what he or she *conceives* the other's position to be. More often than not, both husband and wife come away from the encounter enlightened and edified.

If you are having a human relationship problem with someone who is making your life difficult, maybe you should consider a period of role playing. Consider the other person's viewpoint or what you think his or her position to be. Does it have merit? Have you been selfish or inflexible? Is there some compromise you should propose? Does the other person agree that you have understood his or her position? Pray about the matter. Ask God to give you the wisdom and the words to heal any broken or strained relationship that can be mended. If you've done all that you can and the situation has not changed, trust God and His timetable. Perhaps it will take more time.

Lord, help us see that being a healing agent of Yours is more important than being right.

2 "And be not conformed to this world: but be ye transformed by the renewing of your mind, that ye may prove what is that good, and acceptable, and perfect, will of God."

Romans 12:2

During a recent cold wave, we have been using the fireplace every night after dinner. This is a pleasant family time to sit around a warm fire, drink a cup of coffee or cocoa and discuss events of the day.

Once upon a time I thought I was conserving fuel while burning logs, but a recent news story informed me that between 90 and 97 per cent of the heat from logs goes up my chimney. Old pot-bellied, wood-burning stoves were much more practical, losing only 30 to 40 per cent.

Many Christians are like my fireplace, I suspect. They burn brightly and appear to be operating efficiently. But much of their energy is being lost, wasted on minor church issues and sectarian debates that divide and confuse. Meanwhile, people who need the warmth of God's good news go cold.

If you would be a more effective worker for Christ, concentrate on the loving and serving aspects of His ministry. In Matthew (23:12) Christ told His disciples "whosoever shall exalt himself shall be abased; and he that humbles himself shall be exalted." When we serve each other, we witness to the transforming love of God, and our actions will not go unnoticed by a hungry world.

Lord, help us burn with passion for Your work and keep us from getting sidetracked.

"What makes the difference is not how many times you have been through the Bible, but how many times and how thoroughly the Bible has been through you."

Gipsy Smith

Eldridge Cleaver, whose recent conversion to Christianity surprised believers and non-believers alike, made an interesting statement about the Bible following his turnaround.

Said Cleaver: "My mother always has been very religious and she encouraged me to read the Bible, which I did as literature, a book of stories, parables, folklore, but not as a guide nor as the word of God. Now its truths leap from the pages. It's the difference between a dead Bible and a living Bible."

When we come into the saving knowledge of Jesus Christ, everything becomes new, including us. We become new creatures in Him. (II Corinthians 5:17) Suddenly, the scales fall off our eyes, and we see things in a new, more vivid, more revealing light. Eldridge Cleaver's discovery, the melting of his "soul on ice", is as old as Zacchaeus, as new as today. And every day others find the path that changes everything. It's verification that both the Word and its Author are alive and well in this 20th century.

Thanks be to God for His unspeakable gift. (II Corinthians 9:15)

 "Blessed are those who have not seen and yet believe." **John 20:29**

"I only believe in what I can see," a brash, young sailor once told a minister who tried to talk to him about God. Then, on his next voyage the sailor's ship was sunk by a mist-shrouded iceberg, most of which floated beneath the surface of the water. Fortunately, he was rescued and lived to reconsider his views on the reality of unseen things.

Some of the most real things in life are invisible and untouchable until they become manifest in people's lives. Redemption and atonement were empty words until God sent His only Son to earth. Christ's birth, His preaching, His teaching, His healing, His ministry and His sacrificial death brought new meaning to them as well as some other abstract words—faith, hope and love.

If you have come into the saving knowledge of Jesus Christ, nothing is more real than His love, nothing more essential to your present and future well-being. It's as the old hymn says, "Once I was blind, but now I can see; the light of the world is Jesus."

When doubts assail our faith, Lord, send Your revealing light.

5 **"A faithful friend is a strong defense; and he that hath found such a one hath found a treasure."**
Aprocrypha

The late Senator Everett Dirksen of Illinois was a man of strong opinions, and he often expressed them forcefully when debating proposed legislation on the floor of the Senate. Yet despite his outspokenness, he was well respected by the "Loyal Opposition," and he had deep affection for friends "on the other side of the aisle."

While writing a book about the senator several years ago, I asked him how he'd been able to maintain such good relations with his opponents.

"Because," he explained, "I make it a point to separate a person from his politics."

There is much wisdom in that statement. Too often we are alienated from others because we wrap them and their viewpoints in the same blanket. Christ was one who could separate the sin from the sinner, and we need to learn to do the same.

When someone's words or actions offend you, try to see the reason behind them. Don't write off a person just because you disagree with him. Depersonalize debates and you'll win much more than an argument.

Lord, help us see the Christ in others,
Give us love for them like brothers.

 Be Thou my vision, O Lord of my heart;
Naught be all else to me, save that Thou art. ·
                                        Irish hymn

Speaking of Senator Everett Dirksen as I was yesterday, I am reminded of a personal experience of spiritual healing that he told me about. It occurred in 1948 while he was still in the House of Representatives. One day he noticed that the sight in one eye was blurred, so he went to a specialist and learned it was serious. In fact, consultation with more specialists resulted in the unanimous conclusion that he would lose the sight in the ailing eye, and that it should be removed.

When the time came for the operation, the Senator took a train from Washington to Baltimore, but when he got to John Hopkins Hospital, he told the surgeons he was not going through with the operation.

"Why?" they asked disbelievingly.

"Because I've been to another doctor."

"Who?" they inquired.

"The Big Doctor," said Dirksen. "Coming over on the train I got down on my knees and had a little talk with the Lord, and I am not going through with this operation."

After a period of rest, Dirksen's sight improved, and he decided to run for the Senate. He won not only that battle, but also the one for his sight. The eye that doctors had wanted to remove was fully restored.

The Psalmist wrote, "he that dwelleth in the secret place of the most High shall abide under the shadow of the Almighty." (Psalm 91:1) If you ever have been tested to the limit, you know how true that verse is. If not, take it from those who have trod that dark valley, God is more than able to sustain you.

Help us see beyond the superficial things of life, Father, and give us an inner vision that results in deeper faith.

7 "Be ye strong therefore, and let not your hands be weak: for your work shall be rewarded."
II Chronicles 15:7

One thing is for certain—no, two. Everyone alive has problems (they are a condition of being alive) and some people cope with problems better than others.

A friend in Ohio tells me she uses the "cookie jar" method of dealing with her concerns. "Whenever something is bothering me, I go to the cupboard and take down my cookie jar. That's where I keep my problems—on little slips of paper." The woman explained that whenever she is anxious about something, she makes a written note of the worry, prays about it and places the note in the cookie jar.

"About once a month, I sort through the problems and remove the resolved ones. I mark them P.T.L. (Praise the Lord). Then, I tear them up and throw them away. It's amazing how many of my prayers are answered in a month."

Today, write some worry or concern or need that you have in the space below (or begin your own cookie-jar collection). Then pray about it. A month from now we'll look back and see what's happened.

Father, I know You love me and want to free me from worry, so show me how to handle this problem.

 The greatest sermon I ever heard
Was sung to me by a wounded bird.
F.B.

"I have been sick most of the winter," a DAILY GUIDEPOSTS reader wrote me recently, "and spiritually I had hit rock bottom. My prayers didn't seem to reach any higher than my head. Then one cold day, returning from the mailbox, I saw something strange in the yard. Looking closer, I discovered several *snowdrops*, those little white bell-shaped flowers with bowed heads, blooming in the middle of a patch of ice. Suddenly, God spoke to me through those flowers: 'Keep going even though it's difficult,' I heard Him say. 'It wasn't easy for these flowers to make it through the ice, but I sustained them, and I will do the same for you.' "

Nature has a way of articulating some of life's greatest truths. German theologian Paul Tillich said that God is "the ground of all being," (which I interpret to mean that God is at the root of all life) and nothing witnesses more to that fact than a fragile snowdrop fighting through frozen soil. When you are ill or worried or depressed, remove yourself from people and the noise of the world long enough to hear God speak through flowers and trees, sky and sea, animals and birds. You may find in them a parable applicable to your problem.

Lord, give me the discernment to recognize Your many faces.

 **"Though I am weak, yet God, when prayed,
Cannot withold His conquering aid."**
Ralph Waldo Emerson

The cost of sending a first-class letter has risen in my lifetime from three cents to five cents to eight cents to ten cents to thirteen cents. I hesitate writing this because, before the ink is dry on this page, the price may escalate further. In fact someone recently predicted that if things continue the way they are, a 50-cent letter may come to pass.

Last week while on a speaking trip, I tried to make a local phone call, but was unable to complete it because I had deposited only a dime. The rate had been increased recently to 20 cents. Inflation seems to spare nothing or no one. Still, there is one form of communication that has never known a rate hike: and that is the charge for praying to God.

It doesn't cost any more today to send a prayer than it did 100 years ago or 5,000. And there has been no cutback in service. God is on call 24-hours a day for all customers. Considering the help available and the bargain it represents, it is surprising more people don't try to reach Him more often.

We need Thee every hour, most precious Savior.

 "The beauty seen is partly in him who sees it."
Christian Nevell Bovee

A statue honoring Anne Frank, the Dutch teenager whose World War II diary won her worldwide fame, was unveiled last year in Amsterdam near the canal house where she and her Jewish family took refuge with sympathetic Christians. After two years of hiding, the Otto Frank family was discovered, captured and imprisoned by the Nazis. Anne died in 1945 in the Belsen concentration camp at the age of 15.

Several years ago I recall visiting the house where the Franks hid out and reading photostatic copies of pages taken from the sensitive and courageous girl's diary. Of all the things she wrote, nothing has stayed with me as much as this line: "In spite of everything, I think people are really good at heart."

That's quite a testimony of faith when one considers the circumstance in which it was written. But it is full of insight. When you begin to think the opposite—that most everyone is inconsiderate, uncaring, unloving, materialistic, self-serving—look again, closer. All about you are people who give of their time, talent and financial resources without thought of return—rescue squad workers, volunteer firemen, church workers, social service aides, Girl Scout and Boy Scout leaders, Little League coaches, school and hospital volunteers. Their treasure is not vulnerable to moth and rust and thieves (Matthew 6:20), and neither will yours if you do likewise.

There is much to be positive about, Lord. Help me see life's bright side.

"Love is an image of God, and not a lifeless image, but the living essence of the divine nature which beams full of all goodness."
Martin Luther

Dwight L. Moody told the story about a man who fell off a bridge into a river and was drowning. A group of hand-wringing people gathered at the scene, but no one made a move to help. Then a young man came by. He looked down into the water, exclaimed, "That's my brother Tom!" Without hesitation, he dived in, swam to the sinking man and saved him.

Sometimes we are guilty of passivity when we see others in trouble—spiritual or physical. We weigh their plights as objectively as a banker would a loan applicant's collateral. Cain's question "Am I my brother's keeper?" (Genesis 4:9) has the same answer today as it did then. "Yes," Christ said when He healed the leper. "Yes," He said when He fed the 5,000. "Yes," He said with the parable of the Good Samaritan.

There are brothers and sisters all around who need your help and love. Because of the light you've received, you have light to share. You can give help without fear of being emptied; you can love without fear of being hurt; and you can serve without any thought of reward.

Remove our chains of self-interest, Father, and inspire us to risk ourselves for others.

The year's at the spring
The day's at the morn;
Morning's at seven;
The hillside's dew-pearled;
The lark's on the wing;
The snail's on the thorn;
God's in his heaven—
All's right with the world.
Robert Browning

"The daffodils are blooming!"
That's what one of my children announced excitedly yester-

day, and sure enough, when I went to the southeast corner of the house, there nestled in a bed of leaves were four beautiful yellow blossoms. Every year about this time my winter-weary soul gets a lift from these early blooms.

Flowers in spring are a symbol of faith for me, a reminder that even though I may be out of synchronization with life on occasion, the earth is on schedule, in order, meeting its annual cyclical timetable. Some flinch at the last two lines of Robert Browning's famous poem above and call him naive. Didn't he see the poverty, the sickness, the hunger, the misery that smothers some of humankind in an endless winter of hopelessness? Of course he did, but it didn't blind him to the breathtaking beauty of God's creations. Hopefully, you haven't lost your ability to appreciate such gifts either.

Still, we all go through periods when our faith is low and hope seems futile. When this happens, remember that like dormant plants in winter, you don't await spring in vain. To all who hold on, persevere in their faith, God promises renewal, rebirth. It is as sure as the return of the daffodils each spring.

Give me the faith to believe, Lord, even when the visible evidence fills me with doubt.

 " . . . For God has said, 'I will never, never fail you nor forsake you.' "
Hebrews 13:5, L.B.

One night about this time last year, the farm house of a plains-state family caught on fire and soon was enveloped in flames. Fortunately, a barking dog roused the parents and the three children, and they all escaped through second-story windows. A short time later, the frame structure collapsed as it burned to the ground.

People who are spiritually attuned might be inclined to thank God for delivering the family, intimating that His hidden hand may have awakened the dog. Agnostics might attribute the result to good luck or fate.

All I know is that my Bible tells me I am a child of God and that my Heavenly Father loves me and will protect me. If you can accept that premise, believe His promise to always be with you, then you need never fear or worry about tragedy in your life again. You can put such thoughts totally out of your mind, because they will have lost their power to frighten you. He is the master of the elements—flames, ice, floods—and will protect you in His everlasting arms.

When I grow anxious and darkness fills my soul, send Your all-pervasive light, Lord.

14

At night, my weary body aches,
My mind is torn by questions deep,
But while I rest my Father takes
And mends my raveled soul with sleep.
F.B.

I am writing this passage in the early stillness of morning. It is a good time to be at my desk before others are up and while my mind is still fresh from the night's rest.

Sometimes I think the Bible gives all the good press, all the good promotion, to light and none to darkness. If I were Darkness, I'd ask for equal time because night does have its virtues. After a long day, it closes off that which has gone before; it blots out unfinished business by drawing a curtain between work and leisure.

Then comes healing sleep. What is more restorative than a sound night's sleep, free of worry and doubt? God was good to light the darkness, but He was wise not to eliminate it, because it is in that blackness that we are rested, restored, renewed. Now in this morning quiet, I am grateful to Him for rest that has cleared my mind and stirred my creativity.

Thank You, Lord, for providing daily the healing touch my body and soul need.

15 Six words are needed
    to keep love in glory,
Three are, "I love you,"
    Three more: "I am sorry."
                                    F.B.

A couple of years ago, I was taking an evening walk with my wife when a jogger ran by. Belatedly, I recognized the man as Erich Segal, the author of the best-selling book LOVE STORY. A professor of English, he was at that time teaching at a college nearby. I'm sorry now that I didn't break into a trot and try to catch up with him because I've wanted to tell him something ever since I read his book, which contained the often quoted line, "Love means never having to say you're sorry."

The truth, I would argue, is that love means always saying you're sorry—today, tomorrow, whenever or however often it is required. The reason is simple enough: We all are guilty of offenses against each other—sins of omission and sins of commission. We commit them every day, even against people we love deeply. Forgiveness—asking and granting—is a part of the prayer Christ taught His disciples to pray, and it should be a part of our daily life. As Alexander Pope noted long ago, "To err is human, to forgive divine."

Today, Lord, give us the insight to see our mistakes and the courage to correct them.

16 Praise God, from whom all blessings flow,
    Praise Him, all creatures here below;
Praise Him above, ye heavenly hosts;
    Praise Father, Son and Holy Ghost.
                                    Doxology

Tomorrow is the date set aside for the wearing of the green, and more often than not shamrocks will be much in evidence whenever people gather to salute St. Patrick, patron saint of Ireland.

Though most view the clover-shaped shamrock as an Irish symbol of good luck, St. Patrick found another use for it as he traveled the length and breadth of Ireland, evangelizing the country for Christ. The famous saint used the shamrock whenever he talked about the Trinity, labeling the three lobes, "Father, Son and Holy Ghost."

Whether or not St. Patrick ever heard this ancient Irish blessing, I don't know, but it is one of the most beautiful adieus ever written. Maybe you can find someone to share it with tomorrow:

> *May the road rise to meet you,*
> *May the wind be always at your back,*
> *May the sun shine warm upon your face,*
> *The rains fall soft upon your fields and,*
> *Until we meet again,*
> *May God hold you in the palm of His hand.*

17

(St. Patrick's Day)
I will sing the wondrous story of the Christ who died for me,
How He left His home in glory, for the cross of Calvary.

F.H. Rowley hymn

When St. Patrick was a boy of 16, he was taken prisoner near his home of Dumbarton, Scotland, by a band of Irish pirates, and sold into slavery. And it was as an indentured servant in Ireland that Patrick worked for the next six years until he escaped and returned to Scotland.

By this time he had decided to enter religious work and began studying for the priesthood. When it came time for an assignment, Patrick chose to return to the country where he'd been imprisoned and his wish was granted. According to Church history, one of the first actions he took upon arriving in Ireland was to go to his old master's home and pay him the price of his freedom. The man was so impressed by Patrick's act that he became a Christian as a result.

Such payment would seem to have a spiritual parallel. God, though creator of man, sent His only Son to reconcile Himself with His creation. Christ's sacrificial death for our sins would seem as unnecessary a payment as St. Patrick's. Yet, in such acts we see the ultimate expression of love. "Greater love hath no man," we read in John (15:13), "than he lay down his life for a friend." Your freedom was bought by such a loving Heavenly Father.

Lord, we realize a love so amazing demands our all.

 "Be not overcome of evil, but overcome evil with good."

Romans 12:21

Not long ago, two prominent athletes interrupted a televised football game to engage in a fight. Millions watched their display of lost tempers.

After they were separated by other players and officials, one of the men yelled after the other, "I'll get even with you later."

His words were a reminder to me of the deep wounds that often result when we let our temper boil over. Whatever the reason for an argument, the more heated the debate, the longer it usually takes to repair the damage.

Do you hold any hatred or ill will for past injustices inflicted upon you? Such feelings are cancerous in that they are consuming diseases, capable of destroying you. Two points could be made about violent behavior, emotional or physical. First, avoid being drawn into it if at all possible. Some people claim to enjoy "a good fight," but in truth there is no such thing. Second, if a battle already has taken place and hard feelings are the result, cut your losses! Don't expand the disagreement, but rather seek ways to contain it, to heal it. If you are even partly responsible for the condition that exists, forget retribution and concentrate on restitution. If that seems difficult, ask God to show you how.

Knocking down walls that divide us is the work of Christians, Lord. Give us the courage to move in where angels fear to tread.

19

(Palm Sunday)
Outside the holy city, unnumbered
    footsteps throng
And crowded mart and streets of trade,
    fling back a swelling song.
The voices echo nearer, in flaming hope
    they sing
"Throw down your branches at His feet,
    Hosanna to the King!"
                    James Gordon Gilkey

When I think of the residents of Jerusalem cutting palm fronds to wave and lay at the feet of Jesus for His triumphal entry into their city (Matthew 21:8), I am reminded of a palm-tree trimming job I undertook one hot summer in Englewood Beach, Florida. Nearly 300 palms stood on our property, and they were badly in need of pruning. Several dead fronds drooped from each tree.

Getting a tall ladder and a cutting tool, I climbed 16 to 18 feet and then chopped loose old branches from each tree. It was long, hot and arduous work. An ecologically wise neighbor advised us to embed the old foliage in the beach as a deterrent against erosion, which we did. Like sea oats and other vegetation, it served as a helpful retainer of sand. And all summer long I saw those dead palm fronds waving in the sea breeze and heard their brittle scraping against each other.

Long after the last hosanna for Christ had faded away and the passion story had run its course, I wonder what kind of memories the people of Jerusalem had when they saw those ragged palm fronds lying about. Did they feel foolish for having taken part in such a celebration? Did they sorrow over Christ's death? Or did they merely look past the dead palm branches to other duties of life?

That's the problem with many of us in our spiritual dedication. We wave our palm fronds zealously for a while and shout lusty hosannas for a season; then we forget their reason until some setback comes that requires a faith greater than our everyday variety. In this high holy season, it is good for you and me to take stock of our commitment and, having done so, to rededicate ourselves to the high calling of Christ.

Give me a steadfast faith, Lord, not one that ebbs and flows like the tides.

20 (Holy Week)
"Except the Lord build the house, they labour in vain that build it."

Psalm 127:1

There is a striking chronology of events that took place the last week of Christ's life, and we will touch on a few of them in the next few days. After Jesus' triumphant entry into Jerusalem, He went to the temple and cleansed it by throwing out the merchants and money changers.

"My house shall be called the house of prayer," He told them (Matthew 21:13), "but ye have made it a den of thieves." Then, He healed the blind and lame who came to Him, and again He was hailed, "Hosanna (which means 'save us') to the Son of David."

Now, it is not hard to imagine the priests' reaction to all of this. They were not impressed one iota by the "wonderful things" He had done. Instead they were "sore displeased." In other words, they wanted this disturber of the peace, this prophet without credentials removed. After all, the temple benefited considerably from the commercial enterprises to which Jesus objected.

There is great insight into human nature in this passage, and the question of how the house of God shall be used is still with us. Obviously, when it becomes a commercial place of business, as the temple in Jerusalem was, its purpose is an abomination. Jesus refers to it as "a house of prayer," and I think we could say without argument that prayer is one of its principal functions. Christ also used it as a house of healing right after upsetting the tables. A third use must surely be as a house of fellowship where believers can gather to meet and worship and hear God's word proclaimed.

If you need direction in your life, if you need strength or healing, chances are good you'll find it where people who love God gather to worship Him.

Give us the right spirit, Lord, when we enter Your house of worship and help us keep it when we leave.

(Holy Week)
" . . . And though I have all faith, so that I could remove mountains, and have not charity (love) I am nothing."
I Corinthians 13:2

The next day following the ruckus in the temple, Jesus returned and spoke with the chief priests and elders. They were bent on trapping Him into committing some blasphemy, because they sought cause to charge Jesus. But Christ, speaking often in parables, saw through their strategy and outwitted them.

One of the questions put to Him by a lawyer was this: "Master, which is the greatest commandment in the law?" (Matthew 22:36) Jewish law was composed of some 3,600 commandments, so Jesus had quite a selection to choose from. But His answer is free of legalistic "thou shalt nots."

Instead He replies with a statement that more than anything else captures the essence of His revolutionary ministry: "Thou shalt love the Lord thy God with all thy heart and with all thy soul, and with all thy mind. This is the first and greatest commandment. And the second is like unto it, thou shalt love thy neighbor as thyself."

In this week of reflection on the last days of Christ's earthly life, it is well for us to examine our lives and measure how close we are living to that injunction.

Fill us with Your Holy Spirit, Lord, otherwise our love will be inconsistent.

22 (Holy Week)
"But of that day and hour knoweth no man
. . . therefore, what I say unto you I say
unto all, watch."

Mark 13:32, 37

As His days dwindled down to a precious few, Christ—like a dying man talking to his children—discoursed with His disciples about the future. One of His admonitions was spiritual readiness, "for in such an hour as ye think not, the Son of man cometh." (Matthew 24:44) Then He told the parable of ten virgins—five wise and five foolish who attended a wedding.

When they went forth to meet the bridegroom, five took oil for their lamps and five did not. So when the bridegroom came, five were ready and five were not. The five foolish virgins went off to buy oil, but while they were gone the other five went in with the bridegroom to the marriage, closing the door on the others. When the unprepared virgins returned and called, "Lord, Lord, open to us," He answered, "I know you not."

Because life is a fragile reed, a flute whose note is of uncertain length, the Bible advises us again and again to be prepared for the future. Every day people come to the end of this road of life. Some are wise like the virgins who came to the marriage prepared. They are the ones who live each day fully, serving and praising God. They are grateful for all His gifts and they trust Him implicitly with their future. "I know not what the future holds," goes the hymn, "but I know Who holds the future." If you do, you have an oil-filled lamp.

You have given us light, Lord; keep us from hiding it under a bushel.

23 (Holy Week)
Love divine, all loves excelling,
Joy of heaven to earth come down,
Fix in us Thy humble dwelling,
All thy faithful mercies crown.

Charles Wesley hymn

The next-to-the-last day of Jesus' life has three principal settings where the drama unfolds. The first is the upper room of a house in Jerusalem where Christ and His disciples have the Last Supper. The second is in the Garden of Gethsemane, outside the city, where Jesus goes to pray and where Judas later betrays Him. The last is in the presence of Caiaphas, the chief priest, who along with other members of the Sanhedrin interrogates Jesus before charging Him with blasphemy, a crime punishable by death.

All of the players in this cast seem to act in character save one. That is Judas. He makes a 180-degree turn. Though it would be easy to write him off as an opportunistic ingrate or one who becomes disenchanted with a Christ who can't or won't set up His kingdom now, these reasons seem too slight, too simplistic.

I read with interest a recent comment of Anthony Burgess, the British novelist who wrote the screenplay for the six-hour TV production "Jesus of Nazareth."

To say that Judas was simply a thief Burgess finds inadequate. Instead he sees him as a complex mix—"sweet innocent, Higher Zealot, indiscreet blabber, disappointed man, but never an easy melodramatic villain."

One thing is for certain: Judas erred and upon realizing his mistake he was so full of guilt that he could not live with himself. What he forgot was that Jesus could have forgiven him even for his betrayal. Apparently Judas had not been listening when Christ gave His Sermon on the Mount and told His listeners, "Love your enemies, bless them that curse you, do good to them that hate you, and pray for them which despitefully use you, and persecute you." (Matthew 5:44)

What about us when we sin and come short of God's glory? "If we confess our sins," we read in I John 1:9, "he is faithful and just to forgive us our sins and cleanse us from *all* unrighteousness." It is important that we note the word "all." It is an unqualified and unconditional promise we should never forget.

Remind us when we fail, Lord, that no sin is beyond Your forgiveness.

73

24

(Good Friday)
"Then said Jesus, 'Father, forgive them; for they know not what they do.' "

Luke 23:34

On the final day of Christ's life, events move quickly to a conclusion. There is a trial which results in Pilate acquiescing to the mob's demand that Barabbas, a murderer, be released, and Jesus, an innocent, be crucified. There is a procession to Golgotha with Jesus at the head of the march followed by Simon of Cyrene who carries His cross and a group of women who are crying over Jesus' sentence. And finally there is the crucifixion at Calvary which Luke describes in just 15 verses (23:32-46).

If one views the crucifixion at face value, it is a tragedy clear and simple, a miscarriage of justice, the death of a good and guiltless man. But in reality, when Jesus went willingly to the cross as a redemptive lamb, the event was God's moment of greatest glory, His ultimate triumph, His completion of reconciliation with His estranged creation, man.

Of all the words Christ uttered at the end, none rings down through history with the thundering impact of His 10-word prayer on the cross: "Father, forgive them; for they know not what they do." This statement tells us like no other that God's love is without limits, that He understands our lack of understanding, that His grace is without equal, that His willingness to forgive us is beyond all human comprehension.

Father, forgive us for our ingratitude.

25

Lift up your heads, ye sorrowing ones
And be ye glad at heart.
For Calvary and Easter Day,
Earth's saddest day and gladdest day,
Were just three days apart.

attributed to Susan Coolidge

Though the Passover feast was in progress (it lasted from sunset Friday until Sunday morning), the day following Jesus' crucifixion must have been a tortuous one for His confused and sorrowing followers. In less than a week their dreams had vanished. What had happened? What had gone wrong? Where would they go from here?

Peter, in particular, must have been beside himself with remorse and guilt. Christ had forecast that Peter would deny Him three times and though the disciple could not believe it at the time, he did indeed disassociate himself from the Master three times.

But Peter was not alone in his mental anguish. It was a dismally long day for all of those who had put their faith in Jesus. Their fear was that it had been a misplaced faith. Wasn't Jesus dead?

When you and I face defeat, loss or sorrow, our faith is apt to flag, too. It is human nature. Yet, we learn from experience that it is darkest before the dawn, and that if we hold on to our convictions just a little longer, God will fill the vacuum. When you feel like giving up, don't. Jesus promised He would not leave us comfortless (John 14:18) and He has kept His promise.

We thank You for Your Holy Spirit, Lord, ever near, ever supporting.

(Easter Sunday)
**Up from the grave He arose,
With a mighty triumph o'er His foes;
He arose a victor from the dark domain,
And He lives forever with His saints to reign;
He arose! He arose! Hallelujah! Christ arose!**
Robert Lowry hymn

Writing for *Guideposts* recently, Marjorie Holmes told about the heartbreak she felt when she looked into her adolescent son's room one morning and discovered that he had run away. She drew a poignant analogy between his empty room and Jesus' empty tomb.

Taken completely by surprise, Marjorie and her husband were filled with guilt and fear and all the empty feelings other parents have experienced under similar circumstances. And it took many months of soul-searching and spiritual growth before they could come to terms with the estrangement. Eventually, Marjorie said, they put the matter in God's hands, and not long thereafter, the son returned safe and unharmed. The depth of joy at such a reunion is hard to comprehend.

On this climactic day in our Holy Week story, Mary Magdalene stood outside the empty sepulchre and wept. (John 20:11-15) Two angels in white were in the places where Christ had lain.

"Woman, why weepest thou?" she was asked.

"Because they have taken away my Lord," Mary answered, "and I know not where they have laid Him." Then Jesus appeared unto her and called her by name.

It's hard to imagine what first thoughts must have passed through her mind. But when she realized that she wasn't dreaming she must have been filled with unparalleled joy. With the father in the Prodigal Son parable, she could have said, "He was dead and is alive again."

That is the victory that we Christians share on Easter, Christ's victory over death.

Because You live, Lord, we have no reason to fear the future.

**Oh, Jesus is a Rock in a weary land,
A shelter in the time of storm.**
Ira D. Sankey hymn

With federal income tax deadline approaching, one reads and hears much about how to figure deductions, write off expenses and protect income from taxation. Accountants and tax experts earn large fees for showing people in high tax brackets how to find good tax shelters.

Now, obviously, there is nothing wrong with knowing and applying tax laws which minimize one's taxes. However, the thought strikes me when I hear a word like "shelter" that many businessmen and women may spend considerably more time looking for a haven for their money than they do for their souls.

Jesus had a distressing report for a rich farmer whose preoccupation must have been material wealth. According to the parable, the man's land was so fruitful that he had to build bigger and bigger barns in which to hold the harvest. "Thou fool," Christ said. "This night thy soul shall be required of thee." (Luke 12:20) The point the Master was making has nothing to do with the evils of money or possessions as some would have us believe, but rather with priorities. When we put other things ahead of Him and take refuge there, then you and I have chosen the wrong shelter.

Lord, help me to look to You for my strength and security, not to the transient treasures of the world.

 "Before God can deliver us, we must undeceive ourselves."
St. Augustine

Not long ago there was a story in my newspaper about a supermarket charged with deceptively labelling packages of meats. According to the story, cheaper grades had been identified as better ones, making the buyer think he or she was getting better quality for the price than was the case.

Unfortunately, Christians are also sometimes guilty of deceptive labelling practices, and too often the object they represent as being of better quality than is the case is themselves. Jesus had little tolerance for people who presented themselves as more holy and more self-righteous than was the fact. You will recall that in Matthew (23:28), He told the Pharisees that though they appeared outwardly righteous, they were inwardly full of iniquity.

There is a thin, but distinguishable, line between healthy

self-esteem and boastful self-aggrandizement. The prophet Micah gave us timeless advice on how we should conduct ourselves when he wrote: "What doth the Lord require of thee, but to do justly, and to love mercy, and to walk humbly with thy God?" (Micah 6:8) That may be a large order, but it is the goal in a nutshell.

Keep us from vain words and actions, Lord, because we know they are barriers between us and You and others.

 "The truest end of life is to know the life that never ends."

William Penn

One of my first jobs on a newspaper was writing obituary notices, an assignment reporters usually try to avoid. But I found the information that summarized a person's life quite fascinating, and to this day I read the obituary columns with regularity.

In today's paper, for example, I read of one Erwin Mueller's death. His name was not familiar to me, and I doubt it was to many outside the scientific community. However, the obituary of the German-born physicist and Penn State professor revealed that he was the developer of a field ion microscope that enabled him (in 1955) to become the first person ever to view an atom.

If your life were to come to an end today, what would be said about you? More important, what would God's record show of your contribution to others? In Matthew (25:31-46) Christ says that on the day of judgment those who fed the hungry, gave drink to the thirsty, clothed the naked, sheltered strangers and visited those in prisons will be rewarded with eternal life.

For many of us, the day is getting late, and it's time we got busy.

Show me how to make each day of my life count for You, Lord.

30

"A poor man served by thee shall make
 thee rich;
A sick man helped by thee shall make thee
 strong;
Thou shalt be served thyself by every sense
Of service which thou renderest."
Elizabeth Barrett Browning

I don't know about groundhogs' shadows, but I do know that when I see a robin this time of year my hopes for warmer weather mount. Yesterday, as I was driving near the lake, I saw one and could not wait to report the news to my children. Speaking of children and robins, there is a little story about this bird which was no doubt written for kids.

According to the fable, a robin was on the scene at the stable, observing the exciting 'activities that surrounded the birth of Jesus. While the newborn baby was sleeping—warmed by a small fire—the undistinguished brown-feathered bird watched in awe. Suddenly, he noticed the fire was dying. The baby would grow cold. Flying to the coals, he hovered over them and began fanning them with his wings. It was tough work, but the flames were revived. All through the night, whenever the fire dimmed, the bird returned; thus the Christ Child stayed warm. When the sun rose, the tired bird flew off to rest, but his friends were amazed. No longer was he a plain brown; now he had a blazing red breast, and that—according to the legend—is how the robin won its colorful marking.

I like the little story not only because it suggests God rewards faithful service (which He certainly does), but because when I look at a robin I am reminded that there are hundreds of little tasks to which I'm called each day. When I respond, they don't always produce an outward change as vivid as the robin's red breast, but they do change me inwardly. When you serve others, your selfless acts witness outwardly to the inward change Christ has made in your life; and you, too, will receive a warm blessing for your gifts.

We realize, Lord, that we can never outgive You; the more we serve, the more we are served.

31

There was ninety and nine that safely lay,
In the shelter of the fold,
But one was out on the hills away,
Far off from the gates of gold.
Away on the mountains wild and bare,
Away from the tender Shepherd's care.

                                    Ira D. Sankey hymn

Stories behind famous hymns are sometimes as moving as the hymns themselves. The famous lines above were found in a newspaper while Dwight L. Moody and his soloist Ira D. Sankey were on a train traveling to services in Edinburgh, Scotland. Sankey showed the poem to Moody, who glanced at it but was unimpressed.

A few nights later, Moody spoke on the subject of "The Good Shepherd" and, after finishing, turned to Sankey for a number on this theme. Sankey shrugged, then remembered the poem. Digging through his notes, he found the clipping and placed it on the organ's music stand. Suddenly, inspiration came to him, and he began to play the tune that has since become familiar to millions. It is a beautiful hymn, full of the love and compassion we know to be characteristic of our Good Shepherd. One cannot sing the lyrics of "The Ninety and Nine" or read the parable of the lost sheep (Matthew 18:11-14) without the realization that we have a personal Savior who cares deeply for each of us.

To know that each of us is important to You, Lord, gives us courage and comfort.

APRIL 1978

S	M	T	W	T	F	S
						1
2	3	4	5	6	7	8
9	10	11	12	13	14	15
16	17	18	19	20	21	22
23	24	25	26	27	28	29
30						

Believe. That one word taken to heart can change your life. Believe in God's power to transform you and situations around you. Believe in yourself and the talents God gave you. Believe and there is no limit to what you can accomplish. This month say, "I believe I can" whenever a challenge arises, and expect spectacular results.

APRIL 1978

1 "The foolishness of God is wiser than men; and the weakness of God is stronger than men."
I Corinthians 1:25

"Your shoe's untied," my young son giggled, trying to keep a straight face and play a joke on me. I went through the motions of looking at my shoes.

"April Fool," he squealed with delight.

No one minds being called a fool on April 1, yet it's something else the other 364 days. In fact, most of us go to great lengths to prove just the opposite. Even so, we all make daily errors in judgment that cost us time or money. Most of them aren't of great consequence, but what of foolish behavior that has "whole life" implications? A case in point is the parable in the New Testament about a farmer who worshiped his wealth. He put his treasure in more barns to hold the tons and tons of grain he must have owned. And most certainly he considered his action wise . . . "just putting a little away for a rainy day," he probably reasoned. But God said, "Thou fool, this night thy soul shall be required of thee." (Luke 12:20)

He apparently was a materialistic fool, one who relished his wealth. If you have become God-conscious and know that His kingdom is built on more lasting things, don't fall into a similar trap. Life is too short for you and me to spend our time hoarding His gifts. It is not just unspiritual, it's foolish.

Give us wisdom, Lord, to separate wheat from chaff.

 "For the thing which I greatly feared is come upon me. . . ." Job 3:25

In *The Wizard of Oz*, the Cowardly Lion tells Dorothy that he is so frightened of things that he hasn't slept in weeks.

"Have you tried counting sheep?" the Tin Man asks.

"No," cries the Lion, "I'm afraid of them."

Though there is great humor in this exchange, there is also a lot of insight. The insight is that many generalizations in life don't hold up. A lion is supposed to be the king of the jungle, afraid of no person or thing, lionhearted, but this particular one was afraid of his own shadow.

Fear is something we all know on a first-name basis. Some of us are afraid to speak in a group, others of us are fearful of new undertakings, still others are frightened by storms, the dark, extreme heights, extreme depths, closed-in places.

Whatever our fears, it is good to know there is someone who understands them and will help us allay them. Your Heavenly Father told His disciples, "Lo, I am with you always, even unto the end of the world." (Matthew 28:20) So, if you know the One who made that promise, you have nothing to fear.

When our hearts beat fast from fear, Lord, quiet us and help us remember that You are in charge.

 "For as he thinketh in his heart, so is he." Proverbs 23:7

Professional hockey goalies (the heavily padded players who guard the goals) have for several years now worn face masks to protect them from fast-flying pucks.

But last season Gilles Gratton, the New York Rangers, goalie, added a new wrinkle, a fiberglass mask which depicts a snarling lion on it. "I feel stronger wearing it," he told reporters, and it did seem to help his play.

Isn't it amazing how our minds can turn superficial things into pluses or minuses? If we see ourselves as stronger or smarter or more poised, that is invariably what we become. The opposite is true when we think on negatives.

The lesson to be learned is that the mind is a fantastically potent tool. It can work for or against us, help us achieve great victories or lead us down the road to inglorious defeat. When it comes to faith, there is unparalleled power in believing. Belief in God can revolutionize your life. Jesus told us that all things are possible to him that believes. (Mark 9:23)

Lord, give us the vision to see ourselves as You would have us be.

 "The Lord God is subtle, but malicious He is not."
Albert Einstein

Once I heard of a naturalist who went in search of the source of a mighty river. High into the mountains he climbed one spring day determined to pinpoint the origin of the flow, the headwaters. What he discovered was a trickle of water here and a trickle there, thousands of small, silent runs fingering their way from patches of ice as winter grudgingly released what it had held captive.

Over the course of human history, each generation has sought the source of its creation. Many have been as unsuccessful as the naturalist looking for the headwaters of a river. In truth, he found the stream's beginning, not in a single emphatic statement, but in a myriad of subtle whispers. That is how God often speaks to us: subtly and·in many diverse ways. It may take practice to hear the shadings and nuances of His voice, but to those who faithfully commit themselves to discovering their purpose and calling, God points the way with unmistakable clarity.

Lord, help me be quiet long enough today to hear Your voice.

5 At the cross, at the cross
Where I first saw the light,
And the burden of my heart rolled away,
It was there by faith I received my sight
And now I am happy all the day.
Fanny Crosby hymn

The story is told of a sudden storm that hit the Midwest one spring, a storm that caused severe flooding and heavy property loss. On one river alone several small bridges were damaged or washed away. At one of the crossings where a bridge had been destroyed, a hiking party searched frantically for a way back. Then one of them discovered that a large cross erected on the stream's bank, near a Christian campground, had been blown down into the water. Crawling on their hands and knees, the hikers were able to use the cross as a bridge and make it to the other side.

Many people stranded by the storms of life have found a way out of their confinement by climbing upon the cross of Calvary. It has served as a rescue point for millions of lost and dying souls. If you feel unbefriended, unappreciated, uninspired, unloved, without direction, you can find meaning and purpose at the foot of the Cross. Jesus can be your bridge over troubled waters.

When we're overwhelmed by life, Father, remind us of what Christ did for us at Calvary.

6 The King of love my Shepherd is
Whose goodness faileth never;
I nothing lack if I am His
And He is mine forever.
Henry W. Baker hymn

86

Recently, I had the pleasure of meeting singer Carol Lawrence, who rocketed to show business celebrity with her memorable performance in "West Side Story" 20 years ago. Since then much has happened to her. She's achieved success with recordings, in television and films, as well as on stage in other musical shows. In her personal life, she has married, mothered two children and, in 1976, been divorced. Most recently, she has made some gospel recordings which have effectively and beautifully witnessed to her new-found faith.

What led to her spiritual awakening? "When I realized my sons were being shortchanged spiritually," she told me, "I turned to Pat and Shirley Boone for advice. They recommended a church, which the boys and I attended and liked. But I did more than give my sons a church experience; I found a personal relationship with Christ that I'd never known before. It has revolutionized my life."

People search the world for something authentic, real, relevant, meaningful, fulfilling, without any luck. Then, they make the life-changing discovery that Carol did. If there is a vacuum in your life or in the life of someone you love, the emptiness may be a spiritual one. Neither riches nor fame nor anything else can provide the fulfillment that Christ can. Faith is the victory that overcomes the world.

You are the missing ingredient in many lives, Lord. Help us witness to the change You make.

7 **"Prayer is not conquering God's reluctance, but taking hold of God's willingness."**

Phillips Brooks

A month ago, I told you about the Ohio lady who writes all her prayer concerns on slips of papers and places them in a cookie jar. Then once a month she reviews her petitions to see how God has answered them.

On March 7, I asked you to write down some problem or need and pray about it. Now I'd like you to turn back to that page (or if you wrote your note on a separate paper, please find it.) Has the problem been resolved? (My Ohio correspondent marks her answered prayers P.T.L.—Praise the Lord—and throws the papers away.)

If the answer is yes, I'd like to hear about it. Write me in care of Guideposts, Carmel, New York, 10512. If your need has lessened only slightly or is still unmet, restate it again on paper and ask God if there is some action you should take to help. Believe the problem is going to clear up; anticipate its resolution. If you have faith as a grain of mustard seed, the Bible says, nothing is impossible. (Matthew 17:20)

Thank You for answered prayers, Lord.

 "A foolish man . . . which built his house upon the sand: And the rain descended, and the floods came, and the winds blew, and beat upon that house; and it fell: and great was the fall of it." Matthew 7:26,27

A friend of mine talked of building a house on a low-lying piece of property that bordered a beautiful tumbling brook. On the face of it, the idea seemed like a good one, but a surveyor advised him that the land was on a flood plain and that he would be wise to choose higher ground. The following spring, when the snows were melting, I drove past the plot and observed that it was under water. The banks of the little stream had not been able to contain the torrent.

Some people build their lives on flood plains, gambling that the waters of adversity will not touch them. They ignore the counsel of time-wise friends and jump headlong into questionable endeavors.

How can we be sure whether or not some undertaking is right? First, we need to gather all the available information and weigh it. My friend was advised not to build on a flood plain, and by heeding a knowledgeable person he avoided much grief. God expects us to use the heads He gave us and exert all the common sense we have.

But sometimes problems are more complex and our counsel contradictory. What then? Wise Christians turn to their Heavenly Father for His direction and guidance. Is that always forthcoming? Seldom in signs as clear as burning bushes or wet fleeces (Exodus 3:2, Judges 6:38), but given time, every committed believer I've known has received help from the still, small voice that prompts all who listen. When you have a difficult decision, one that presents pluses and minuses on both sides of the question, petition God for help. He specializes in sticky wickets.

Help us wait patiently, Lord, when problems appear and ready answers aren't available.

 "Let us run with patience the race that is set before us, looking unto Jesus the author and finisher of our faith." Hebrews 12:1,2

When I was growing up there was a preacher-track star whom I idolized. His name was Gil Dodds, the holder of the world's indoor record for the mile run. He set the mark in 1948 (4 minutes, 5.3 seconds) and it stood for six years.

But what stands out in my mind is the exemplary Christian life he led. As a young man absorbed by sports, my loyalty to the church was being tested. There were so many other activities at school and in the community that vied for my time. Then I remember seeing a film in which Gil Dodds gave his testimony. "Though I love to run," he said, "Christ comes first." It helped me put things in perspective.

In February 1977, Dodds died at age 58, but many people's lives were touched by "The Flying Parson." Many young people treasured his autograph, which he always signed with the addendum, Philippians 4:13—"I can do all things through Christ which strengtheneth me."

You and I can, too, if we put our minds on the One who gives the power.

Remind us of the goal, Lord, and help us keep our eyes on it.

10

> Safe in the arms of Jesus,
> Safe on His gentle breast,
> There by His love o'ershadowed,
> Sweetly my soul shall rest.
>
> **Fanny J. Crosby**

Dr. Harry Peelor, minister of the First United Methodist Church, Palo Alto, California, tells a reassuring story of faith, helpful to anyone who is gripped by a fear of death.

It is about John Todd of Rutland, Vermont, a Congregational minister of the mid-1800's. One day he received a letter from his aged aunt, who had raised him from age five when he was orphaned. In the letter, the woman expressed her fear of impending death. When John replied, he told of the trepidation he had felt when he was on the way to live with her, years before.

"Night fell before we finished our journey. As the darkness descended, I became more and more afraid. Finally, I said anxiously to your hired man, 'Do you think she will go to bed before we arrive?' 'Oh no,' he answered. 'She'll certainly stay up for you. When we get out of these here woods, you'll see her candle shining in the window.' Presently we did ride out of the woods and there was your candle. I remember you putting your arms around me and lifting me down from the horse, a frightened and lonely little boy. There was a fire on your hearth and warm supper on the stove. After supper you took me to my room and, after hearing my prayers, sat beside me until I went to sleep.

"You undoubtedly realize why I am now recalling all these things for you. Someday soon, God may send for you to take you to a new home. Don't fear His summons. At the end of the road you will surely find love and a welcome. You will be safe there in God's love and care. Surely He can be trusted to be as kind to you as you were years ago to me."

When we put ourselves in Your hands, Lord, we know You'll take care of us.

"There is only one real failure in life that is possible, and that is, not to be true to the best one knows." Frederick W. Farrar

Without question, failure is one of the most difficult things on earth to deal with. It fills us with inferiority feelings. It immobilizes us, hurts us, embarrasses us, costs us. Furthermore, we are likely to reject people that we consider failures for fear their circumstance is contagious and on a par with some incurable disease.

The truth is that you and I and everyone else are failures. We fail at something every day—unless we do nothing at all, and even that (doing nothing) is a form of failure. The really important thing is our average.

Experienced salesmen know that they must make a certain number of calls to reach their goal. Successful fishermen (and fisherwomen) persevere even when the fish aren't biting; they go back the next day, knowing that things average out. A baseball player will tell you that three hits in ten times at bat is excellent hitting—and that averages seven failures against three successes!

So don't get discouraged today if you make a mistake or two. Say a little prayer and launch into the next challenge. If you keep trying, you'll win on perseverance. It all averages out.

We know that faith and love make us vulnerable, Lord, but give us the courage to chance both.

 "Winter is past, the rain is over and gone: flowers appear on the earth: the time of the singing of birds is come."
Song of Solomon 2:11,12

My wife took a class recently in which the students were taught the Ukrainian way to decorate eggs for Easter. The art of coloring and making designs on eggs, I learned, is called *pysanky* and is a spring ritual that predates Christianity. But the influence of Christian symbols is readily apparent to anyone who studies the Ukrainian art. There are crosses and fishes and stars and triangles (which stand for the Trinity), crowns, nets (for fishers of men) and prayer ladders (the kind Jacob saw leading to heaven).

All around us this time of year we see symbols reminding us that we serve a living God. The greening grass, the budding trees, the migrating birds, birth and rebirth. Though there is much disorder in the world, we should take note in this most triumphant of seasons that things are in order with God. Spring is on time. God is good. Life is good.

Renew our spirits, Lord, as You do the earth after a long winter.

13

To take the prize a great thing,
To take it graciously greatest,
'Cause nothing's quite so deflating
As winners detailing their latest.
                                        F.B.

"I'm the greatest," proclaims heavyweight boxing champion Muhammad Ali with tongue-in-cheek (I think).

"World's greatest golfer," says the message on my son's T-shirt.

"The greatest daredevil in the world," says the announcer of motorcyclist Evel Knievel.

And up until quite recently, the *Chicago Tribune* hailed itself as "The World's Greatest Newspaper." For some reason, the publishers have decided to drop this self-congratulatory motto from the paper's front page.

Being the best at something may be a worthy goal in areas of measurable competition, but generally speaking doing one's best is more important. One sure way to alienate yourself from others is to intimate you are better or more intelligent or more talented than they. More often than not people who need to flaunt their superiority aren't superior. Modesty and humility are garments that never go out of style—or to draw on some timeless wisdom from the Bible, "Pride goeth before destruction and an haughty spirit before a fall." (Proverbs 16:18)

Father, help us see that there is no contradiction in being both heirs of the Kingdom and servants of the King.

14

"Alienation from self and from one's fellow man has its roots in separation from God."
Fulton J. Sheen

Nearly an acre of our lot is covered with trees, and every spring there are a few which don't leaf and need to be taken down. I cut them into sections and split the wood into fireplace logs. That's what I was doing yesterday, splitting some maple logs.

To halve a log, one needs a sledgehammer and some steel wedges. While I was pounding the wedges into the wood, the thought came to me that while wedges work to an advantage in log splitting there are other kinds of wedges that work to our disadvantage—the negative ones which come between us and God. And without exception, we are the ones who drive the wedges that separate us from our Father.

Were we to label the dividers, their names might be Jealousy, Selfishness, Greed, Dishonesty, Disobedience, Lust, Arrogance, Pride. Whatever, we must stay alert to both sins of omission and commission which open breaches between us and God. The best precaution, of course, is a close walk with the Shepherd of our faith. He knows the safe paths as well as the perilous pitfalls. Give God first place in all areas of your life, and you can keep things from coming between you and His love.

Lord, don't let anything come between You and me today.

15

"No man is really consecrated until his money is dedicated." Roy L. Smith

While in England last year, I toured a museum which had on display a wooden lectern once used by evangelist John Wesley.

It brought to mind a story about a sermon Wesley once made on stewardship. Like all good sermons, it contained three points. The first was, "Make all the money you can."

A well-to-do farmer who served the church as a deacon said, "Amen."

Point two was, "Save all the money you can."

"Amen," said the deacon even more emphatically.

"And," concluded Wesley, "give all you can."

The deacon frowned and muttered, "That spoiled the sermon."

When it comes to money, most find it more fun taking in than paying out. But the Scriptures tell us that of him who has been given much, much will be required. (Luke 12:48) I suspect that includes money as well as time and talent.

Knowing You, Lord, is knowing the Source of an unlimited supply. Teach us to share the blessings You've given us.

 "Take therefore no thought for the morrow: for the morrow shall take thought for the things of itself." Matthew 6:34

When I was a boy, the famous baseball pitcher "Satchel" Paige came to town with a barnstorming team of ballplayers for a game, and I was there to get his autograph. Though well along in years, the crafty pitcher was more than a match for any of the locals, and as I recall he struck most of them out. In addition, he entertained everyone with his droll humor.

Never at a loss for words, Satchel Paige was forever supplying sportswriters with quotable quotes. Probably his most famous one went like this: "Never look back, something may be gaining on you."

Now, you might want to challenge that thought on the grounds that looking back on pleasant happenings is great enjoyment. I certainly believe that the gift of memory is one of God's great blessings to man. But Satchel Paige was talking about worrisome glances over the shoulder. God wants us forward looking, dealing with tasks and needs at hand. When you are in the center of His will, you don't have to concern yourself with who's gaining on you or even with who's passing you. The Lord will show you when to speed up and when to slow down. If you're on His team, then you'll finish a winner and He will get you where you're supposed to be on time.

When I grow anxious about life, Father, still my heart and fill me with Your unparalleled peace.

It's giving up thoughts that breed discontent
And accepting what comes as a gift
    heaven-sent,
It's giving up wishing for things you have not
And making the best of whatever you've got.
              Helen Steiner Rice

Many months ago, I wrote to Helen Steiner Rice when I learned she was in a Cincinnati hospital. When her stay lengthened, I inquired about her progress by phone and received it through her secretary. Finally, America's most widely read inspirational poet was released, and in no time at all she sent me a long letter. She is a dedicated and indefatigable correspondent and I always enjoy hearing from her.

Her letter was filled with typical H.S.R. faith statements, among them this memorable line: "I keep struggling and striving to be worthy of the cross God has fashioned just for me." Here is a woman who has accepted the good and the bad of life with an unshakable faith. Her steadfastness may well be her greatest virtue; she certainly has communicated this message often in her poems. The excerpt above from "How to Find Happiness" is but one example.

If you spend valuable time fretting about the hand you've been dealt, wondering about the missing elements you think would make you happier, Helen's counsel may be just the thought you need. Try today to accept the good and bad, the pluses and minuses, with equanimity—that is, evenness of mind, composure, balance, self-control. The Lord is gracious and merciful (II Chronicles 30:9) and if you are faithful through thick and thin, the scales will balance in the end.

Teach us to thank You for everything, Lord, even for the crosses we must bear.

18 Finish then Thy new creation,
Pure and spotless let us be;
Let us see Thy great salvation
Perfectly restored in Thee.
Changed from glory into glory,
'Til in heaven we take our place,
'Til we cast our crowns before Thee,
Lost in wonder, love and praise.
Charles Wesley hymn, "Love Divine"

How fully are you living? Are you enjoying every day of your life or are you merely existing, waiting for some problem to clear or some good fortune to befall you? "This is the day which the Lord hath made;" we read in Psalm 118:24, "we will rejoice and be glad in it."

"Oh, that's easy for you to say, Mr. Bauer," I can hear someone replying, "but I'm old " or "I've got this troublesome mate " or "I'm suffering from arthritis " or "I'm broke " or "I'm worried." I know how difficult some problems are to overcome, but the truth is, all of life contains some elements of discord or disharmony. The difference between people is that some cope with adversity and some don't. Problems are either saddled and ridden or they saddle us. Some people have a genius for living, and they seem to find joy even when discomforted or defeated. How?

Their secret is that they're very creative, and they have fertile imaginations. When problems knock them down, they refuse to stay down. "Just you wait," these people say "I'm going to go to Easter services if I have to crawl." Or "I'm going to plant the garden come May." In other words, they refuse to give up or give in. These are the people who know "the abundant life" Christ promised to all believers. (John 10:10)

George Bernard Shaw once said that the words on the tombstone of many people should read: "Died at 30, buried at 60." Don't be one of them.

Help us take a positive view of life, Lord, positive because we have life in You.

My life is but the weaving
    Between my God and me;
I only choose the colors
    He weaveth steadily.
Sometimes He weaveth sorrow
    And I in foolish pride,
Forget He sees the upper
    And I the under side.
        Anonymous

The problems in life often drop a roadblock between us and our plans. As a result, we are left wondering, frustrated, depressed. "Why?" we ask God.

Dr. Kenneth Taylor, author of THE LIVING BIBLE (Tyndale), was an editor and minister when he inexplicably lost his voice several years ago. It curtailed his speaking and, for a while, he thought it might end his ministry. But because of this physical roadblock, he was able to concentrate on his paraphrase of the Bible and complete it much sooner than otherwise would have been the case. It is now the most popular book of our time with sales approaching 20 million at last count.

"God never closes a door, but what He opens a window" goes the old saying. Think about that today if some desire of yours seems delayed because of a lingering personal problem. Pick up the pieces of your life and reassemble them. It's never too late if you include God in your plans. He may have some new endeavor or new direction for you, one that is a thousand times better than the course you'd have selected.

When things go wrong in my life, Lord, teach me to look for blessings in disguise.

"Trust in Him at all times; ye people, pour
out your heart before Him: God is a refuge
for us." Psalm 62:8

Once there was a man who was involved in an unethical and
dishonest business venture. Eventually the law caught up with
him, and he was arrested and convicted of bribery. He admitted his guilt and threw himself on the mercy of the court.

The man's lawyer, hoping for a reduced sentence, brought
witnesses to attest to his client's character. In the course of such
laudatory evidence, it was revealed that the man tithed 10 per
cent of his ill-gotten income.

The judge interrupted upon hearing this news, asking incredulously, "You mean the defendant tried to bribe God, too?"

It is a memorable line. Sometimes in our prayers many of us
get close to bribery, trying to influence or sway God's mind,
trying to bargain with the Lord by promising something in
return for His favor.

When we engage in such prayers, we are skating on thin
spiritual ice. Mature Christians seek to know God's will, not to
impose their wishes upon Him. Remember, your Heavenly
Father loves you and wants the best for you. If you ask for bread
He will not give you a stone. (Matthew 7:9) Bribes aren't
required from children who have loving fathers, just requited
love.

Give us understanding hearts, God, so we pray wise prayers.

 "You must do the thing you think you cannot
do."   Eleanor Roosevelt

A good many professional writers that I know collect meaningful quotations and post them near their typewriters. Maybe
it is because writing is a difficult occupation, filled with its share
of criticism and rejections.

My friend Marjorie Holmes has written since she was very
young, but it wasn't until her book I'VE GOT TO TALK TO

SOMEBODY, GOD (Doubleday) was published that her popularity as a writer was achieved. She told me that once when she was struggling along she tacked up on her wall a little note of encouragement that a favorite teacher had written:

"You must make the most of your talent. If you have a strong enough desire, you can write beautiful things for people who crave beautiful things."

"A strong enough desire" is the phrase that jumps out at me because I know it can make a difference between success or failure in everyone's life. If you want to achieve some goal, some place, some pinnacle in life, you need a strong inner compulsion coupled with a strong faith to reach it. Reversals, temporary setbacks and discouragement usually come along the way, but you cannot let them derail you. If your aspirations are worthwhile and your commitment firm, you can succeed despite the hurdles. In fact, once you've reached your dream, it is the obstacles you have defeated that will make your accomplishment all the more sweet.

Reassure me that I'm on the right track, Lord, even when my wheels seem to be spinning.

22 "Speak to Him, thou, for He hears,
and Spirit with Spirit can meet—
Closer is He than breathing,
and nearer than hands and feet."
Alfred, Lord Tennyson

While working in my New York City office located on the 23rd floor of a midtown building, I recently watched two men on scaffolding wash the windows. Though dangling hundreds of feet over the street below, they seemed oblivious to any danger.

Then I noticed that each wore a safety belt that was connected to a rope independent of the scaffold. Should the cables supporting the scaffold give way, they had a lifeline that would keep them from falling.

As I watched, my palms perspiring, it came to me that you

and I have a supporting lifeline, too. It is from God, wrapped around our waists, ever present, ever protecting. Some people become aware of it only when an emergency arises. But those whose spiritual antennae have brought them into a deep consciousness of their Heavenly Father know that He is with them each day, each hour, each minute of their lives. If you are one that possesses this divine wisdom , you have a priceless possession that gives you perfect understanding of Christ's promise: " . . . My peace I give unto you: not as the world giveth, give I unto you." (John 14:27)

> *Lord, keep me daily in Your care,*
> *Free of worry and despair.*

"Nor love thy life, nor hate;
but what thou liv'st
Live well; how long or short
permit to Heav'n."

John Milton

As the town sage grew old, he was heard to express concern about death and heavenly judgment. "You are a good man, John," a friend told him, "the most honest and fair in all of Edinburgh, as wise as Moses. Why should you of all people be fearful?"

"When I die and face God in judgment," the wise man answered, "I will not be asked, 'Why were you not Moses of Israel?' but rather, 'Why were you not John of Edinburgh?' "

When it comes time to sum up our lives, to total the pluses and subtract the minuses, the only standard that counts is how well we measure up to our own potential. Christ's parable of the talents (Matthew 25:14-30) gives us a clue to the Lord's yardstick. Those who bury their assets in hopes of protecting them against loss are fools. Christ bids us invest the gifts He has given us, serving and giving to others without restraint. If we do, after we die the bottom line will report our lives profitable on all counts.

Lord, show us how to use the time You've given us wisely.

'Tween optimist and pessimist
The difference is droll:
The optimist sees the donut,
While the pessimist sees the hole.
Anonymous

The woman at the checkout counter today was beside herself with frustration. Because the line was too long, she was going to be late for her hair appointment and that would result in her being too late to get the car repaired, which would make her husband angry.

"Everything has gone wrong today," she sputtered. And in her state of mind, I doubt that she was exaggerating.

In truth, however, whether today is a good day or a bad day will depend to a large extent on the attitude you and I wrap around it. If we choose to see a broken glass, an interrupting phone call, a missed traffic light or a torn newspaper as signs that everything is going wrong today, then we will surely find much evidence throughout to support that premise.

It is to our advantage to overlook the little problems and annoyances that are part of every day for everyone and to concentrate on the reasons it is good to be alive. "This is the day which the Lord hath made; we will rejoice and be glad in it." (Psalms 118:24)

Today is full of possibilities, Lord; give me an attitude that will help uncover them.

"Come ye, and let us go up to the mountain of the Lord, to the house of the God of Jacob; and he will teach us of his ways . . . "
Isaiah 2:3

One of the toughest mountains to climb in the Appalachian chain that stretches from Alabama to Maine is Mt. Katahdin in Baxter State Park, near the Canadian border. The day my family and I tried to scale it, it was blistering hot and we were tested to the limit. Several times we thought we had reached the summit, but each time we got to what we'd figured was the end, another peak came into view. Finally, after six hours we reached the top, exhausted but proud of our accomplishment.

Often since when I've come up against difficulties that seem to string out interminably, like Mt. Katadin, I've thought back to that mountain-climbing experience. It has reinforced something I know to be indisputably true: perseverance wins. If you are having difficulty with some unreachable star, some unrelenting problem, don't lose faith. Keep climbing and keep praying, and you'll come out a victor.

In our walk with Thee, O Lord, lead us on to greater and greater heights.

 "Bless the Lord, O my soul, and forget not all His benefits: Who satisfieth thy mouth with good things; so that thy youth is renewed like the eagle's." Psalm 103:2,5

"How'd you like to take a ride on my new bike?" an enthusiastic eight-year-old asked his grandmother.

"No, I'm afraid I'd fall off," she answered.

Discretion may have been the better part of valor in this situation, but the remark brought to mind an observation someone once made about aging: *One of the reasons people fail less as they get older is that they risk less.* In other words, they stay away from chancy endeavors. This can be both positive and negative.

In order to learn, we need to expose ourselves to unknown subjects and situations. For some people with fragile self-images such probing may be too threatening, so they avoid anything new and as a result miss many growth opportunities. Humorist Will Rogers had some advice for such folks when he said, "Remember, we're all ignorant, only on different subjects."

Be careful saying no to new opportunities. New books, new flavors of ice cream, new friends, new styles of clothing, new forms of worship, new games, new ideas, new roads—any of these may offer you enriching, undreamed-of rewards. Keep alive the spirit of adventure, no matter what your age. It will help keep you youthfully alive all your life.

A life of faith is a daily adventure, Lord. Keep us from seeing it as ordinary or commonplace.

27

The kiss of the sun for pardon,
The song of the birds for mirth—
One is nearer God's heart in a garden,
Than anywhere else on earth.

Anonymous

Life, it seems to me, is filled with thousands of simple pleasures. Little joys that don't have any value in the marketplace, but that are priceless when your world's gone stale. Maybe I'll write a book someday listing the little happenings that can take an ordinary moment and put a halo around it. Examples abound: keeping tabs on the eggs in a bird's nest, anticipating the day when they hatch into furry, all-mouth babes; watching a forsythia bush progress from green buds to one golden sun; listening to a brook run carefree over glistening rocks.

What brought all this to mind was a trip I made a few minutes ago to my wife's flower garden that is surrounded by fresh, green mint. Before I poured my mid-morning cup of tea, I went out and plucked a couple of sprigs and added them to the pot. Such an aroma, such a delicious brew. I have no idea how the mint came to grow there. It has been there every spring since we've lived here. All I know is that I liked the taste treat very much. So in the absence of any other one to thank, I thank God today for supplying the extra ingredients in my tea—and for all the other little pleasures that I experience and forget to thank Him for.

You, Lord, are the Giver
Of sunshine and rain,
The Planter of seeds,
The Gardener of grain.

"Thy word have I hid in mine heart, that I might not sin against thee." Psalm 119:11

Jerry Lucas was an all-American basketball player in high school (Middletown, Ohio) and college (Ohio State) and an all-star in the professional ranks (Cincinnati, San Francisco and New York) as well, but says he, "the most exciting things in my life have come since I retired from basketball." What has he found that is more satisfying than winning basketball games? The answer is winning souls and teaching Christians how to memorize important passages of Scripture. In fact, Jerry has written a book on the subject: REMEMBER THE WORD (published by Acton House).

How did a star athlete who had no interest in religion get into such a ministry? First, he has been practicing memorization techniques since he was young, and he had a reputation for having a fantastic memory. But his interest in the Bible and the Christian faith didn't occur until he started dating a young lady who was the daughter of an evangelist. When their relationship grew serious, she asked Jerry to read the Bible, and as a result he found the Lord.

"We want people to hide God's word in their hearts," say this Van Nuys, California, couple. No one who has learned favorite Scripture verses will argue with that goal. Memorizing significant passages of the Bible is a good way to strengthen your spiritual life and to grow in faith. When serious problems arise, the Bible can be a great source of help and if you carry His word with you—in your mind and heart—you'll always have it handy.

Teach us to rely on You and Your word, Father, in both fair times and foul.

 Thro' days of toil when heart doth fail
God will take care of you;
When dangers fierce your path assail,
God will take care of you.
                              C.D. Martin hymn

Three years ago this day, a 51-year old Vietnamese journalist, his wife and a two-year old daughter were caught in a panic-stricken mob on a riverside dock in Saigon. Behind them, North Vietnamese troops were streaming into the city. In front of them, South Vietnamese marines were firing shots over the heads of people in the desperate crowd, trying to turn them away from the U.S. Navy ship that already was full to overflowing with fleeing families. Somehow, the trio made it on board and eventually came to America.

The man is Tu Ngoc Bich, who helped design and arrange the layout of the pages of this book. He is employed by *Guideposts*. He, his wife and three children (two who were entrusted to another family have been reunited with their parents) make their home in Mount Vernon, New York.

Leaving everything behind in Vietnam, fleeing for one's life, struggling to get a job and a foothold in a strange country might be more than some of us could handle. But Bich looks on the whole experience with gratefulness. "No one who has been through what we have could ever again doubt that God loves us and watches over us."

If you have faced faith-testing tribulation before, then you know your God is able to help you deal with it. If you've lived a life relatively free of upsetting reversals, then it's good to hear confirming evidence that God doesn't change, no matter how much the world around does.

Sharpen my eyes, Lord, to see You even in the darkest of days.

We all get the same, no more,
Each hour 60, each day 24.
Anonymous

Today, most of us around the country will be turning our clocks ahead one hour ("spring forward, fall back") as we begin Daylight Savings Time.

Do you know who first thought of the idea? Ben Franklin,

while he was U.S. Minister to France some 200 years ago. Ever the penny saver, Franklin figured residents of Paris could save 1,281 hours of candle burning a year if they'd adopt his plan. But alas, his idea came too early to be appreciated.

Saving time should be of interest to us all because, as a philosopher once noted, it is the stuff of which life is made. If you find yourself short on time for life-enriching activities, maybe you should make a "time-use study," as the efficiency experts call it.

Perhaps you'll discover ways to eliminate unnecessary motions, to combine things, to rearrange schedules and to standardize work habits so you can spend your hours more meaningfully. Ask God's guidance in the matter. Remember, there is a difference between leisure time and wasted time.

Lord, show us how to pace ourselves so we balance work with play, activity with rest.

MAY 1978

S	M	T	W	T	F	S
	1	2	3	4	5	6
7	8	9	10	11	12	13
14	15	16	17	18	19	20
21	22	23	24	25	26	27
28	29	30	31			

For the weary and discouraged, Christ said, "Come unto me all ye that labour . . . and I will give you rest." (Matthew 11:28) This month rely on Him for your strength. Ask Him to lift any burden that weighs heavily on your mind and experience the joyous freedom that results.

MAY 1978

1 More like the Master I would ever be,
More of His meekness, more humility;
More zeal to labor, more courage to be true,
More consecration for work He bids me do.
Charles H. Gabriel hymn

While I was driving to an appointment today, another motorist in a hurry to get around me made a dangerous pass in heavy traffic. In fact, he nearly ran me off the road pulling in ahead. As he sped off, I noticed a bumper sticker that said "Honk if you love Jesus." I was tempted to honk, but for another reason.

I would submit that this driver is a poor advertisement for his faith. If a person decides to be a quiet, passive, underground professor of Christianity, his personal lifestyle will neither add nor detract from it. However, those who overtly call attention to the fact that they are followers of Christ, as the motorist did, must show a little more Christian courtesy if they are to be effective witnesses.

Remember, when you lose control of your temper (or worse your tongue), when you act in ungenerous or unjust ways, when you fail to show humility, when you forget to take others' feelings into consideration, you are not being Christ-like, and—in the last analysis—that should be our primary goal.

Help us, Lord, to overlook and to understand.

"God's gifts put man's best dreams to shame."
Elizabeth Barrett Browning

An old man and his son were making a long journey on foot. One afternoon, hot and tired, the father motioned that he must stop and rest. So they sat down along a dusty road.

"Oh, for the cooling shade of a tree," the young man said.

"Yes, that would be heavenly," the man responded. "Let us plant one."

"You are overcome by the sun, Father. It would not spring up this hour and provide us with cover."

"No," said the old man, "but if I plant a seed today, future travelers will rest here in comfort. Remember, my son, to always give more than you take from life. It is the secret of happiness."

The man was wise indeed, for it is true that the givers in life are the real livers of life. The Bible admonishes, "Cast thy bread upon the waters: for thou shalt find it after many days." (Ecclesiastes 11:1) It means that you cannot outgive God, you cannot bless without being blessed, you cannot love without being loved.

Lord, make us free-flowing rivers of Your love,
not restraining reservoirs.

 "Whoso offereth praise glorifieth me: and to him that ordereth his conversation aright will I shew the salvation of God."

Psalm 50:23

When it comes to compliments—either giving or receiving them—most of us need improvement. Why do people have trouble handling this important area of human relationships? For one reason, many are suspicious of those who pay compliments to them. ("This is really soft soap . . . It isn't true . . . I'm not that good . . . What do they want?") And when words of praise are on their tongues, their souls often fear they will be misunderstood.

Is there a test for measuring the validity of compliments?

Yes, and that test is whether or not the complimenter is sincere in his or her praise, not flattering us in hope of gaining favor. Our word *flatter* comes from a French word which means "to caress, soothe, stroke." The Psalmist David suggests an ulterior motive in Psalm 12:2 when he admonishes those who speak "with flattering lips and a double heart."

A genuine compliment, however, is heartfelt recognition of something worthy, beautiful, virtuous, delightful, pleasing. Furthermore, it is good to be on either the giving or the receiving end of such expressions. Today, look for opportunities to praise people who need and deserve encouragement. Often it's only a matter of taking the focus off ourselves and putting it on others.

Lord, help us find loving words that will increase another's self-esteem.

Does the road wind up-hill all the way?
　　Yes, to the very end.
Will the day's journey take the whole day?
　　From morn to night, my friend.

But is there for the night a resting-place?
　　A roof for when the slow dark hours begin.
May not the darkness hide it from my face?
　　You cannot miss that inn.

Shall I meet other wayfarers at night?
　　Those who have gone before.
Then must I knock, or call when just in sight?
　　They will not keep you standing at that door.

Shall I find comfort, travel-sore and weak?
　　Of labor you shall find the sum.
Will there be beds for me and all who seek?
　　Yea, beds for all who come.

Christina Rossetti has long been one of my favorite inspirational poets, but it was only recently that I learned a few details of her life. Born in 1830 to a London family of modest means, Christina's life was filled with struggle. Her principal assets seemed to be a strong, dedicated faith and a facile mind that she focused on devotional poetry. Her lines often spoke of personal, spiritual imperfections which she implored God to correct.

Two romances fell short of marriage (both men failed to meet her spiritual requirements), and as Christina grew older she devoted herself to her mother and to her verse, the latter slowly winning her critical recognition. Her legacy when she died in 1894 was a sheaf of beautiful poems such as the one above, entitled "Up-Hill."

Like Christina Rossetti, Lord, help us make a contribution that will inspire others who follow.

5 **Thank You, God, for little things**
    that often come our way,
The things we take for granted
    but don't mention when we pray.
                  Helen Steiner Rice

Today I watched Daniel, my youngest son, ride his bicycle up the street on his way to a friend's house. There was nary a waver in his balance as he pumped away on the pedals, his mind no doubt on other things than the mechanics of bicycle riding.

Only a year ago, he was having all kinds of trouble learning to stay upright on his bike. In fact, he was so frustrated that a practice session often ended in tears. Now it is all taken for granted.

What blessings, skills, talents or accomplishments are you taking with a grain of salt today? I'd imagine there are many. Other than life itself, you must have a relative degree of good health, the use of your senses, a mind that works, a viable faith, friends and loved ones, shelter, food. You can no doubt add to the list. The point is, don't be a possessor of blessings without acknowledging them. Thank God for them daily. Then demonstrate your thanks by reaching out to somebody who has less.

Give me a grateful heart, Lord, so grateful that my hands

won't be content holding themselves, but are compelled to reach out and serve others.

"He went into a ship with his disciples . . . and there came down a storm of wind on the lake: and they were filled with water, and were in jeopardy. . . . Then he arose, and rebuked the wind and the raging of the water: and they ceased, and there was a calm." Luke 8:22-24

A friend of mine is in the oil tanker business, and he has been responsible for building, leasing and operating some of the largest vessels afloat. Recently, we were talking about super-tankers (some of which are 900 feet long) and how bulkheads separate the many tanks inside these ships, minimizing the danger of huge oil spills.

"Bulkheads," he explained, "compartmentalize a ship, closing off one section from another should the hull be punctured. They are safety precautions against a ship sinking."

Thinking about his explanation, I see an analogy between faith and bulkheads. When we get into trouble, when we make mistakes that threaten to sink us, our faith in God can limit the loss, minimize it, contain it.

All we need do is call on Him. His protecting power can rescue us from any mortal danger. No matter what our offense, He is faithful and just to forgive us (I John 1:9) and return us to His fellowship in good standing. He is a life preserver that will hold us up in any storm, a bulkhead that will never fail.

When we are in danger of sinking, Lord, remind us that Your lifeline is just a prayer away.

"The light of the eyes rejoiceth the heart."
                    Proverbs 15:30

Yesterday, I went through the woods cutting out dead trees. This is a good time of the year for it when all the live trees are leaf green. A small locust tree that stood like a skeleton in the middle of a grove of healthy trees was felled by my bow saw and sectioned for winter firewood. As I was piling the pieces, I studied the end of one of them, counting the rings. By my estimate, the locust was about 15 years old. One who is a forester can tell the history of a tree, I'm told. Droughts, fires, disease and age are all there for the seasoned eye to read.

In one respect, people are like trees, but their "ring count" is recorded in their eyes. Eyes—the windows of the soul, according to one poet—report ecstasy, sorrow, despair, loneliness, worry, weariness, illness, horror, enthusiasm, surprise, hopelessness and dozens of other interior feelings.

Beauty as the world judges it is fickle, and I suppose most of us feel rather average in that regard. But if you are at peace with God, if you are sure of your stand with Him, your eyes will report it whether you're nine or ninety. Eyes that turn their attention regularly to Him reflect the inner satisfaction and peace that He alone can give. Like the rings of a tree, your eyes reveal whether your heart is young or old.

Give me that sparkle, that joy of living, Lord, that comes from knowing You.

 "Help thy brother's boat across, and lo! thine own will reach the shore." Anonymous

Once I was talking with professional basketball star Bill Bradley, a consummate team player. Among other character-revealing things he told me was: "I get a bigger kick out of making a good pass that results in a basket than I do scoring one myself."

Over the course of years, I have interviewed hundreds of athletes, and a statement such as that is unusual, believe me. Why? Because athletes like the rest of us are human, and we all enjoy the limelight, the glory, stardom. Furthermore, on the stage of life we tend to worship people whose names are in lights, often forgetting the ones who made the costumes, fashioned the scenery, directed the play, wrote it and so forth.

I'm on a little campaign to praise and compliment the "behind-the-scenes" workers of the world. Maybe you'd like to join me. If so, you must look harder and search out the people who made the table decorations, the ones who publicized the successful meeting, the people who design book types, the frame-makers who enclose beautiful paintings, the seamstresses who sew straight hems, the athletes who don't score the baskets but make the passes that lead to them.

After you have complimented the Marys of the world, go a few steps further—backstage—and give the Marthas a pat on the back, too.

Point to the ones who need encouragement, Lord, and give me the words to lift their spirits.

 "Pray as if everything depended on God and work as if everything depended on you."
Anonymous

A midwest farm had fallen into disrepair after the last of the Browns had died, leaving it to the starlings and weeds. Then, Tom Austin bought it and through months of back-breaking work transformed it into a place of beauty. The barn roof was repaired, the house was refurbished, fences mended, outbuildings painted, the weeds mowed and the fields pregnant with maturing wheat and corn.

One day, the minister came along and, with one foot on the fence, observed, "God and you have sure made a big change in the place, Tom."

Tom said he was certainly grateful to God for His goodness. Then he added drily, "But you should have seen this place when He was running it by Himself."

Humor aside, God doesn't do for us what we should do ourselves. Furthermore, we wouldn't want it any other way. Satisfaction from a job well done is one of life's richest blessings. There is truth in the statement that God feeds the birds, but He doesn't throw the food in their nests.

Lord, show us how to make our little corner of the world better than the way we found it.

10
On Christ, the solid Rock, I stand;
All other ground is sinking sand.
                                    Edward Mote

Once, while hiking high in the mountains, I came upon some
scraggly pines—dwarfed, gnarled, struggling for a foothold
among rocks and lichens. A strong wind was blowing and they
yielded willingly to the force, bending to avoid being torn from
their stand. Looking below, I saw large healthy trees. They had
found a more cooperative climate, a more agreeable soil in
which to sink their roots. Above me there were no trees at all. I
was at the timber line, that place of demarcation on all towering
mountains where the last life-giving nutrients are available to
sustain plantlife.

   You and I have, or will have, times in our lives when we stand
at the timberline, lonely, anxious, tested. Like the pines, we
will need to be limber to deal with adverse winds, flexible in
the face of problems, able to bounce back after a storm has
passed. By ourselves we might have trouble enduring. But if
we rely on our Heavenly Father, we can handle any difficulty.
He is the Rock to which we can root our lives with assurance.

*Keep me from giving up, Lord, when the winds of trouble
rage.*

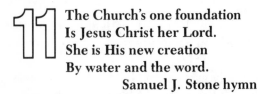

11
The Church's one foundation
Is Jesus Christ her Lord.
She is His new creation
By water and the word.
                                    Samuel J. Stone hymn

My friend and associate Norman Vincent Peale says there is a
simple six-word formula for succeeding in any business endeavor. It is this: *Find a Need and Fill It.*

   If I were the inventive type, I'd try to develop a non-
streaking window cleaner, something that would make a window sparkle with one swipe. After doing the porch windows
yesterday, I am positive there is a need for such a product. I
went over the panes three times each, but this morning I
noticed they looked as if I had used neet's foot oil.

However, I feel there are more pressing problems to be dealt with by the creative minds of the world. For example, I read recently that no more than 25 per cent of the population is in church in the course of any given week. I am sure more than 25 per cent have spiritual needs. Apparently, many people don't feel the solutions to their problems can be found in church.

Is it a correct assumption? It is if the specific church has a focal point other than Christ. But there are dynamic churches in every community whose ministers and parishioners are serving the Lord with dedication. How can you get the word out that your church is God's feeding station? The best way is the witness you make with your life the other six days of the week. Whether you realize it or not, you are a walking advertisement for your church and your Lord.

Make us worthy of being called Your disciples, Lord.

12 "He that endureth to the end shall be saved." Matthew 10:22

Once I visited the famous Stedelijk Museum in Amsterdam, Holland, which houses paintings by some of the world's greatest artists. I was particularly fascinated by the works of Vincent Van Gogh (1853-1890). I remember his renowned "The Potato Eaters" and "The Sunflowers" and his self-portraits. All told, Van Gogh is believed to have created about 700 drawings and 800 oils. But—and this is a footnote worth remembering— he is said to have sold only *one* painting in his lifetime!

When you question your progress, when you grow depressed from failure, when you don't seem to be reaching your goals, it is important to remember people like Van Gogh. Recognition of his talent came after his death. Mature Christians know that not all the seeds they plant will reach maturity in their lifetime, yet they press on in faith, knowing that God promises ultimate victory to those who keep His commandments.

Whether the world recognizes your contributions or not,

you can be assured that God does, and He will reward you for your steadfastness.

I know You have a plan for each of our lives, Lord.
Reveal it to us.

13 Creator Spirit by whose aid
The world's foundations first were laid,
Come, visit every pious mind.
Come, pour Thy joy on humankind;
From sin and sorrow set us free
And make Thy temples worthy Thee.
John Dryden

The red peony bushes in our backyard have an abundance of buds, and the ants that help soften them and enable the flowers to bloom are busy with their annual spring chore.

Tomorrow is Pentecost or Whitsunday (so named because people who come for baptism traditionally wear white) when we commemorate the descent of the Holy Spirit upon the apostles and disciples, and I am reminded that in German-speaking countries the red peony is called *pfingstrose* which means "rose of Pentecost." I suppose by this time of year in most European countries this magnificent flower is in bloom. Whatever, it is a worthy symbol to remind us of what happened 50 days following Christ's resurrection.

In Acts 2:2-4 we read, "And suddenly there came a sound from heaven as of a rushing mighty wind, and it filled all the house where they were sitting. And there appeared unto them cloven tongues like as of fire, and it sat upon each of them. And they were all filled with the Holy Ghost, and began to speak with other tongues, as the Spirit gave them utterance."

The miracle that occurred on this day in church history is an ongoing miracle. God's power sent from Heaven that day has not dissipated over the intervening years. It still is available to all who seek to serve Him with their whole selves. That includes you and me.

We ask for the indwelling of Your Holy Spirit, Lord.

14 (Mother's Day)
"Mother is the name for God in the lips and hearts of little children."
William Makepeace Thackeray

All mothers are special, but some are super special. I suspect that Susanna Wesley, the mother of John and Charles Wesley, fell into the latter category.

Mother of 19 children, 11 of whom survived infancy, she apparently had a monumental influence on her children, two of whom gained worldwide prominence. We get some insight into the dedication she brought to her maternal role from a practice she instituted for each child. According to John, his mother scheduled one hour a week for each of her children. When that hour came, she put aside everything else and devoted it to that child alone, listening and talking about his or her special concerns. One hour may not seem like a lot, but with 11 children to care for, this wife of a minister no doubt had her hands full, and busy mothers can appreciate her self-discipline.

The most basic unit of society is the family and how our culture fares depends to a large extent on the strength of the home. Loving parents who give their children a sense of self-worth and make them feel special are engaged in a godly calling. On this day when we salute mothers, it is good to remember the Susanna Wesleys in history. They are gems of purest ray serene.

It's also good to recall the positive influences of our own mothers and the sacrifices they made for us. If possible, thank yours personally; if not, thank God.

For the love and guidance of a wonderful Christian mother, I thank You, Lord.

15 "Cast away from you all your transgressions . . . and make a new heart and a new spirit. . . ." Ezekiel 18:31

My friend Watson Spoelstra, former major-league baseball writer for the *Detroit News*, once was a captive of alcohol. His addiction spanned many years. Then, one day his 18-year-old daughter was rushed to the hospital with a brain hemorrhage.

"Please, Lord," Waddy cried out to a God he had been estranged from since his youth, "do something about Ann and I'll let Jesus do something about me."

The Lord worked two miracles—Ann's recovery and Waddy's conversion. Since that day, Watson Spoelstra has used his talents for the upbuilding of the Kingdom, founding the now-flourishing baseball chapel program that organizes Sunday worship services for all 24 major-league teams. Hundreds of big league ballplayers meet in prayer every Sunday during the season. The guiding hand behind this work is a guy who calls himself "a broken-down baseball writer."

All I can say is that Waddy may have been broken down, but he has been mended and lifted up to new heights since he was reborn in Christ. That's the amazing thing about the reach of our Lord. No one's ever so low that He cannot lift them up and give them new life.

Even when we fail You, Father, it's reassuring to know You're always ready to forgive us.

16 "So we, being many, are one body in Christ, and every one members one of another. Having then gifts differing according to the grace that is given to us . . . ."
Romans 12:5,6

Sometimes we look on famous men and women as persons born with special talents, unique skills and unusual intellect. In truth, most were not endowed with extraordinary gifts nor were they particularly outstanding among their peers until they found their place, their niche, their calling.

It is good to remember that Winston Churchill—despite special tutoring—flunked qualifying exams three consecutive years when trying to enter Sandhurst, the military institution. In particular, he could not seem to grasp Latin, which is astonishing when one reads the books of this masterful practitioner of the English language. But then, Thomas Edison was once at the bottom of his class, Albert Einstein flunked math and was called "mentally slow," and Henry Ford was written off by one teacher as "a student who shows no promise."

Each of us has special God-given gifts, but not all are equally successful at discovering them or using them. Sometimes we speak disparagingly of our gifts, viewing them as inferior to others' gifts.

How faithful are you in performing the tasks God has given you to do? If you are frustrated, feeling depressed or unappreciated, begin serving God today in the place you are. No matter how humble or unimportant your assignment seems, do it with your whole heart. If it's a cup of cold water that you're asked to deliver in His name (Matthew 10:42), do it willingly. Using the gift God has given you may be the portal through which you must pass before new opportunities are revealed. Performing your present duties well could be the key to finding an exciting new spiritual dimension in your life.

You made each of us unique, Lord. Help us use that uniqueness to serve You.

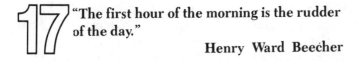

17 "The first hour of the morning is the rudder of the day."
Henry Ward Beecher

One of the pleasures of spring is walking warm. With the sun's life-giving rays striking the earth's northern hemisphere more directly again, Nature invites us outdoors, and I accept its invitation as often as possible. Yesterday I walked long enough to irritate the heel of my left foot, a predictable happening when one rushes the breaking in of new hiking boots.

Many things in life require a "breaking-in" period. New shoes, new cars, new friendships, new jobs, new disciplines. Someone wrote to me a short time ago and said that he felt a need for more "daily worship time," but that he could never find enough minutes in the day's busy schedule. One effec - tive method is setting your alarm 15 minutes earlier in the morning and using that period to frame your day. Consider what you want to accomplish. Ask God's blessing. Read some Scripture. Meditate upon its application to your life.

It may take some getting used to—this earlier rising regimen—but after a breaking-in period the habit will grow and become a treasured beginning of each day. Like a new pair of hiking boots, it won't make you uncomfortable for long.

After a good night's rest, Lord, give us grateful hearts and renewed spirits.

 "Cast thy bread upon the waters: for thou shalt find it after many days."
Ecclesiastes 11:1

In her book, THE ADVENTURE OF BEING A WIFE , Ruth Stafford Peale has some very pointed and practical advice for wives. When one woman complained that her husband worked all the time, even at home ("He always brings a full briefcase home for evenings and weekends "), Mrs. Peale counseled:

"If his work is the most important thing in your husband's life, learn to take an interest in it. Urge him to talk to you about it. Instead of resenting it, try to be a part of it."

One wife who did just that, Mrs. Peale writes, was Mrs. Alfred P. Sloan, whose husband once headed General Motors. By taking a deep interest in her husband's business, Mrs. Sloan developed an understanding of her husband's special problems. And though he was not lacking in expert business counsel, the president of the world's largest automobile company once paid his wife the unusual compliment of being "the best business adviser I've got."

The point is a simple one. When we take the focus away from ourselves and put it on another, a relationship always deepens. It is the same whether the liason is husband-wife, parent-child, preacher-parishioner, boss-employee, you-God. When we quit asking and begin giving, the result is always the same: we receive something in return. More often than not, that something is love.

Lord, help·us see that when we give of ourselves to help another, we are twice-blessed.

**Oh, blest are they who walk in love,
They also walk with God above.
Helen Steiner Rice**

Speaking with a group of young people recently, I asked about their areas of recent spiritual growth.

"One of the things I've learned to do is pray for people who bug me," said a young lady named Jeanine.

"That's a giant step for anyone to make," I responded. "Tell me, how did you do it?"

"Oh, I didn't. The Lord did," she explained. "There were several people I couldn't stand to be around. I knew that wasn't right so I asked God to help me defeat my problem, and He did. His grace is sufficient to lick such things."

What else can one add to such a mature analysis of how to deal with a problem we all experience. A wise minister once told a Bible class, "Face the fact that there are some people you just won't be able to love on your own, but they need loving and you've got to love them. And if you try, God will provide the means to overcome your resistance. Then you'll discover something else—after you've really gotten to know them and have found the Christ in them—they're a lot more lovable than you thought."

Blind us to the faults of others, Lord, and magnify their virtues.

"If God be for us, who can be against us?"
Romans 8:31

Catherine Marshall was telling me about a serious operation she had faced a couple of years ago.

"I was full of fear initially," she said. "Then God sent all kinds of support to assure me of His love and power." She went on to enumerate the ways God spoke to her—through the Bible, through meditation, through family, friends and doctors.

This phenomenon of God responding to our need always is forthcoming. Still, it is our nature, no matter how long we have walked in the Spirit, to question whether or not He will respond "this" time. The disciples were fearful when Christ's departure was imminent, but He told them not to be afraid, that God "shall give you another Comforter, that He may abide with you forever." (John 14:16)

If today you are faced with something that you dread, something that causes your palms to perspire and fills your heart with tremors, something that gives you such anxiety that your stomach churns and you can't think straight, stop right now and clear your mind of all negatives and doubts. Your Heavenly Father is perfectly able to give you, right now, the wherewithal to deal with any problems. Has He failed you in the past? No, of course not. He never fails and He won't today either.

When we leave You out, Lord, life is a puzzling equation.
When we include You, our confusion disappears.

"Search the scriptures . . . which testifieth of me."
John 5:39

Once a group of seminarians were discussing conflicting viewpoints on Scripture. One authority believed this, and another that. One commentary said this, another that. One translation interpreted a Biblical phrase this way, another that way.

"We are totally confused," said one of the young men to his professor, "we are completely in the dark."

"Perhaps," the gray-haired scholar said with a wry smile, "you all should read the Bible. It has been known to throw light on the subject."

Some people read the Bible as if it were an opponent, an adversary, something to debate and challenge, while others see it as a friend, a companion, a source book of wisdom and answers. Of course there are obscure and complicated parts of the Bible, but there are also passages as clear as a crystal pool, as lucid as a cloudless day. "It's not the parts of the Bible I don't understand that give me trouble," a wise Christian once said. "It's the parts that I do."

If you're having difficulty with some decision in your life today, isolate the problem spiritually. Does it concern obedience, wisdom, love, selfishness, worry, fear, trust? Whatever, look in the concordance of your Bible. (If it doesn't have one, you need such a Bible.) Then read some of the verses that speak to that theme. Like the seminarians who were in the dark, you too can find light for your life in the Book of Life.

When we can't find answers for our problems, Father, direct us to Your illuminating word.

22

"Let there be no strife, I pray thee, between me and thee; for we be brethren."
Genesis 13:8

Writing in *Guideposts*, schoolteacher Wanda Jones of Jackson, Tennessee, told about one of her very early classroom experiences with a farm boy named Homer. "He was clumsy, slow and indifferent," she recalled. Furthermore, Wanda suspected that he was lazy. But one day she gave him the assignment of composing a poem. To her amazement, she discovered a depth and beauty in the boy she never imagined. He knew much about the out-of-doors and wrote of water and birds and trees with moving gratitude and insight. "He taught me," Wanda concluded, "that there is beauty in every human soul. It's always there, a well within; in some people bubbling to the surface, in others lying still and quiet deep inside."

Sometimes we are tempted to make snap judgments about

people on the basis of superficial impressions. Subconsciously, we insist that they match some arbitrary, but exacting formula that we may use to classify individuals. The result is that we miss many opportunities to "entertain angels unawares."(Hebrews 13:2) Keep your eyes and heart open today for people who need your acceptance. A world that is too often distant and cold could be warmed several degrees by Christians willing to look beneath the surface for "the beauty in every human soul."

Give me an understanding heart, Lord, and an open mind.

 "Go to sleep, God is awake." Victor Hugo

A woman from Arkansas writes that she has been suffering from insomnia for several months. "I know I shouldn't be anxious about things, that God will take care of me, but my married children—a daughter and son—seem to have lost their faith, and I'm worried about their souls."

There are dozens of over-the-counter prescriptions available to people suffering from sleeplessness, and hundreds of home remedies for insomniacs (e.g., warm milk before bed, long walks, hot baths). But when one's mind is agitated all night long like butter in a churn, nothing seems to help. Nothing, that is, except thoughts that calm, soothe and relax. Where do these thoughts come from? Two sources, I believe. One is experience. After you've lived a few years and been through a few of life's hurricanes, you come to see that "this, too, shall pass away." Time does heal. It erases, smooths, restores, replenishes.

The second source of a tranquil mind is God. When you can't sleep, turn your thoughts toward Him. Pray for relief from the anxieties that trouble you. Ask Him to shoulder your load. He will—whether the problem is a personal one or one that concerns another, such as a wayward son or daughter (as in the case above). Remember, parents, they are His children, too.

To serve You I need rest, Lord, so tonight I put all my worldly concerns in Your hands.

24 " . . . My grace is sufficient for thee: for my strength is made perfect in weakness. . . ."
II Corinthians 12:9

In Greek mythology, the entrance to the city of Thebes was guarded by the sphinx, a winged monster with a woman's head and a lion's body. Nobody entered or departed without her permission. When wandering Oedipus approached the city's gates, she asked him a riddle. If he answered it, he would be allowed to enter. If not, he would be killed.

"What creature walks on all fours in the morning, on two legs at noon and on three in the evening?" the sphinx asked.

After thinking a while, Oedipus replied, "A man. As a child he crawls, when he is grown he walks upright and when he is old he uses a cane." Thus, Oedipus gained entrance to Thebes.

Life is an unsolved riddle for all of us until our estrangement with God ends and we become part of His family. That was the mission of His Son, Jesus: to point the way to life with the Father, abundant life, eternal life. What must we do to find such life? In Mark (1:15) we are told "the Kingdom of God is at hand: repent ye, and believe the gospel." When we accept Christ's sovereignty as Lord and Saviour—whether we are young, standing on two legs or three—we no longer need worry about the future.

Supply us with Your wisdom, Lord, the wisdom that solves all of life's puzzles.

25 "Unto thee lift I up mine eyes, O thou that dwelleth in the heavens." Psalm 123:1

There was a guy named Alfred in my hometown who always walked the streets looking at the ground. He was one of those individuals some call a ne'er-do-well. I don't think he ever married or ever held a job or ever caused anyone any trouble. He just walked back and forth between his parent's home and the pool hall looking at the ground, all hunched over, arms locked behind his back. Sunshine or rain, heat or chill, he always took the same posture. I suppose he found a few coins and, on occasion, a comb and a nailclipper or two, but can you imagine what he missed? I'll tell you. He missed seeing a lot of smiles, he missed a lot of rainbows, he missed a lot of flowering trees and birds on the wing.

But the Alfreds of the world have lots of company. Not all of us stare at the ground all the time. But a good many of us plod right through life missing half the fun, half the joy and half the beauty, because we're too busy concentrating on our little world of problems, problems related to children and school and money and health and politics and growing up or growing old.

Today, wash your eyes with ice cold water and vow to take a new look at life. There are things we all are missing because we're looking down instead of up. One thing you should know, no matter how worried or how discouraged or how sick you are. That is, God loves you. A whole bunch.

Lord, don't let us become so preoccupied with life's problems that we miss life's beauty.

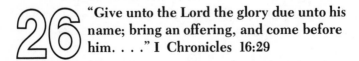

"Give unto the Lord the glory due unto his name; bring an offering, and come before him. . . ." I Chronicles 16:29

Thomas Beecher, brother of preacher Henry Ward Beecher, was once called upon to be a substitute speaker for his famous relative. Naturally, people who had come to hear Henry—some from long distances—were disappointed when they learned of the switch. In fact, during the singing of the first hymn a few of those present sidled toward the nearest exit. Motioning the pianist to stop, Thomas announced, "Those who came to worship my brother may leave now. Those who came to worship God are invited to join me in the singing of the rest of the hymn."

The story reminds me that we need to be sure the focus of our church attendance, of our worship, is God. Those of us who are guilty of putting ministers on a pedestal have missed the point of Martin Luther's crucial phrase: "the priesthood of us all."

That means each of us is a minister in our own right. We may not be called upon to teach or preach, but we all have been given spiritual gifts (I Corinthians 12) and we all are required to use them fully. You may think your talent small and your contribution smaller , but God's criterion is faithfulness. Give willingly and wholeheartedly and you will please the Lord. Serve Him with gladness (Psalm 100:2) and receive a blessing of joy and peace.

Teach me that worship isn't a one-hour-a-week duty to You, Lord, but a seven-day-a-week opportunity.

27

"But the word of the Lord endureth for ever. And this is the word which by the gospel is preached unto you." I Peter 1:25

A recent article in the *New York Times* noted the great "book hunger" that exists today in Russia. Even in Moscow's largest bookstore, copies of books by Pushkin, Dostoevski and Tolstoy are seldom available according to the report. The story did not mention Bibles, which are suppressed by the government and must be smuggled into the country. Underground Christians, spiritually hungry for copies of God's word, look to outsiders to supply them.

What a privilege it is to live in a country where one of our basic human rights is a free press. It is a blessing that often goes unappreciated. Can you imagine what it would be like to be denied ready access to your favorite books, newspapers or magazines? And what if you had no Bible? Go to God's word today—right now if possible—and open it to a favorite passage. Read it gratefully. It is another gift to you from God.

Thank You, Lord, for the printed word, especially Your printed word.

28 "But they that wait upon the Lord shall renew their strength; they shall mount up with wings as eagles; they shall run, and not be weary; and they shall walk, and not faint." Isaiah 40:31

Lou Gehrig earned the nickname "Iron Man" because of his durability as a baseball player for the New York Yankees. In fact, he set a major league record by playing 2,130 consecutive games over a 15-year period. Had it not been for a fatal nerve disease, the number would have been even greater.

Consistency, steadfastness, faithfulness are virtues we all admire. They are marks of well-disciplined people. But how do we develop such worthy character traits in ourselves and our children? One way is to practice what we preach. Setting high goals is not enough. Calling yourself a Christian is one thing; living a life of faith is another.

To be an iron man or an iron woman of faith—one who is consistent in his or her witness—one must rely on more than a desire for the good life. We must call upon God's grace to keep us from faltering and giving up. It is His indwelling Spirit that makes the difference.

Live in me and through me, Lord, so I may witness for You.

 29 (Memorial Day)
"His heart was as great as the world, but there was no room in it to hold the memory of a wrong." Ralph Waldo Emerson.

On this slow-news day, one story will certainly get plenty of attention from the media. That will be the number of tragedies that befall holiday revelers. Highway deaths and drownings always receive considerable time on radio and TV and space in newspapers.

Being extra careful, even cautious, is the first rule if you must travel this busy weekend. If you're driving, do it defensively.

But even defensive driving isn't enough to avert some accidents. The truth is brought home with dramatic impact when someone you know is seriously injured or tragically killed. In an instant, life can be gone.

My mother always told me to "keep short accounts." She meant don't let ill will, bad relationships, unresolved differences fester over long periods of time. The reason being that life can end very unexpectedly. As we get older, the odds increase.

On this day when we honor the memory of our war dead, it is good for the living to take inventory of their spiritual health. If you have any concerns or conflicts that need resolution, today might be a good day to attend to them.

Show us where we've erred, Lord, and how to make amends.

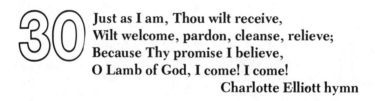

Just as I am, Thou wilt receive,
Wilt welcome, pardon, cleanse, relieve;
Because Thy promise I believe,
O Lamb of God, I come! I come!
                                    Charlotte Elliott hymn

"We are going to write it off as a loss," I heard a financial officer of a large company say one time, referring to a new product line that had failed and was being taken off the market.

"What does that mean?" I asked.

"That we are going to take it off our books, consider it finished, eliminate it, cancel it," he answered.

If a company can wipe its books clean of miscalculations, errors or reversals, I got to thinking later, why can't individuals? The answer is, of course, they can—but the difference seems to be in emotional involvement. The officers of the company I mentioned above were being dispassionate, logical, objective about their mistakes; but generally speaking, individuals have more trouble accepting failure with such detachment.

Do you have difficulty admitting errors, shortcomings, wrongs? If so, the problem may be in understanding the anatomy of such transactions. To forgive ourselves, to "write off" a mistake, we must first realize that such things happen to everyone. Falling down isn't an indication of inadequacy or clumsiness or inferiority or anything else except that we mis-stepped. Failing is part and parcel of being an active human. The second step is to admit our faults and, if necessary, try to correct them or make amends for them. If our actions have moral or spiritual connotations, then we will want to ask God's forgiveness and sometimes the forgiveness of others.

An amazing thing happens in human relations when we take responsibility for some error. The other person invariably tells us to "forget it." And that is exactly what God does when we seek His pardon.

Soften our hearts when we're slow to forgive, Lord, and remind us of Your willingness always to forgive us.

31 " . . . Lord, I believe: help thou mine unbelief." Mark 19:24

"You can't make a silk purse out of a sow's ear," goes an old maxim, but it pays to look behind timeless wisdom before accepting it. Demosthenes, the famous Greek orator, stuttered as a young man and must have been told by someone that he should consider becoming a scribe or sculptor rather than a senator. But Demosthenes was not deterred. He had things on his mind that he wanted to say—emphatically, dramatically.

So, he walked the beaches practicing his words over the roar of the waves. To help him overcome his speech impediment, he placed pebbles in his mouth. It worked. Demosthenes, whose name today is synonymous with *orator*, lived to hear this encomium from a contemporary: "When I speak, the people say, 'How well he speaks,' but when Demosthenes speaks the people say, 'Let us march!' "

The most effective preachers I've heard have had two things in common. First, they have believed 100 per cent in their messages. Second, they have been good communicators, technically skilled speakers. If you want to be an articulate spokesman for your faith, it will be to your advantage to be a practiced speaker; but more important you need to believe in what you're saying. If you do, God will help make marchers out of your listeners.

Lord, help us to be doers of Your word, not just speakers and hearers.

JUNE 1978

S	M	T	W	T	F	S
				1	2	3
4	5	6	7	8	9	10
11	12	13	14	15	16	17
18	19	20	21	22	23	24
25	26	27	28	29	30	

When you face difficult decisions this month, turn to God and draw upon His incomparable wisdom. "Trust in the Lord with all thine heart; and lean not unto thine own understanding. In all thy ways acknowledge him, and he shall direct thy paths." (Proverbs 3:5,6)

JUNE 1978

1 'Mid all the traffic of the ways
Turmoils without, within —
Make in my heart a quiet place,
And come and dwell therein.

John Oxenham hymn

Today, I am writing this page at a lake cottage in Indiana. It is a modest little house that has been in our family for 60 years, and I have come here most every summer for as long as I can remember. The place provides some wonderful memories, especially of my father who has been gone for nearly 15 years. In my mind's eye I see him at the dock beside a boat, hear him telling a fishing story, feel his touch when I grip one of his hammers or rakes.

Ostensibly, my purpose for coming here this week — alone — is to write, but it's also to clear my mind. The restorative properties of this setting border on the miraculous. I can come here mentally fatigued and within a day or two feel renewed in body, mind and soul.

I suppose everyone has a place that they go to recharge their batteries. If not, I recommend trying to find one. The world is full of mini-retreat centers to which you can withdraw for a few minutes to get away from the confusion when it becomes too much.

Any place will do where you can shut out the noise of the world and let your mind run in neutral for a few minutes. It is in meditative times such as these that we get in touch with ourselves and with God. They are golden moments that strengthen and revitalize us.

Show us how to use moments of quiet, Lord, to find ourselves—and You.

2 "For as he thinketh in his heart, so is he."
Proverbs 23:7

Ruth Gordon, that inveterate and seemingly indestructible actress, has written spiritedly (how else?) the story of her first 80 years in an autobiographical book called MY SIDE (Harper & Row). She has much to say in her 502-page *tour de force*, but nothing capsules the book or the woman as much as this statement:

"I believe in God, Jesus, Life Eternal, people, luck, my voices and myself. Pan me, don't give me a part, publish everybody's book but this one, and I will *still* make it! Why? Because I *believe* I will. If you believe, then you hang on."

Can one have any doubts why this irrepressible woman has succeeded to the degree she has? Quite simply she always has been a believer, and believers triumph where doubters fail. If you have some lofty goal, some dream that you hope will come true, remember that all things are possible if you can believe.

We know that enthusiasm comes from a Greek word meaning "full of Spirit, full of God." Lord, fill us with this elixir of life.

"If a house be divided against itself that house cannot stand." Mark 3:25

One day while we were on vacation, a sink hole developed near where I was staying, and within a few minutes a three-bedroom home dropped intó the hole 60 feet below. Fortunately, the family that occupied the house heard the walls cracking and was able to escape unharmed. Outside, they watched helplessly as the hole expanded·and the house dropped.

Though not common, the phenomenon of sink holes can occur, I am told, when underground streams dry up and the earth above falls in the void.

When I hear of such things, I am reminded of Christ's statement, "Heaven and earth shall pass away, but my words shall not pass away." (Matthew 24:35) That verse should clue us as to where we need to place our trust. Certainly not in material things, for they may not survive the various upheavals that come and go. Rather, we need to build our spiritual house upon the Rock of Ages. For when we do, we secure ourselves to the one sure thing in life.

> *Help us keep our trust in Thee,*
> *Today, tomorrow, eternally.*

 "Bloom where you are planted."
Anonymous

One of my wife's favorite flowering plants (and mine, too) is fuchsia, a member of the evening primrose family. Named for a German botanist by the name of Fuchs, the red-purple flowers that cascade from a back-porch pot all summer long are a never-ending source of beauty and pleasure. As one flower fades and falls from its stem, another seems to magically re-place it.

There are people who have the characteristics of fuchsia. They never stop blooming month after month. They keep giving even when they suffer losses. They spread beauty and fragrance, and all who come in contact with them are the better for it.

Such behavior has a source, I have discovered, and that source is a deep and abiding faith. Such faith helps its possessors take the long view of things and keeps them from retreating when temporary setbacks come their way. Where does this faith come from? From God, the One who lovingly sustains flowering fuchsia and fuchsia-like people.

Help us, Lord, to be reflectors of Your beauty and love.

 "Jesus said unto him, 'If thou canst believe, all things are possible to him that believeth.' " Mark 9:23

As a young man, I attended many baseball games at Detroit's Briggs Stadium, and though Ty Cobb had long before retired, his legend was very much alive. At one time he held more hitting and base-stealing records than any player in the game. But the statistics don't reveal his greatest asset: a never-say-die, competitive spirit.

When I think of Ty Cobb, I am reminded that his baseball career almost died aborning. In his first season, he played in only 41 games for the Augusta, Georgia, team and hit a measly .237. The management saw no great talent in him and told him he was through.

Cobb was discouraged and wrote of those feelings in a letter to his father. The elder Cobb was unsympathetic in his curt reply. The essence of it was: "Don't come home until you've given it your all."

Ty Cobb took his dad's advice. He got another job in baseball, and the following year drew raves wherever he played. In a few short years, he was the most heralded player in the major leagues. Eventually, he was enshrined in baseball's Hall of Fame.

When you face setbacks and think there is no hope, be

careful not to give up too soon. Many a success story has been built on a foundation of early frustration and failure. "Sweet are the uses of adversity," wrote Shakespeare, and he was right. Out of ashes came the phoenix. Out of darkness God made light. Out of clay He shaped man. And out of a borrowed tomb came the Savior of the world.

When our hopes resemble dying embers, Lord, fan them with Your love.

Like mechanized carnival ducks,
We move along a pre-set track,
Until one discovers wings
And flies off, never to come back.
F.B.

An ornithologist who has observed and photographed exotic birds all over the world told me this story about a common wren. Recently, a mother wren attracted him to his backyard where she was angrily scolding someone or something. At first he thought a cat might be the subject of her chatter, but when he drew closer he saw that the bird was directing her shrill notes to her young inside a birdhouse.

When a fluffy, fat offspring finally stuck its head partway through the small opening, my friend understood. The babies had grown to the point it was time for them to fly and begin foraging for food. They themselves had been fed and protected all their young lives, and they were reluctant to come out of their secure birthplace. But Mother knew best. "Now!" she seemed to be saying.

People are a lot like these baby wrens. We like secure places, too, places where we are safe, hidden, protected, untroubled. But the Bible says that if we are to mature as Christians, we must give up babies' milk and eat grown-ups' meat (Hebrews 5:12-14); there comes a time in our growth when we must serve, teach, give, witness. If we are to grow in things of the

Spirit, we must test our wings. When we do, we risk falling, of course, but we also have the possibility of reaching the heavens.

When we shy away from opportunities for growth, O Holy Spirit, fortify us with Your matchless power.

7 "All that glitters is not gold."
Shakespeare

A graduation speaker once told his young audience, "The message life repeats over and over is that you and I can achieve most any single thing we set our minds to. I underscore *single* thing."

What keeps people from reaching their goals? Several things, no doubt, but vacillation is one of the leading barriers. Impatience is another.

There is a story told about a California rancher who sold his property to a retired Army colonel. The year was 1847. The rancher, then, went off in search of gold. When the area began to develop, the colonel decided to build a new mill on the property. In order to power it, he had to dig a mill race. It was while men were digging that gold was discovered and soon people all over the country were talking about the find at Colonel John Sutter's mill, including—no doubt—the former owner of the land who had sold it in order to go off in search of gold.

Generally speaking, God put most of the tools we need to succeed in life close by. The problem is that our perspective is often clouded by the familiar. Ask the Lord to give you new eyes to evaluate the harbor at hand before you sail off in the direction of some distant rainbow. Your pot of gold could be right under your nose.

I believe You have a plan for each of us, Lord. Help us find it.

**This is my Father's world:
I rest me in the thought,
Of rocks and trees, of skies and seas
His hand the wonders wrought.**

Maltbie D. Babcock hymn

Several people unknown to each other were walking on a public beach near sunset. When the dome of the sun dipped behind the horizon like a child pulling his head beneath the covers, magnificent golds and oranges reflected on the clouds and across the water.

"No one paints like God," one gentleman remarked to no one in particular.

"*Res ipsa loquitur*," said another, remembering his Latin. The phrase means " the thing speaks for itself," and no question about it, the setting sun was making quite a speech.

All about us are beautiful things that testify to a Creator's hand: sun, stars, moon, tides, seasons, harvests, birth and rebirth. Only a person with a blindfolded mind could believe that all this beauty is happenstance. *Res ipsa loquitur.*

Remind us, Father, when we would witness for You that actions often speak louder than words.

**On the cross He sealed my pardon,
Paid the debt, and made me free.**

Philip P. Bliss hymn

Before a person in ancient Greece was buried, it was the custom to put a gold coin under the tongue of the deceased. Thus, when the woman or man reached the River Styx which led to Hades, he or she would have fare for the boat trip across.

Christians won't need a token or ticket or money to enter Heaven when they die. According to Scripture, their price of admission was paid by Christ when He endured the Cross. (Hebrews 12:2)

If you have accepted the Lord, you already are living in the Kingdom, because eternal life begins the very moment you come into the saving knowledge of God. From that time forward, you can forget about death and can concentrate on the joy of living. That's the good news of Christ: death has been defeated. As a result, you and I can devote all our time and thought to life — and all its magnificent possibilities.

Because You have redeemed us, Lord, we can face the future unafraid. Remind us of this inheritance when we forget.

10

" . . . because they are brethren, do them service . . . "   I Timothy 6:2

A fellow I know (call him Jim) opened a new business the other day. It is his sixth try, maybe seventh. He goes through businesses like a porpoise through water. He hasn't exactly failed at everything he has tried, but usually after frenetic promotion and advertising, some great enthusiasm and lofty predictions, the bloom fades and Jim begins looking for his next enterprise.

"Jim has never learned about the *serve curve*," a friend told me.

"The serve curve?" I asked.

"It's essential to all successful businesses," he answered. "Selling is only one side of the coin. You have to give enthusiastic service, too. When you do, one satisfied customer tells another and up the way old customers return to buy again. You can chart it. Instead of business declining because of poor or inadequate service, a graph would show an upward and improving trend as time goes on. I call it the serve curve."

I don't know anything about serve curves, but I do know life has takers and givers. The takers are collectors, hoarders, keepers. Though they often consider themselves shrewd in business, they are really rather pitiful creatures for they miss much of life's joy. The givers on the other hand receive most of their pleasure from helping and serving others. They measure riches in the form of thoughtful children, of loyal friends, of loving mates, of warm homes, of a solid faith.

In Galatians 5:13 Paul admonishes us: "By love serve one another." When we do, we are most Christlike, and when we are most Christlike the windows of Heaven open to us.

Help us realize, God, that in Your service we find perfect freedom.

11

"Nothing is so much to be feared as fear."
Henry David Thoreau

A reader tells me there is a treacherous, narrow mountain road near Colorado Springs, Colorado, that fills many a driver with fear. In fact, more than a few motorists, afraid their cars would go over the edge, have decided to retreat rather than continue.

But an unusual road sign planted at the most nerve-jangling spot advises, "Yes, you can." To their surprise, wary drivers discover they can indeed as they inch forward and succeed in making it through the dangerous pass.

When you face obstacles in your life, ones that test your faith and fill you with action-freezing doubt, remember that the biggest obstacle is usually your own fear. When Moses was 120 years old and unable to continue into the Promised Land, he encouraged his people with these words, "Be strong and of a good courage, fear not, nor be afraid of them: for the Lord thy God, he it is that doth go with thee; he will not fail thee nor forsake thee." (Deuteronomy 31:6) If you believe in God and are able to say "Yes, I can" to the roadblocks that come your way, there is nothing that can keep you from going forward.

Your perfect love, Lord, does indeed cast out our fear.

12

"For God so loved the world, that he gave his only begotten Son, that whosoever believeth in him should not perish, but have everlasting life." John 3:16

Her name was Joanne and she had gone to church all her life. She taught a Sunday school class and was an officer in the women's society. She was active in her community — PTA, hospital, United Fund. She had a loving husband who was a successful businessman and three bright, attractive children. They lived in a four-bedroom ranch-style house in one of the better sections of town, drove a new car and last winter vacationed in the Caribbean. Everything was about perfect. Then one day her husband dropped dead at work. Joanne was shattered, and even after several months she was still unable to overcome her grief. She came to church less frequently, quit some of the work in the community and stayed at home most of the time.

One day her minister called and after hearing about her continuing depression, he asked Joanne a strange question.

"Have you been born again?"

"Why I've gone to church all my life," she said. "My mother, my father . . ."

"But have you really been born again? Accepted Christ and turned your life totally over to Him?" She wasn't sure.

Opening his Bible to the story of Nicodemus (John 3:1-15), the minister read that moving story. When he finished, he prayed. Then, Joanne prayed and asked Christ to come into her life. From that day forward, her life took on new excitement. She overcame her grief and rejoined the human race.

After President Carter's public declaration of his faith, people are asking in increasing numbers, "What does it mean to be *born again*?" If you know and have experienced it, then you have a great opportunity to help others to become a new person in Christ. If you aren't sure that you have been born again, then today would be a good day for asking God to take over the management of your life. A beginning point would be saying a prayer along these lines:

God, I believe You sent Your Son, Jesus Christ, to save me from my sins. I accept Him as my Lord and Savior.

13 "A man there was, though some did count him mad,
The more he cast away the more he had."
John Bunyan (PILGRIM'S PROGRESS)

On Carnegie Lake near where I live, some of the country's outstanding eight-oared crews race against each other each spring. What an exciting sight watching those sleek shells knife through the water, propelled by the rhythmic rowing of young men who put everything they have into this demanding sport. After one close race, I talked with a member of the winning crew.

"What is the single most important thing in crew racing?" I asked him.

"Teamwork," he replied without hesitation. "Everyone must pull together."

Whatever the goal—a successful business, a loving family, a good school, a strong church—team work is essential. Unless we pull together, the chances of getting the job done are greatly reduced.

Are you a good team player? If you are on Christ's team, you should be, because self-sacrifice is one of the tenets of your belief. Christ's word on the subject was: "It is more blessed to give than to receive." (Acts 20:35) But the amazing thing about giving selflessly is that you always receive something in return. Today, try thinking and acting in terms of others' wants and needs, and you'll reap some unexpected rewards.

Channel our lives, Lord, into ever-flowing rivers of service.

14
I'll go where you want me to go, dear Lord
O'er mountain or plain or sea;
I'll say what you want me to say, dear Lord,
I'll be what you want me to be.
Mary Brown hymn

In her illuminating and instructive book, FOR SUCH A TIME AS THIS (Revell), Vonette Bright, wife of Campus Crusade for Christ president, Bill Bright, says that when she and Bill were first ministering to college students, she found herself more often than not in the kitchen preparing refreshments while the others were in the living room talking about the Christian life.

"And I resented it terribly. I wanted to have the glamour of being in the forefront," she writes. But Vonette Bright is bright. She prayed about her Martha role and saw that she was serving God in the kitchen. "Little by little I began to experience real joy—God-given joy—in preparing punch and cookies for Him."

Today, my friends Vonette and Bill are both being used in a mighty way because they were willing to humble themselves for Him. When we are willing to do any job God asks of us, the result is predictable. He smiles upon us and commends us as the Lord did in Christ's parable: "Well done, good and faithful servant; thou hast been faithful over a few things, I will make thee ruler over many things. . ." (Matthew 25:23) When you feel a job is beneath you, a wise person once advised, get down on your knees and pray about it. There it won't look so lowly.

Lord, give us willing heads, willing hearts and willing hands.

We give Thee but Thine own,
Whate'er the gift may be;
All that we have is Thine alone,
A trust, O Lord, from Thee.
William W. How hymn

A few weeks ago we planted our garden—tomatoes, potatoes, green beans, carrots, peppers, eggplant, squash and radishes. Yesterday the first fruits of our efforts were realized when we enjoyed several tender and succulent radishes at dinner.

The growth of a seed is still a miracle to me. Horticulturists can explain hybrids and mutations and the effects of chemicals and fertilizers upon a seed, but still one needs a seed to begin with. How earth, water and sunlight can change a tiny brown seed into a succulent radish is incredible.

Life is full of God-affirming miracles. The evidence of His hand upon our world is so overwhelming it humbles all else. Our very existence, our birth and growth, are further testimony to His power and beneficence. The least we can do is acknowledge our gratitude for His gifts. The most we can do is serve Him daily with our lives. Neither is enough, but they are all He asks.

All things come of thee, O Lord, and of thine own have we given thee.(I Chronicles 29:14)

16 **Through waves, and clouds, and storms,
He gently clears thy way;
Wait thou His time: so shall this night
Soon end in joyous day.**
**Paul Gerhardt (translated
by John Wesley)**

When one of my sons was young, he was afraid to put his head underwater while learning to swim. As a result his progress in swimming reached a certain plateau and stopped. Nothing I could say or do would embolden him to get his face wet. Then his mother bought a pair of plastic goggles. With these, she told him, he could open his eyes under water and see where he was going. He bought the idea, and in no time at all lost his fear. From that point forward, his swimming improved dramatically.

We all know what it is to be afraid. Venturing into new territory — be it a dark street in an unfamiliar town, or learning to drive a car, or making a speech before an audience of strangers—can fill us with a certain amount of apprehension. But in most cases our fears dissipate when we challenge them. Once we see the anatomy of a problem it becomes less imposing and less frightening.

Faith is a tool that helps us deal with the unknown. It helps light up dark places. But even when we cannot see where we are stepping, we learn from experience to trust God to keep us safe. Like my son's swimming goggles, your faith can give you the courage to go where you haven't ventured before. "I will lead them in paths they have not known; I will make darkness light before them, and crooked things straight." (Isaiah 42:16)

When we are frightened by what lies ahead, Lord, it is helpful to know that You have gone before us.

17 "God shall supply all your needs according to his riches in glory." Philippians 4:19

The wages of sin is death, the Bible tells us (Romans 6:23). Have you ever thought about the wages of worry? Unless you are vastly different from most people, you are anxious about something today, something that you needn't be. Some people who are reading these words are so upset, so uptight, so distracted by their concern that they cannot concentrate on anything else. Thus they are immobilized, unable to perform anything but the simplest duty.

I would submit to you that the wages of such deep worry are also death—if death can be defined as an "absence of life." When worry consumes all of our thoughts and time and energy, it is sure that we are not "living." Do me—and yourself—a favor. If you are really worried about something today, write your problem in capsule form below. Do it in as few words as possible.

Now write your ideal solution to the problem (also as succinctly as possible).

Now pray and ask God for His counsel. Last, copy the above verse from Philippians (change the pronoun *your* to *my*) and take it with you wherever you go. Repeat it until you know it by heart.

I believe You will supply all my needs, Lord, and today—this moment—I commit them all to You.

18

(**Father's Day**)
Lord, teach me understanding
That I may know the way to my child's
    heart and mind;
Give me strength,
That I may not fail him in minor tragedies
    or in great crises;
Give me courage,
That I may stand firm when he is wrong, or
    wayward, or heedless;
Grant me humility,
That I may acknowledge my own mistake
    when he is right.

**Gordon Phillips,
A Father's Prayer**

"Could I use the car Friday night to go to the concert?" I asked my dad. He hesitated. I was 16 and hadn't had my driver's license very long. Finally, he agreed.

A whole carload of friends went along and it was a great evening until on the way home the motor overheated and quit, miles from town. I feared I'd done irreparable damage.

We caught rides home without any trouble, but I remember how worried I was about my dad's reaction. *He might not let me use the car again for months*, I thought. But to my relief, he only said, "Don't worry about it. We'll get it fixed tomorrow." Then he laughed and recalled the first time he'd used his father's car, a brand new Model A. "I sideswiped a pole and tore off a fender," he said. The reason for telling me the story was obviously meant to make me feel better.

I've never forgotten his reaction. It's helped me deal with

similar problems involving my own children.

When I think about my dad's strengthening and encouraging love on this day that we honor fathers, I am reminded that my Heavenly Father's love matches and surpasses anything I've ever known. That is good to know when I fail and need His understanding and forgiveness.

Father, we thank You for our fathers and their love. They give us an idea of the depth of Yours.

19

"Before the mountains were brought forth . . . thou formed the earth, from everlasting to everlasting, thou art God."
Psalm 90:2

Once when a thunderstorm began, a little girl raced inside the house of her grandparents and threw herself into the arms of Grandpa, who was sitting in his favorite chair.

"I hate storms," she said, closing her eyes tightly and burying her face against his chest.

"Why?" he asked.

"Because of all that lightning. I'm afraid I might get hit."

"You're safe here," Grandpa said giving her a squeeze. "Lightning's not all that bad. In fact it's part of God's plan." Then he explained to her that lightning heats the atmosphere which is full of nitrogen. Once dissolved, the rain carries it to earth where the chemical, essential to plant growth, feeds the earth and nourishes crops. Thereafter, his granddaughter had a new understanding of lightning and its purpose.

So many things in life have two or more sides to them — weeds blossom into beautiful wildflowers, uncomfortable body temperatures destroy harmful bacteria, bone-chilling cold that causes heat bills to sky rocket also cracks seeds and enables them to grow, and poisonous snakes destroy rodents and figure in the balance of nature.

God created a wonder-filled universe, full of secrets, many of which have yet to be unlocked. Before you complain about some condition in your life, some excess or some shortage, consider how it may figure in God's design. The key to happi-

ness is accepting things we cannot change, and the key to
spiritual growth is thanking God for His many gifts—sunshine,
rain and even lightning.

*Help me to remember, Lord, that in Your world everything
has a purpose.*

20

Come to the Light, 'tis shining for thee,
Sweetly the Light has dawned upon me;
Once I was blind, but now I can see,
The Light of of the world is Jesus.
Philip P. Bliss

"More than half the people who come to me seeking help," a
local minister said, "come because they are suffering an identity crisis." He explained it as being a time when people ask:
What do I want to do with my life?

Those who have lost interest in their work or are searching
for occupational direction, those who feel listless, unimportant, drifting, bored—all could be said to be having an identity
crisis.

Some people need professional help for such psychological
maladies—especially if problems persist unabated for lengthy
periods of time. Most pastors today have training in counselling, and can either offer help or refer a troubled person to
someone who can.

But many times our difficulties are ones with which we can
deal ourselves. When we are depressed, fearful, unsure and
just generally unable to cope with life, we need two things—an
understanding of our problems and a plan for dealing with
them. The Greek word *metanoia* means "change of mind,"
which is what Christ helped Zacchaeus accomplish. Zacchaeus,
you remember, was a dishonest tax collector. Jesus confronted
him with his negative, destructive way of life and helped him to
see how he could turn from his old ways and become a new
person.

The Bible says, "Ye shall know the truth, and the truth shall
make you free." (John 8:32) Christ releases us from a useless

existence and frees us for a fulfilling life of commitment. Accepting Him and servingHim are the surest cures for an identity crisis that I know.

All that we have is Yours, Lord, a paltry sum considering what You give in return.

"Now I lay me down to sleep
I pray the Lord my soul to keep."
A child's prayer

"How do you sleep when the wind blows," a plains state farmer inquired of a man applying for a job.

"Fine," he replied. "I once slept through a tornado."

"Good. You're hired," said the farmer. "We get lots of heavy wind this time of year. Anybody skitterish about storms would be awake most nights and be too tired to work the next day."

How do *you* sleep through storms? Your answer may say something about the depth of your faith. If you have accepted Christ, then you have nothing to fear from external forces. As a child of God, you are protected forever by His invincible power. You are eternally safe from all harm and nothing will ever be able to separate you from the love of God. You can sleep easy knowing those great verses from Romans (8:38,39) are not idle promises:

"For I am persuaded that neither death, nor life, nor angels, nor principalities, nor powers, nor things present, nor things to come, nor height nor depth, nor any other creature, shall be able to separate us from the love of God, which is in Christ Jesus our Lord."

Fill us with the peaceful reassurance that You are our guardian, Lord, whether we're awake or asleep.

"Better to light one candle than to curse the darkness."   **The Christophers' motto**

The late Father James Keller, founder of the Christophers, once spoke to a large gathering in the Los Angeles Coliseum. At a certain point in his talk, he motioned for a technician to turn out the lights, and the vast stadium was left in darkness. Then, Father Keller lit a single match, and urged the audience of 100,000 to do likewise. In a few seconds, the great arena was illuminated by light from thousands of matches, and the crowd was amazed at the amount of light produced by their mutual effort.

There are many times when we feel small and insignificant, unable to make any impact on people or events around us, but we should remember that together in communion with other Christians we can do mighty things. Jesus told His followers not to hide their light under a bushel (Matthew 5:15,16) and we shouldn't either. As a child of God, created in His image, you are important to Him and His work. Don't put yourself down as insignificant or untalented or of little worth. When you are on fire for God, your efforts are magnified many times and you can do mighty things in His name. Don't curse the darkness, but light the way for those lost in the shadows.

This little light of mine, Lord, I'm gonna let it shine.

 "Not by might, nor by power, but by my spirit, saith the Lord of hosts."
Zechariah 4:6

My son Steve, who is home from college for the summer, had a problem getting his car started the other morning. It had rained and the dampness had affected the ignition. Eventually, his battery went dead.

"May I hook up the jumper cables to the station wagon, Dad?" he called up the steps.

"Yes," I shouted back. In a couple of minutes, he had connected the two batteries and when he tried to start his car this time he was successful. Power from my stronger battery had been transferred to his weaker one, and as a result of the "boost" his car was running and regenerating lost energy. In a short while, his dead battery was full of power again.

Like my son, we have to turn to our Heavenly Father when our spiritual batteries need recharging—which is every day. Trying to operate on our own power is like pedaling a bicycle up a steep hill. It's exhausting. But when the Lord is our helpmate, the effort isn't half as bad. Before we know it, we've reached the top and are coasting down the other side.

If you've got an energy shortage in your personal life and you can't seem to generate enough power to get moving and get the things accomplished that you should, then call on the Lord. He is a specialist in regenerating spiritually dead batteries.

Empower us, O Holy Spirit, to accomplish things that by our own strength would be impossible.

24

God moves in a mysterious way
His wonders to perform;
He plants His footsteps in the sea,
And rides upon the storm.

William Cowper

Last year in these pages, we told the story of English poet William Cowper's unsuccessful suicide attempt. (See DAILY GUIDEPOSTS, 1977, page 51) In that episode, Cowper's hansom driver got lost in London fog and, instead of taking him to the Thames River, unknowingly deposited the poet back on his own doorstep. It was an occurrence Cowper found too mysterious to call "coincidence."

Now a reader points out that the lines above were included in the famous Olney Hymns collection (1779). Titled "Light Shining Out of Darkness," Cowper's hymn was published by the Reverend John Newton, who ministered to Cowper at his country parish in Olney, northwest of London.

Newton knew about God's mysterious ways himself. Son of a sea captain, his mother died when he was 6, and at 11 he joined his father at sea. His early life as a sailor was a failure, sin-filled and pointless. Then he read Thomas á Kempis' book, THE IMITATION OF CHRIST, which impressed him greatly. When

. a ship upon which he was serving encountered a violent storm a short time later, Newton accepted Christ and eventually became a minister. Like Cowper, he wrote poems that were set to music. One which recounted his miraculous story goes like this:

Amazing grace, how sweet the sound
That saved a wretch like me.
I once was lost, but now am found
Was blind but now I see.

"For thou shalt be his witness unto all men of what thou hast seen and heard."

Acts 22:15

A good many of us are assigned life roles that seem to require our working behind the scenes, off camera, in the wings. Someone like this was Edward Kimball who lived in Boston in the 1850's. There isn't much known about Kimball except that he taught Sunday school classes and that he was a very dedicated teacher.

One day Kimball called on one of his students who worked in a shoe store. It was apparently a slow day, for the two of them had time to talk about the young man's future when he wasn't waiting on customers. Before Kimball left, he had prayed with his student and the young man had accepted Christ and God's sovereignty for his life. It was quite a decision for the new convert who was to become the foremost evangelist of his time. His name was Dwight L. Moody.

If you sometimes think your role is insignificant, not very important, remember that God's work is the most vital of any. If we follow His leading and do the best that we can, we will be blessed for our faithfulness and others around us will be blessed, too. Whether the world recognizes your contributions or not, God does. Of that you can be sure.

We have many opportunities to tell others about You, Lord. Help us make the most of them.

Courage, brother! do not stumble,
Though thy path be dark as night;
There's a star to guide the humble,
Trust in God and do the right.

Norman MacLeod

There is a tree that grows in the arid lands of southwestern Arizona and southeastern California known as the Joshua tree. A member of the yucca family, it reaches a height of 15 to 30 feet and produces pointed green leaves and clusters of white flowers. But my interest in it was historical, not botanical. *Why*, I asked, *was it named after Joshua?* In Hebrew, his name means "the Lord saves." *Did the Joshua tree provide nourishment or shade for some desert traveler?* I wondered.

Research reveals that the tree was named by early Mormon settlers in the West who, when crossing this rugged terrain, commented that the yucca's angular branches looked "like the outstretched arms of Joshua leading us out of the wilderness." One would be hard pressed to find a better symbol of faith than Joshua, the successor of Moses who led the Israelites on their invasion of Canaan and was in command at the famous battle of Jericho.

The Lord's words to Joshua (1:9) when he assumed leadership are ones that all believers should memorize. They assure anyone called to new duties or sent on new missions of God's backing. "Be strong and of a good courage;" the Lord said, "be not afraid, neither be thou dismayed: for the Lord thy God is with thee whithersoever thou goest."

He makes that same promise to you and me when we commit our all to Him.

Give us, like Joshua, Lord, obedient hearts and minds.

"The hope of the righteous shall be gladness." Proverbs 10:28

I was on a speaking trip today, and at breakfast in a restaurant was served by the most outwardly happy person I've come upon in a long time. Smiling, effervescent, bright, the young woman simply bubbled over with pleasantness.

"Tell me," I finally asked, "why are you so happy?"

"I'm always this way," she answered with a laugh.

"Well, you're very unusual," I told her.

"I've got a lot to be happy about," she added. "I like my job. It helps me earn money for college. I'm studying to be a speech therapist. Also, I'm engaged to a wonderful guy. And to top it off, I'm a Christian."

How happy are you? Once upon a time it apparently was fashionable for Christians to go about with long faces as a way of showing how pious they were. I'd submit that my waitress today will attract more people to her faith than a hundred self-righteous stiffs. There's an old saying that a drop of honey will attract more flies than a gallon of vinegar. It must apply equally well to bringing people into the Kingdom.

You have given us reason to have happy hearts, Lord. Make it show on our faces.

Sitting still and wishing
Makes no person great.
The good Lord sends the fishing,
But you must dig the bait.

Anonymous

Poet John Masefield was a struggling writer, beginning to doubt that he had it in him to succeed in his chosen profession, when he came upon the quatrain above. He credited this simple verse with helping sustain him through his darkest days. As a result, he kept digging, kept working, kept trying, kept hoping. In time, he found a publisher for his poems, his work was read and his talent recognized.

What dreams and goals hold a lock on your heart? Do they seem a long way from realization? If so, don't trade them in for lesser ones until you have exhausted every avenue that might lead to their fruition.

"Pray as if everything depended upon God and work as if everything depended upon you" was the advice of a saint. That's a no-lose formula. If you pray and work with all that's in you, the odds for winning are in your favor. But even if you fall a little short, you can live with the results if you've given your all.

Lord, help us discern the difference between pipe dreams and God-inspired ones—and guide us to hug the latter.

"Chance is the pseudonym God uses when He doesn't want to sign His name."
Anatole France

The work of THEOS, a national organization (11609 Frankstown Road, Pittsburgh, Pennsylvania, 15235) dedicated to helping widows and widowers, has long had my admiration. Recently, I received a personal letter from its talented director, Bea Decker.

Mrs. Decker wanted to tell me, among other things, that one item in particular from last year's DAILY GUIDEPOSTS had helped her immensely. It was contained in a devotional on the subject of "the courtesy of Christ." (The point being that courtesy and kindness are Christlike virtues that we should practice diligently.)

"The message came at the exact time I needed to hear it," she wrote. "I had come home deeply disturbed by a cutting remark a man had made to me. I was tempted to write a curt note, setting him straight. Then I read your words, and suddenly I was filled with understanding and peace. A reply was unnecessary."

Like Mrs. Decker, several others have written to me, surprised that a devotional fell on a date that coincided with a specific personal need. Christians of long standing have come to believe that what the world calls "coincidence" is only God working in another miraculous way, sending specific people, words, healing, encouragement at a time when they are desperately needed.

If you are at wit's end today, troubled by some current problem that doesn't have a ready solution, ask God for His solution. When we remove our preconceived ideas of how we want a difficulty resolved and let the Lord intervene, inspiration which borders on the miraculous often results. It is indeed amazing what God can do—and what He's done for others, He'll do for you.

Lord, give me insight to recognize Your hand in things others may call coincidence.

"Therefore if any man be in Christ, he is a new creature: old things are passed away; behold, all things are become new."
II Corinthians 5:17

A recent study of top management people in some of the nation's leading companies revealed one constant factor. In almost every case, the men interviewed said they owed a great debt to their wives' support. "Without my wife standing with me, advising and supporting me," one executive stated, "I'd have failed miserably."

There is no question that we all need the love and understanding and support of others if we are to succeed at anything. The expression "self-made person" always has been a misnomer. No one is self-made unless it be a fool.

In addition to human support of mothers, fathers, relatives, friends, neighbors, co-workers, fellow church members, we all need God's backing, and the Bible promises it to all who believe in Christ, no matter what their race, age, creed, sex or station in life. The thief on the cross told Jesus, "Lord, remember me when thou comest into Thy kingdom," and Christ answered him, "Today shalt thou be with me in paradise." (Luke 23:42,43) His support can turn anyone's life around. All we need to do is turn to him.

Thank You, Lord, for the loving people You've sent into my life.

JULY 1978

S	M	T	W	T	F	S
						1
2	3	4	5	6	7	8
9	10	11	12	13	14	15
16	17	18	19	20	21	22
23	24	25	26	27	28	29
30	31					

"For as he thinketh in his heart, so is he." (Proverbs 23:7) Ask God to help you think and act positively in all your dealings this month. Expect your words and deeds to produce good results and they will.

JULY 1978

1 "I have lived, Sir, a long time, and the longer I
live, the more convincing proofs I see of this
truth—that God governs in the affairs of men.
And if a sparrow cannot fall to the ground
without His notice, is it probable that an empire
can rise without His aid?"

Benjamin Franklin

While the delegates to the Constitutional Convention at
Philadelphia were struggling to reach a consensus that would
lead to our Declaration of Independence about this date in
1776, the bespectacled printer-author-statesman-inventor-
philosopher Ben Franklin made the statement above, im-
ploring his colleagues to ask God's blessing upon their
deliberations. Otherwise, he pointed out, their dreams for a
free republic had little likelihood of success.

When we plan new undertakings, it is likewise important
that we ask God for His guidance. If we are really serious about
wanting His input, however, we must be open to His leading.
Sometimes that means delaying or altering our ideas to con-
form with God's. "Being sure of God's marching orders is easier

said than done," I can hear a skeptic say. The answer is to see for yourself. If you are willing to accept His sovereignty in your life and earnestly seek His will, you can be assured of the Lord's help in making any decision.

Father, we aren't trying to build empires, just lives that are centered in You. Help us.

2

"O God, our help in ages past, our hope for years to come."

Isaac Watts

A teenager nearly lost his life in a nearby river not long ago because he forgot one of the cardinal rules of water safety: never swim alone. Fortunately, a passerby heard his cries for help and saved him.

Youngsters need to be taught to use the buddy system when swimming because one never knows when he or she might get into trouble and need help. This is especially true when one is swimming in new or unfamiliar waters.

The buddy system has a spiritual parallel. All of us get into water over our heads from time to time, and we need a buddy to throw us a lifeline. Jesus Christ promises His followers that He will be that buddy, that friend, that brother, if we but ask. In John 15:7 He makes a wonderful sustaining promise, "If ye abide in me, and my words abide in you, ye shall ask what ye will, and it shall be done unto you."

Take my hand, Lord; lead me through the difficult, uncharted waters of life.

3

"One cannot control the length of his life, but he can have something to say about its width and depth."

Anonymous

At a baseball game once, I watched a fight develop between a runner and the catcher when they collided at home plate. In an instant, the two teams swarmed out onto the field and a free-for-all ensued. When that fighting ended, people in the stands began fighting among themselves, and the police were needed to restore order.

It seemed to me a simple case of "monkey see, monkey do"; and face it, the behavior of people sometimes seems little removed from the jungle.

Whether we realize it or not, our actions do have a contagious effect on others. One only need observe men's and women's clothing to see an example. When the designers of the fashion world decree longer hemlines on dresses or wider lapels on suits, style-conscious people adapt to these trends. By the same token, language is contagious. Sloppy English by adults begets the same from children.

But positive things are contagious, too. You can have a good influence on others by the moral and ethical quality of your life. Honesty, fairness, generosity, helpfulness, justice, kindness, all send ripples across the waters of life, and as a result others are prompted to do likewise. So set high standards for yourself and stick to your guns. There's nothing square about being a square shooter.

When we are tempted to give less than our best, Father, remind us of our high calling in You.

(*Independence Day*)
**My country, 'tis of thee,
Sweet land of liberty
Of thee I sing:**

Samuel Francis Smith

One of God's most thoughtful gifts to His children is memory, and on a holiday such as today my mind wanders back to the excitement this day held for me as a child . . .

The big Fourth of July parade always formed at the town hall. There, freshly polished fire engines gleamed apple red under a sky unblemished by clouds. Kids on bikes decorated with red, white and blue crepe paper rode dizzying figure-8s around the cordoned-off street. Drum majorettes in spotless white boots with red tassels practiced twirling their batons, and the reflection off those silvery sticks danced merrily across faces in the crowd. The crowd held no strangers, just mothers, dads, grandparents, aunts and uncles who always came "downtown" to watch. The horsemen, astride their well-brushed steeds, were at attention, and so were the gray-haired men in khaki, blue and green uniforms which had been cut for more svelte physiques than the ones they now draped.

I always started early enough, right after lunch, to be where the police chief turned on his flashing light and led the marchers up Main Street toward the high school—but I had to cross Cranbury Run on the way, and it had a special magic, too. Filled with all the country things God made to entertain a boy—melodic meadowlarks, hopscotching butterflies, sunning turtles and darting tadpoles—that meadow so gently parted by a brook could steal my mind in a minute. Only the sound of a band off in the distance, striking up some heartstopping march like "Stars and Stripes Forever" would remind me of the celebration and of time passing. Then, I'd run for blocks to bring up the rear of the big parade.

We thank You, Lord God, for Your truth which makes us free in every sense of the word.

 "He giveth power to the faint: and to them that have no might he increaseth strength."
Isaiah 40:29

The other day when we were preparing to go on a trip, I pushed the generator button in our motor home and blew out a giant fuse. Carelessly, I had forgotten to turn off an appliance, and the quick call for power had knocked out the electrical system. The mistake proved to be a costly one timewise because few businesses carry this type of 30-amp fuse, I discovered, and I must have made a dozen calls before I found a replacement.

There is one obvious analogy between electrical systems and people, namely that both have limited capacities. When you and I go too long without food or water or rest, or when we undergo too much emotional or physical stress, a breakdown is likely to occur. We overload our circuits, so to speak, and our systems malfunction.

Periods of shutdown, when we have little or no power, are times for healing in healthy minds and bodies. And given time, God can heal us. He has engineered a miraculous recovery mechanism in man that enables him to come back from devastating setbacks.

If you have had some physical problem that has left you without enough energy or power to accomplish what you feel you must, turn to the Source of all power, Jesus Christ. "I am the light of the world," He said in John 8:12. It is a scientific fact that where there is light there is power.

You are a never-ending source of power, O Lord. Remind me when I search elsewhere.

"The best way out is always through."
Robert Frost

Once a man was walking through the woods when he came upon a butterfly struggling to be free of its cocoon. Taking a knife from his pocket, he cut the shell and the butterfly emerged free to take flight. But it didn't. Suddenly, as the man studied the fragile insect he realized why. It was in the struggling that the butterfly developed and matured to the point that its wings were strong. Without this exhausting exercise, the insect would be earthbound.

When we long for shortcuts to the fulfillment of some ambition or dream, it might be helpful to remember this simple little illustration. As someone once said, "Nothing worthwhile was ever accomplished without work." God gave us the tools with which to make our sandcastles real, but we must put them to work or otherwise our dreams will never take shape. Time may be required, study may be needed and struggle will no doubt be involved, but the view from the mountaintop always erases the pain of the climb.

Lord, we know that with You on our side nothing is impossible.

7 **"Let the moment come when nothing is left but life, and you will find that you do not hesitate over the fate of material possessions."**
Eddie Rickenbacker

Encircling walls were one of the principal defenses of military powers during the city-state rivalries in ancient Greece. So it was that a visitor to Sparta in those times was surprised by the absence of such protective barriers. "Where are your walls?" he asked incredulously.

"I'll show you later," said the general who was conducting his guest around the city. In time they came to high ground that offered a panoramic view of a vast plain below. Thousands of Spartan soldiers, their armor gleaming, stood shoulder to shoulder, row upon seemingly endless row.

"There," said the general, pointing, "there are our walls, every man a brick."

Security always has been a dominant concern of man. Protecting one's life, one's family and one's possessions, a heavy responsibility. But Christ urged His followers to put Heavenly matters first . . . to put their treasures where moth and rust cannot corrupt and where thieves cannot steal. (Matthew 6:20) When you invest your life in spiritual instead of material things, you won't have to rely on walls or locks or safes or guards to protect your most valuable possession. That's because your faith is thief-proof.

You are our protection, Lord, our security in every trial, our rescuer from every danger.

For the beauty of the earth,
For the beauty of the skies,
For the love which from our birth
Over and around us lies;
Christ, our God, to thee we raise
This our hymn of grateful praise.

Folliott S. Pierpont hymn

While we were driving in the Allegheny mountains of Pennsylvania recently, my wife, Shirley, called my attention to the flowering crown vetch that covers most hillsides along the highway. Crown vetch (or *coronilla*) sends out runners in the manner of strawberry plants, spreading its cover over a wide area. It is particularly valuable along highways because it helps prevent rockslides and soil erosion.

As I drove along, the thought came to me that people need something to slow the erosion or aging process, too. Otherwise, as we move through life many of us become blasé about the beauty around us. Even Christians who should have spiritual immunization against such mind deterioration fall into old B.C. (Before Christ) habits. When I was a kid it was called *backsliding*, an expression I don't hear much anymore.

If you feel yourself getting ultra-critical of things or if you find yourself no longer marveling at the wonders of life, step back from what you're doing. You may be pressing too hard. Lie down on your back in an open field and study the vastness above. Frederick M. Lehman in his beautiful hymn "The Love of God" wrote, "Were every stalk on earth a quill/And every man a scribe by trade/To write the love of God above/ Would drain the ocean dry." Thank God for all the good and all the beauty and all the love He's put into your life. Chances are you are way ahead of the game.

For eyes to see golden sunsets, for ears to hear meadowlarks sing, for tongues to taste just-picked strawberries, and for a million other pleasures, we thank You, Father.

**My hope is built on nothing less
Than Jesus' blood and righteousness;
I dare not trust the sweetest frame,
But wholly lean on Jesus' name.**

Edward Mote hymn

Cathy Rigby, the talented gymnast who was on the U.S. team in the 1972 Olympics in Munich, recently recalled for *Guideposts* magazine readers a memorable piece of advice from her mother.

When she failed to win a gold medal and was feeling miserable because of it, Cathy's mother told her: "Doing *your* best is more important than being *the* best."

We all need to remember the truth of that statement when we stumble and fall. Not everyone can be first all the time. In fact, most of the lessons life has to teach come from defeats, not victories. For it is out of adversity that we advance, out of setbacks that we are seasoned, and out of struggle that we find the strength to continue. Doing your best won't insure a prize, but it will enable you to look others and yourself in the face.

God, give us the courage to go on when we fall short of our goals.

**"All things bright and beautiful,
All creatures great and small,
All things wise and wonderful,
The Lord God made them all."**

Cecil Frances Alexander

A DAILY GUIDEPOSTS reader from Detroit, Mrs. Russell Miller, wrote and shared a little story about an old Scottish Highlander who rose early every morning and walked off a little distance from his cottage. There he stood by himself and quietly watched the birth of a new day.

'Once a friend came by and asked, "What might ye be doin'?" The man answered, "I've come here each day for years and taken my hat off to God's beautiful world."

If you haven't taken your hat off lately to the beauty of God's magnificent creation, then you're overdue. It has never been equaled by anything man-made.

Open wide our eyes and minds, Father, to Your priceless gift of life.

 "Oh, God, Thy sea is so great and my boat is so small."
Old fisherman's prayer

Once not long ago, I took my children to Washington and one of our stops was the Smithsonian Institution. I have visited the great exhibits of that organization before and never had enough time to appreciate all of its many artifacts, and we only saw a fraction of them this time. But while we were there, Chris—10 at the time—marveled at the Spirit of St. Louis, Charles Lindbergh's famous plane, which hangs high overhead.

"That's a pretty small plane," my son said. I studied it and had to agree it was no 747, but then I realized it was not the size of the plane that was important. It was the size of the dream and the size of the faith of the man who flew it that made the difference. These were the ingredients that carried Lindbergh across the Atlantic.

Whether we succeed or fail in this mutual adventure of life depends not so much on our vehicle—we all are flying pretty small ships when we think of the size of the universe—but on the size of our dreams and our faith. If you're having trouble making your dream come true, perhaps your God is too small. Remember He specializes in lost causes. But with Him there is no such word as "impossible."

Give me the faith, Lord, to trust You in this sometimes overwhelming adventure of life.

12

Love ever gives—
Forgives—outlives—
And ever stands
With open hands.
And while it lives,
It gives.
For this is Love's prerogative—
To give, and give, and give.

John Oxenham

In the musical "Fiddler on the Roof," Tevye asks his wife, Golde, in song, "Do you love me?" She suggests that the answer is obvious. Hasn't she tended his children, milked the cow, washed his clothes and fixed his meals for 25 years? "Yes," Tevye answers, "but do you love me?" Again, she is circumventive in her answer, and again Tevye presses his query. Finally, Golde gives in. "Yes," she says, "I love you." A huge smile crosses Tevye's face, and he concludes, "After twenty-five years, it's nice to know."

Why do we sometimes withhold our love from each other? Why are we often so vocal in our criticism, but so restrained in our statements of affection? Apparently, some of us have been conditioned to be sparing with our love. Maybe our parents weren't demonstrative with their love. Maybe we fear rejection or maybe some (many men, apparently) are uncomfortable giving voice to endearments they feel. Though tangible caring, giving, helping and supporting may be the best evidence of true love, all of us like to hear the words, "I love you." Why not say them to someone dear to you today.

Lord, the Scriptures tell us that man does not live by bread alone (Deuteronomy 8:3). Help us remember this when it comes to expressions of love.

13

"The sea is His, and He made it; and His hands formed the dry land."

Psalm 95:5

While swimming in the Gulf of Mexico off the coast of Florida last summer, I felt my foot touch something rough on the bottom. At first I thought it was a scallop shell, but when I brought it to the surface, I discovered it was a sand dollar, a flat round sea urchin that lives in sandy ocean beds.

Showing it to my children, I told them there is a Christian legend about the sand dollar. The story is related best in this poem:

> Upon this odd shaped sea shell
>   a legend is told
> About the life of Jesus
>   the wondrous tale of old.
>
> The center marking plainly shows
>   the well known Guiding Star
> That led to tiny Bethlehem
>   the Wise Men from afar.
>
> The Christmas flower, Poinsettia
>   for His Nativity,
> The Resurrection too is marked,
>   the Easter Lily, see.
>
> Five wounds were suffered by our Lord
>   from nails and Roman's spear
> When He died for us on the cross;
>   the wounds show plainly here.

Within the shell, should it be broke
    five Doves of Peace are found
To emphasize this legend
    so may Peace and Love abound.

O Lord of heaven, and earth and sea,
To Thee all praise and glory be.
        Christopher Wordsworth hymn

14

"Think that day lost whose slow descending sun
Views from thy hand no noble action done."
        Jacob Bobart

Let me serve up some figures upon which you can chew today. According to the latest statistics on church membership, 131 million people—better than 61% of the U.S. population— belong to Christian churches,and 94% of the U.S. population according to the most recent Gallup poll, "believe in God."

Those are impressive figures indeed, and the moral and spiritual impact of the people behind them is tremendous. Yet, one wonders about the degree of dedication and commitment they represent. How much spiritual power for good lies dormant or sits impassive in the pews? Or to put it as an old evangelist once did: Are you standing on the promises or just sitting on the premises?

Christ, quoted by John in Revelation 3:16, speaks of His disdain for the lukewarm . . . "I will spew thee out of my mouth." If you call yourself a Christian, a believer in Jesus, then there are inheritant costs of discipleship. One of the costs is serving your fellowman whenever and wherever you discover needs. Don't be just a number, a statistic, a person on the roll, receiving God's dole. Be a giver, a shaker and mover, an active member of the Church universal.

When another is suffering, Lord, help me remember there is never an excuse for passing by on the other side of the road.

"Judge not, that ye be not judged. For with
what judgment ye judge, ye shall be
judged. . . ."

Matthew 7:1,2.

It takes experience to weed a garden, I've discovered. A few
weeks ago I was working with my wife, Shirley, in our little plot
and I came to some lacy, green plants that had sprung up near
the eggplant. I knew they weren't supposed to be there, so
impetuously I yanked out a handful and threw it aside. Just
then Shirley looked up from where she was working on her
knees.

"That's a wildflower," she said. "Butter-and-eggs, I think." I
disagreed. "Well, anyway, don't pull any more," she scolded.
Reluctantly, I gave the rest of the stuff a reprieve.

Today, when I went to the garden, I noticed several sprigs of
variegated yellow and gold-orange flowers on the stalks of the
"weeds" I almost pulled. It *was* butter-and-eggs, a colorful
member of the figwort family.

More often than you and I like to think we place people and
things into higher and lower categories—sometimes with the
capriciousness of a tyrant. Like weeding a garden, we are often
guilty of placing judgmental labels on human beings, a practice
that must grieve our Heavenly Father considerably. Why?
Because it isn't our job to vote on the worthiness or unworthi-
ness of others. Our job is to be agents of God's love. One of the
most desirable fruits of the Spirit is to be longsuffering. (Galatians 5:22) When you allow room in your garden for
different—and sometimes difficult—people, you will often
discover flowers growing where you expected to find weeds.

Make me as tolerant of others, Lord, as You are of me.

"I am come that they might have life, and
that they might have it more abundantly."
John 10:10

For more than a dozen years, a group of touring golf profession-
als have been meeting one night a week for Bible study. It was

begun by my friend, Jim Hiskey, a former touring pro. The fact that players meet for prayer and Bible study only becomes news when one of the young men in the group (which numbers about 15) does well and wins a tournament or two. And last year, after more success than he had known in four previous years, it was 30-year-old Rik Massengale's turn to tell reporters how his faith in Christ had turned his life around.

"Both my golf game and my marriage were falling apart," he recalls. "Then I heard Billy Graham speak. His people gave me some literature, which I studied. It wasn't long until I entered into a personal relationship with Christ. Now I'm at peace. The pressure's gone."

How does he explain his dramatic improvement on the tour? "I've got the same old swing I had when I wasn't winning," he says, "but now golf isn't the most important thing in my life. The Lord comes first."

No matter what our line of work, we always have more success when the Lord is in it. When we take Him on as our playing partner, we find new power, new strength, new perspective. The result inevitably manifests itself first in our attitude, and that new frame of mind allows us to relax and do our best. If you're having trouble performing some task, ask God to guide your thoughts and actions.

The results may surprise you.

Help us put You first, God, others second and ourselves last.

**Open my eyes, that I may see
Glimpses of truth Thou hast for me.**
Clara H. Scott hymn

Yesterday, a friend that I'd not seen in some time hailed me as I was walking up the street and asked if I'd have a cup of coffee with him. I really wanted to pass. There were several things yet to accomplish before dinner and I knew I'd never get finished if I accepted his invitation. But . . . I did. And I'm glad.

He had family problems he wanted to discuss with someone

who'd give an attentive ear. That's about all I provided. But it was enough because as he talked I observed his thoughts tilting toward what I felt was a proper solution, and when we parted he had decided on that course of action.

Unspoken calls for help come to us most every day, but unless we are careful we will miss a good many, and as a result miss an opportunity to serve. Sometimes those pleas are camouflaged or disguised in innocent or casual-sounding phrases such as "Got time for a cup of coffee?" If you keep your spiritual antenna pointed toward your Heavenly Father, He will help you receive His signals and teach you to "read between the lines." You'll then not only be a giver of blessings, but also a receiver of them, too.

> *Lord, give me a heart unspurning*
> *A mind both wise and discerning.*

18   **"Therefore if thou bring thy gift to the altar, and there rememberest that thy brother hath aught against thee; leave there thy gift and go thy way; first be reconciled to thy brother, and then come and offer thy gift."**

Matthew 5:23,24

The story is told that while working on his painting "The Last Supper," Leonardo da Vinci had a violent argument with a friend. Bitter words were exchanged, and the two parted in anger.

Returning to his canvas, the artist put his brush to work on the face of Jesus, but after a few poorly executed strokes he quit. The argument had unnerved him and he was too upset to continue. Instead, according to the story, he went to his friend's house and asked his forgiveness. Then he returned to his work and was able to continue painting the face of Jesus.

When we are upset by external problems, there is often a pronounced internal reaction. Some doctors believe that as much as 75 percent of physical illness is psychosomatic (mentally induced). Headaches, stomachaches and rising blood pressure are only a few of the maladies that can occur when worry or anger take hold of us.

If you are tense or anxious about something in your life today, try to isolate the reason. Perhaps you are just exhausted from continual pressure of duties and responsibilities. Whatever, take a few moments to quiet yourself. Some people do this by taking a walk, or reading from a book, or listening to quiet music, or working in their gardens. I'd suggest a few minutes of meditation. Ask God to calm you. Repeat a favorite verse of Scripture. Breathe deeply and go back to your work determined to pace yourself better. If there is some guilt or resentment that needs to be dealt with, take care of it. Like Leonardo da Vinci, you won't be able to do your best until you can concentrate fully on the work at hand.

Quiet my heart and calm my soul, O Lord of peace.

"Speak Lord for Thy servant heareth . . . "

I Samuel 3:9

Not long after I graduated from college, a radio station in Ohio (WONW, Defiance) hired me as an announcer. One of my assignments was to do the play-by-play descriptions of any athletic contest the station covered—football, basketball, baseball, track.

When a broadcast was scheduled, I would accompany an engineer to the site of the sports event and we would set up our microphones and amplifier and check the transmission lines back to the station. Then when it came time for us to go on the air we knew for sure everything was ready to be transmitted. Once we had made connections we kept an open line between our broadcasting point and the station. That way either party could contact the other on a moment's notice.

An open line is important in personal relationships, too. People who depend on each other—husbands and wives, parents and children, bosses and employees, fellow Christians—need to be able to communicate freely and frequently if they are to stay on the same wave length and be supportive of each other. And when it comes to spiritual growth, it is imperative that we keep an open line between ourselves and God. In that manner, we can express our concerns whenever they arise and our Heavenly Father can give us His counsel and guidance. Like Samuel, we need attentive ears that are attuned to God's voice, ready to receive His messages at any time, day or night.

Guide us in making difficult decisions today, Lord.

"Happiness adds and multiplies as we divide it with others."
Anonymous

When I hear people say they aren't needed, that they have nothing to give, I'm reminded of the story that is told about a totally defeated man who decided to take his own life. *I am going to jump off the bridge into the river*, he said to himself, *unless someone I meet on the way gives me some recognition, some sign of caring.*

Thus he set out across the city to the river. A truck driver honked a warning to him at one intersection, and a policeman directing traffic held up a halting palm at another; otherwise no one paid him any attention whatsoever. No one spoke, nodded or even smiled. That is, not until he reached the bridge and walked out on it. There a freckle-faced young boy trying to unsnarl his fishing tackle asked, "Mister, could you help me?" The man looked at the line. It was a hopeless tangle. "It can't be fixed. You'll have to throw it away," he said sourly.

"I can't," the boy said. "It's all I've got and I don't have money to buy any more."

For a moment the man studied the lad's anxious face. Then, he looked at the line. "In that case," he said softly, "I guess we don't have any choice but to untangle the mess." And together they worked for nearly an hour until the last knot came free.

Watching the boy joyfully cast out his line, the man suddenly realized that he had untangled a lot more than a fishing line. In helping the boy with his problem, he'd forgotten his own.

When we get depressed, Lord, point us to the needs of others.

"I know whom I have believed and am persuaded that he is able to keep that which I have committed unto him against that day."

II Timothy 1:12

Paul Tillich, the brilliant German theologian, wrote that all men are interested in salvation, all have ultimate concerns.

"What is your ultimate concern?" a seminarian was once asked.

"That the Ultimate is concerned with me," he answered.

Do we serve a personal God, one who is intimately concerned with our needs, our safety, our spiritual well-being? Christ answered that question with His parable about the lost sheep. (Matthew 18) Even if a shepherd had 99 animals safely in the fold, He explains, the shepherd would be worried about the missing one and would go and search for it. If successful, Christ said, the shepherd would "rejoiceth more of that sheep than of the ninety and nine which went not astray."

So it is with our Heavenly Father. We serve a God who loves us and wants us for His own. Such love should not go unrequited.

Bring us safely into Your fold, Lord, where there is perfect peace.

"With men this is impossible; but with God all things are possible."

Matthew 19:26

"I can't do it," my youngest son said the other day when I asked him to guide the sailboat with the rudder.

"Sure you can," I answered. "Try it." A few minutes later he was proudly steering the boat across the lake.

Whenever I hear someone say "I can't," I want to look behind the statement. More often than not, people don't mean that they are incapable, but that they are afraid to try, afraid to risk, afraid to fail.

Dr. Sara Jordan of the Lahey Clinic in Boston once prescribed a "mind shampooing" for one of her patients imprisoned by negative thinking. And that's what you and I need whenever we cower in the face of a challenge. "The difficult we do immediately, the impossible takes a little longer" was a famous World War II motto. The Bible says, "If you can believe, all things are possible." (Mark 9:23)

If you're bogged down by some problem that won't go away, put it under a microscope today. Don't say "I can't" until you've exhausted every possibility. Pray about the obstacle. Ask God to give you a new insight into the difficulty. Then, attack it anew—with faith.

Lord, help me remove the "im" from impossible.

"If we discovered that we had only five minutes left to say all we wanted to say, every telephone booth would be occupied by people calling other people to stammer that they loved them. Why wait until the last five minutes?"

Christopher Morley

While driving in the car yesterday, I had the radio tuned to a country-and-western station. The lyrics to one song were about the vitamins one needs to stay healthy—A, B, C, D, E and so on.

"But," the singer drawled, "the vitamin you need most is Vitamin L (love)."

I certainly subscribe to that, and so do thousands upon thousands of psychiatrists, psychologists, ministers and doctors who do a land-office business counselling people who are undernourished when it comes to love. And I'm talking about love in its fullest dimension, the kind that connotes deep commitment, lasting involvement, total concern and caring.

When people feel unloved and/or feel they have no one to love, they suffer a spiritual and psychological death. And only love can resurrect those lifeless souls.

As I'm sure you know, the New Testament was first written in Greek, and there are three words for love used. They are *eros* (erotic love), *philos* (brotherly love) and *agape* (Christian love). The first has a self focus, the second and third have others as their focus. When we practice *philos* and *agape* love, our Christ-likeness is revealed. We all need to give and to receive Vitamin L daily. Without it, Paul said in I Corinthians 13:2, "I am nothing." And so are we.

Fill our hearts, Lord, with a love that overflows to those around us.

24

"A wise man will make haste to forgive, because he knows the true value of time, and will not suffer it to pass away in unnecessary pain."

Samuel Johnson

The middle-aged woman was afflicted with arthritis in her hands and wrists, and it was so painful that she gave up playing the piano at church. Medication helped some, but the pain persisted and even seemed to grow worse. One day her doctor asked a very personal question:

"Ruth," he began, "you may choose not to answer this question, but I'm going to ask it anyway. Do you have some deep resentments or hatred in your life?" At first, the woman denied that she had any such feelings. Then her eyes filled with tears. Yes, she had a sister whom she felt had cheated her in a business venture. The two women had not spoken to each other in years.

"Your physical problem could be related," the doctor told her. "Even if it isn't, you are carrying some self-destructive seeds. Why not talk the matter over with your sister?"

The woman took the physician's advice, went to her sister, forgave her and reaped all the rewards of a healed relationship. But there was more. To her surprise, her arthritis improved remarkably. Oh, it didn't go away entirely, but she began playing the piano at church again. Some say better than ever.

Never let us forget, Lord, that good health is a symphonious concert of body, mind and soul.

25

"Ask, and it shall be given you: seek, and ye shall find; knock and it shall be opened unto you."

Matthew 7:7

A reader of something I had written dropped me a note to take exception. "You say that God answers prayer, and give many convincing examples by way of proof. But I would contend that for every incident that you give, there must be millions of unanswered prayers. By showing the exception to the rule, you are misleading people for whom prayer is not answered into thinking something is wrong with *them*."

Reading between the lines, I'd guess that my correspondent has had some series of problems and/or disappointments that have left him or her (the letter was unsigned) disillusioned with God. It is easy to come to the conclusion that He doesn't answer prayer when we fight a virulent problem for a long time without making headway. Job had every reason to feel deserted, unloved, uncared for, but he continued to pray, to remain loyal and faithful through an ordeal that would have consumed a lesser man of faith. His example should be a memorable lesson for us all.

It has been said that God answers prayers in three ways: yes, no and wait. Don't yield to unbelief in the face of unresolved conflict, but "pray without ceasing" (I Thessalonians 5:17). Your faith will not be in vain.

Sustain our faith, Lord, when doubts assail us and discouragement grows.

 "If the Son therefore shall make you free, ye shall be free indeed."

John 8:36

Bill was a successful stockbroker in New York City, a young man with an unlimited future. Then he started drinking heavily and he became an admitted alcoholic. Though he wanted to stop drinking and he tried with all his might, nothing worked. He thought his condition hopeless. Then, a friend, a former drunk, told him how he had defeated his drinking problem through a new-found faith in God. Bill wasn't interested in religion and rejected the idea. But the next time he was in a hospital "drying out," the friend came to see him and suggested again that he turn to God. Later, alone, Bill got to thinking about "this God business."

"I realized that I was powerless," he recalled, "that I couldn't help myself and and nobody else could help me . . . I sat up in bed and said, 'If there be a God, let Him show Himself now.' All of a sudden there was a light, a blinding, white light that filled the whole room. A tremendous wind seemed to be blowing all around me and right through me. I felt that I stood in the presence of God. I felt a sense of peace, and I was sure beyond all doubt that I was free from my obsession with alcohol."

That was how a man named Bill Wilson found his way back to health. But that is only part of the story. From that hospital vision sprang an organization that over the years has helped thousands of Bills. It is called Alcoholics Anonymous.

We may not be slaves to alcohol, Lord, but we may be in bondage to other things that separate us from You. Help us overcome them.

"Study to show thyself approved unto God, a workman that needeth not be ashamed . . . "
II Timothy 2:15

When I was in the Army, K.P. (kitchen police) was a much-dreaded assignment. One of the chores of such a detail was peeling potatoes. Until recently, I had never heard of anyone who liked the job.

English-seaman Gerald Pereth was the exception apparently. Instead of approaching a mound of unpeeled potatoes with disdain, this merchant marine took on the task with great enthusiasm, and the results showed it.

Potatoes peeled by Pereth were unbelievably smooth, according to my source. All eyes and blemishes were scraped away. So exceptional was his work that he was hailed as a peeler *par excellence*. No one could hold a blade to his spuds.

When it came time to retire, Pereth went to London and opened a business of his own. Doing what? You guessed it, peeling potatoes. Today, he owns a small but profitable business selling perfectly peeled, fancy, select potatoes to the best restaurants in town.

If you are faced with some lackluster job or task today, try throwing yourself into it with enthusiasm. Seek out ways to do it with a little imagination, a little flair. If you do, you may discover more fulfillment in a task than you imagined. You might even learn to like it. Barring that, you'll at least finish quicker and be able to go on to other more satisfying pursuits.

Remember, when faced with a boring job, foot-dragging won't accomplish anything except, perhaps, give you holey shoes.

Open our eyes, Lord, to the hidden joys of our daily work.

"For God hath not given us the spirit of fear; but of power, and of love, and of a sound mind."
II Timothy 1:7

A few miles from where I live is a peaceful little crossroads known as Grovers Mills, New Jersey, the site of a fictional Martian attack in an H. G. Wells story. Actor Orson Welles' famous 1938 radio dramatization of the "invasion" sent listeners into instantaneous panic. The phone lines of fire departments, hospitals and rescue squads were jammed. Police and national guards were alerted. Fear-stricken residents fled into the streets. Only repeated disclaimers by authorities over a period of several hours were able to convince people that the whole thing was an unintentional hoax.

Fear is a contagious disease, and only faith can immunize a person from it. If in an emergency you are unsure of yourself and unsure of your standing with God, you are likely to be a "carrier" of the germs that spread fear. But if you have put your life in His hands, if you are committed to trusting Him in all things—big and little—you have a built-in governor that will throttle runaway emotions. The source of courage is faith; the source of unjustified fear, doubt. You can do all things through Christ who strengthens you (Philippians 4:13)—even remain calm and composed while others are losing their cool.

We believe that nothing can separate us from Your love, God, not even death. Help our lives witness to that truth.

**Among the great and glorious gifts
Our heavenly Father sends
Is the gift of understanding
That we find in loving friends.**
Helen Steiner Rice

A favorite story of mine that Norman Vincent Peale tells concerns an aging minister who lost his wife of many years. Upon hearing the news, a friend of the bereaved man went to him and persuaded the preacher to go with him to his lake cottage nearby. After a simple meal and a little conversation around a roaring log fire, the friend put the minister to bed, tucking him in with the care a mother would give to a sick child.

"Aren't you going to bed?" the minister asked.

"No," said the friend. "I think I'll sit by the fire for a spell."

Several times through the night, the broken-hearted pastor awoke. Each time, he saw his friend sitting across the room, silhouetted by the fire he'd kept burning. It was his friend's reassuring vigil, the minister recalled later, that helped sustain him through that long, painful night.

He also said something else: "I'd always wondered what Christ looked like. That night it came to me that He must look just like my friend who sat up all night by that open fire."

Trying to find words to console a bereaved friend is one of the most difficult things we are called upon to do. Invariably, we feel awkward and helpless. But more than our words, friends and loved ones need our presence. That single gesture is often enough to reassure them that they are not alone in the loneliest hours of life. So be there—it is the most Christlike thing you can do.

Make me sensitive to the hurts of others, Father, and use me as Your healing agent.

"Better to do a good deed near home than travel a thousand miles to burn incense."
Chinese proverb

Sir Arthur Conan Doyle, the creator of the Sherlock Holmes mystery stories, gained fame as a writer by the exploits of his intrepid detective; but after a while he grew tired of the series and decided to devote his talents to more erudite literature. To free himself of mysteries, he wrote a final chapter in which Inspector Holmes was killed in a fall off a cliff. However, fans of Sherlock Holmes were so unsettled by Doyle's decision that they prevailed on him to resurrect his leading man. Thus, another story was written, one that began by explaining how Holmes was saved from the fall, and the series continued *ad infinitum*.

In real life, people grow tired of others, too, and they would like nothing better than to write them out of their lives as Doyle did Sherlock Holmes. In essence, that's what a woman once told me she'd like to do with her alcoholic husband. But unlike fictional characters in a book or a play, real people can't be walked on and off stage on a whim. Each of us knows individuals who have problems too heavy for them to carry alone. When they are friends or loved ones or neighbors, the responsibility for helping them may fall on us. How you and I respond to these people, how willingly we carry these "spiritual bundles" God gives us, says much about our Christian maturity. Jesus instructed us on such matters when He concluded His parable of the Good Samaritan with these words: "Go and do thou likewise." (Luke 10:37)

When we grow weary and footsore from the journey, Lord, remind us that we can find rest at Your doorstep.

 "It's good to remember that not even the Master Shepherd can lead if the sheep do not follow Him but insist on running ahead of Him or taking side paths."
Catherine Marshall

Yesterday I was reading the story of Balaam (Numbers 22:5-35) to my son Daniel, and he was quite amused by the fact that the ass could see the angel who stood in their way while Balaam could not. You'll recall that Balaam got so angry with the animal that he beat it three times—once for running off into a field, once for crushing its master's foot against a wall and finally for falling down in a heap with Balaam astride. Then, to top it all, the animal talked. I submit that this is indeed a story with a lighter side.

But it also has a serious point. Finally, Balaam's eyes were opened, and he saw the angel, who impressed upon him the importance of obedience to God's instructions. Balaam, as we know from the rest of the story, followed the Lord's directions.

Now, you and I are not likely to meet up with any talking donkeys today, but the truth is the Lord sometimes uses unusual means for speaking to His children. If your plans are met by repeated roadblocks, ask God for reconfirmation of your directions. His voice is clearest to those who seek to do His will.

Keep us from talking so much, Lord, that we miss Your still small voice.

AUGUST 1978

S	M	T	W	T	F	S
		1	2	3	4	5
6	7	8	9	10	11	12
13	14	15	16	17	18	19
20	21	22	23	24	25	26
27	28	29	30	31		

When you are feeling unloved or unappreciated, as we all are from time to time, remember that God's love for you is constant, unwavering, everlasting. You are special, unique and worthy in His sight, so don't despair. Instead, reach out to others who are feeling low and show them the love you have found in Him.

AUGUST 1978

 "For by grace are ye saved through faith; and that not of yourselves: it is the gift of God: Not of works, lest any man should boast."

Ephesians 2:8-9

When Christopher, my 12-year-old son, was given permission to go with some friends on a bike trip and his brother Daniel, 8, was not (because he was too young), the latter complained, "It isn't fair." He went off to his room in tears until his mother mollified him with a piece of chocolate cake and an understanding ear.

Daniel's beef was that his parents were playing favorites, and he wanted a fair shake. Justice is something we all seek—in our families, on our jobs, from the state, from God. When we don't receive a fair deal, we are upset.

Jesus told a parable about laborers in a vineyard (Matthew 20:1-16) that offended some of His listeners' sense of justice. The story, you'll recall, was about laborers who came to the fields at different hours in the day. But when quitting time came, the owner of the vineyard paid them equally. An open and shut case for a labor relations board, right? Wrong. Jesus' story wasn't about justice, but about God's grace. The Lord will forgive people of their sinfulness and accept them into His Kingdom whenever they're ready, be it "the morning side of the mountain or the evening side of the hill." That's justice, love, understanding and mercy rolled into one.

Give us understanding of Your Word, Lord, understanding and the will to live by it.

 "I will lift up mine eyes unto the hills, from whence cometh my help."

Psalm 121:1

One of the scariest jobs a novice seaman was asked to do on old-time ships was to climb the mast and unfurl or repair the sails in the top rigging. Riding high above a swaying deck tested the courage of any neophyte. Even worse was going up to lower a sail that had gotten caught in a storm.

The advice captains often gave young trainees was this: "If you lose your nerve and become afraid, don't look down, look up."

That's a good piece of counsel for us all. When trouble bares its long fangs and we don't know what to do, looking up to the Lord and asking His help is the wisest move anyone can make. If you find yourself in a precarious position today, as precarious as on the mainmast of a ship, don't look down, where your fears will only be magnified, look up "from whence cometh my help."

When fear threatens to immobilize us, Lord, remind us that we have a protecting helmet of faith.

 **All hail the pow'r of Jesus' name!
Let angels prostrate fall;
Bring forth the royal diadem,
And crown Him Lord of all.**

Oliver Holden hymn

196

When I hear environmentalists talk about returning to windmills as a viable means of generating power, my mind gallops back to the times I spent as a boy on my Aunt Margaret and Uncle Harold's farm in Ohio. In particular, I remember going to the windmill on hot summer days to drink from a large trough, the water in which was drawn to the surface by a wind-generated pump. How refreshingly delicious was a ladle full of cool water from that well.

Power is a much-sought-after commodity, be it political power, electrical power or spiritual power. All are necessary to create movement, action, vitality. Christians often pray that God will send them the power to accomplish difficult tasks or to overcome enervating problems, and it is right that we should ask for anointing from on high if we feel depleted or inadequate to deal with some obstacle in our lives.

In truth, however, you and I should know that as God's children we have His full power already. The Scriptures tell us that "the Kingdom of God is within." (Luke 17:21) You can draw on this spiritual reservoir 'of power right now and bring it to bear on any problem you face—physical, mental or spiritual. Like the unseen wind that turns the blades of a windmill, His unseen hand can turn you away from any tribulation.

Fill me with understanding, O Holy Spirit, that I may go forward confident of my source of power.

"The earth is the Lord's, and the fulness thereof."
I Corinthians 10:26

It is sweet-corn time, and we had our first crop of roasting ears the other night. What taste treat can compare with tender, hot-buttered sweet corn?

Have you ever wondered about the origin of corn? Botanists have and they are still unsure of its beginning. Their guess is that it came from some wild grass, but which grass and when are unsolved mysteries. We do know from archaeological findings that the ancient cliff dwellers of the Southwest ate corn. And we also know that sweet corn, meal corn and popcorn were being raised by Indians in both Americas when the first Europeans arrived on the continent. It was a good thing for the Pilgrims, for without corn they may not have survived.

All of this only points again to God's creative hand fashioning yet another gift for man's sustenance and enjoyment. Mysteries and questions abound, but for believers they are centered on how, when, why, what and where, not who.

They know that the tides and sun and stars and seasons—and even the first ear of corn—were shaped by God above, the giver and sustainer of all life.

Father, we stand in awe of Your wondrous creation all around us and praise You for Your gifts.

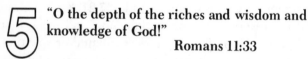

"O the depth of the riches and wisdom and knowledge of God!"
Romans 11:33

A little while ago I got up from my desk and went to the window to see where all the racket was coming from. It was a redheaded woodpecker rat-a-tat-tatting his beak against a tree.

Researchers did a study not long ago to determine why woodpeckers do not get headaches from this activity. They discovered that there is a dense, spongy bone tightly bunched around the bird's brain. To their surprise, little fluid is present to reduce the shock, only jolt-absorbing muscles that hold head and beak rigid. The information gathered may be helpful, it was said, in the construction of helmets for cyclists, athletes, astronauts and the like.

I sympathize with doctors and researchers who must try to keep abreast of the ever-growing body of scientific knowledge. Each day, it seems, we learn something new about God's magnificent universe and I marvel at the puzzles that are solved. Still, there is much we don't know. The Bible tells us that "Now I see through a glass darkly; but then face to face:

now I know in part; but then shall I know even as also I am known." (I Corinthians 13:12) Until that day, it's good to be alive. We live in an exciting time.

For the wonderful gift of life, abundant life, beautiful life, Father, our hearts are filled with gratitude.

"Better the world should know you as a sinner than God know you as a hypocrite."
Danish proverb

Niccolo Machiavelli (1469-1527), a Florentine statesman and philosopher, won himself a permanent place in literature with his writings about political opportunists of his time, leaders who would stoop to most any form of deceit or duplicity to hold or increase their power. So cynically graphic was Machiavelli in books like THE PRINCE and THE MANDRAKE that his enemies condemned him as being as diabolical and immoral as the subjects he described, thus *Machiavellian*. Though modern scholars praise him for pioneering the field of political science, for his republicanism and for his patriotism, his name connotes political cunning and dishonesty whenever it is used today as an adjective to describe someone's character.

Hypocrisy is a trait which Jesus condemned in his discussions of pharisaical behavior (Matthew 23), admonishing Christians not to flaunt their faith. And to be sure, taking pride in one's relationship with God is not a mark of Christian maturity. Still, we are all guilty of Machiavellian behavior from time to time, presenting ourselves as more righteous than is the case. Because of this we should be careful not to ridicule others for misrepresentation, but rather labor to rid ourselves of the habit. To say what we mean and to mean what we say is a good goal for all of us.

Lord, help us to forgive others of their shortcomings in the hope that they and You will forgive us.

7 "But many that are first shall be last: and the last first."

Mark 10:31

The other day on a neighborhood playground, I watched from a distance as a group of kids chose up sides for a baseball game. The bigger, older boys were selected first, then the middle-sized ones, and finally there was only one boy left. He was about eight, a spindly lad, sixty pounds at most. "You take Bobby," the one captain said, and the other nodded. Thus the sides were filled.

Being the last or almost last in any selection process or contest is never pleasant. And unless you're one of those privileged few, you've been hurt more than a few times when such an incident has left you feeling inadequate or inferior or incapable. And unless you've removed yourself from the "firing line" entirely, you'll be left out again—maybe today. But I know a good way to handle such slights, a foolproof method guaranteed to help you glide right over them. Here's how:

Next time you feel lonely, left out, without much worth or skill, don't fret too long. In fact, the best antidote is not to fret at all. Instead, put aside your self-pity and look about you for somebody else who has been slighted, overlooked, forgotten. Embrace and encourage those who don't feel very good about themselves. Search out their attributes and praiseworthy talents. When you do, you become one of God's chosen people, teaching and preaching the Good News of life.

When we feel unloved, Father, remind us that Your love is never in question.

 8 When you live close to God
And His infinite grace,
Your future's secure,
You don't have to race.

F. B.

There is no question that much of what we worry about is speculative. We don't know that some feared event in the future will take place, but the prospect of it can full us with headaches, stomachaches, heartaches, all kind's of aches. How can we eliminate or minimize worry over things we fear will occur in the future?

The best way is to keep very short accounts with God. The Lord's Prayer says, "Give us *this* day our daily bread." It doesn't ask for food for all week or all month or all year. Your Heavenly Father knows that you'll have needs and He will provide for them through His unlimited riches. Does this mean that we should refrain from making plans or preparations for tomorrow? Of course not. But put tomorrow and its problems where they belong: in God's hands. Say with James (4:13), "If the Lord will, we shall live and do this or that."

Keep my eyes on the ladder's next rung, Lord, not in the
ground below or the sky above.

 "Generosity is giving what you could use yourself."

Marianne Moore

When I was very young, I heard a minister say that Christians have a holy obligation to "share the good news with others. They have a duty to practice *noblesse oblige*." The phrase stuck in my mind, and I went to a dictionary as soon as I got home. It is a French expression which means literally "nobility obligates." Or put another way: one's high birth or rank mandates an honorable, generous, kind behavior.

Christians certainly are blessed in many ways, and their actions and life-styles should reflect the insights and understanding God has given them. Generosity with time and talent and money should be hallmarks of Jesus' disciples. In St. Luke (12:48) we are told: "For unto whomsoever much is given, of him shall be much required."

Be willing today to share His blessings with all who come to you in need. It is a requirement of all the King's children.

You have given us so much, Lord. Show us how to
reciprocate.

> "We then that are strong ought to bear the
> infirmities of the weak, and not to please
> ourselves."
>
> **Romans 15:1**

Homer Rodeheaver, whose musical ministry complemented the preaching ministry of Billy Sunday for many years, once asked a young man who was caddying for him on a golf course near Winona Lake, Indiana, if he went to church. The boy said no, that Sundays were his best days for caddying and that his family needed the money.

"How much will you make tomorrow?" Rodeheaver inquired.

"I'll earn about a dollar," the caddy answered. Rodeheaver reached into his pocket, gave him a dollar and invited him to services the next day. The boy came and found the Lord. But that isn't the end of the story. Many years later Rodeheaver learned that the young man had become a minister.

In the course of a day we have many opportunities to witness to our faith, and the potential influence we have for Christ is much greater than most realize. Often our proclamation of the Good News is made with little deeds—holding a door for someone, taking time to chat with someone ill or aged, paying a compliment, refusing to pass along gossip, apologizing for an oversight, telling a cashier you were given too much change, taking a church job that is hard to fill.

How you handle little daily relationships says much about the depth of your faith. Put yours to work today. Like Homer Rodeheaver, you could change the direction of someone's life.

Our relationship with You, Lord, is reflected in our
relationship with others. Help us strengthen both.

> "Let not your heart be troubled, neither let
> it be afraid."
>
> **John 14:27**

A worried father whose teen-age daughter has run away from

home several times said to me recently, "My wife and I have done everything we know to do, but nothing seems to work. Sleep comes hard. We're at the end of our rope."

Most all parents have had some anxious times dealing with their children and their problems, and even a strong faith doesn't seem enough to quiet uneasy hearts and minds. Some good advice on the subject (which I shared with my troubled friend) comes from the pen of Helen Steiner Rice:

Whenever I am troubled and lost in deep despair,
I bundle all my troubles up and go to God in prayer.
I tell Him I am heartsick and lost and lonely too,
That I am deeply burdened and don't know what to do.
But I know He stilled the tempest and calmed the angry sea,
And I humbly ask if in His love He'll do the same for me.
Then I just keep quiet and think on thoughts of peace,
And as I sit in stillness my restless murmurings cease.

Fill us with Your peace, Lord, the peace that passes understanding.

12   "For the Lord thy God is a merciful God. He will not forsake thee . . . "
                   Deuteronomy 4:31

A DAILY GUIDEPOSTS reader from Oregon writes to tell of a near-drowning several years ago. "A sudden storm developed and we turned back for shore," she recalls, "but the boat capsized in the high waves and my two sons and I were thrown into the water. I was trapped under the boat. A non-swimmer, I should have been terrified, but I was completely relaxed; God was so near. If it were my time to die, I was ready. If God sought to save me, I would go on serving Him.

"After being underwater for what seemed like hours, I surfaced near the boat. With the help of my sons and the fast arrival of the Coast Guard we were all rescued."

In the face of danger people do respond differently. As a result of training, some are better prepared to act wisely in an emergency. But when disaster strikes as in the case described here, the only weapon this woman had in her arsenal was spiritual preparation. She had taken to heart Amos' injunction "Prepare to meet the Lord," and when her moment of truth came, her faith was not wanting.

If you want the assurance of God's presence in moments of calamity, should they come, it is wise to seek Him in moments of calm. That is the best contigency plan there is.

Help us feel Your nearness, Lord, every day of our lives.

13. "For me to live is Christ and to die is gain." Philippians 1:21

This morning before breakfast I went out to the garden and gathered a cupful of wild blackberries for my cereal. There are several blackberry bushes surrounding the garden and every year about this time they bear fruit.

An old-timer once told me that the difference between a good blackberry crop and a poor one is the timing of the spring hoarfrost that falls on the blossoms. Without frost, he explained, the blossoms hang on too long and as a result the plants don't produce fruit.

To the uninitiated, the frost might seem a fruit killer; but to seasoned nature observers, it is a necessary step in the growth process which leads to juicy berries. Most people know what it is to face blossom-killing "frosts" in their lives, too, and they would prefer to avoid such dark nights of the soul. But often the fruits of such tests are stronger character, stronger determination, stronger faith.

When you face difficulties that delay you or force you to detour from your chosen route, be careful cursing the fates. Out of an experience that seems totally negative at the time, may come a marvelous new opportunity. Like hoarfrosted blackberries, God may have a plan that will turn your adversity into a fruit-producing blessing.

Lord, when I get discouraged remind me that out of hardship can come blessings.

14

"Thy word is a lamp unto my feet, and a light unto my path."
Psalm 119:105

Not long ago I was driving in the South, travelling in a part of the country I hadn't visited in some time. Referring often to a road map, I thought I was on the right road, but when I didn't reach my destination after a reasonable time, I pulled into a service station to ask for information.

"Here's where I'm heading," I told the attendant, pointing to a spot on the map.

"Oh," he explained, "you've got an old map. That route has been renumbered." Then taking out a new map, he gave me the right directions.

The incident came to mind when someone took me aside recently and began criticizing a certain translation of the Bible. He had no appreciation of anything but the King James version. Like me, he loves its beauty and imagery and poetry. Yet, I told him, for clearer understanding some people like to also read a more recent translation, one which is written in more contemporary language.

Then, I mentioned to him my trials with an old road map and the need for a newer one to straighten me out. The truth of God's word, of course, is unchanging. The important thing is that we reach our spiritual destination. Whether we get there with an old or new "road map" is immaterial.

Reveal the truth of Your word to me, O Holy Spirit, and inspire me to live by Your light.

15 Hold Thou Thy cross before my closing eyes;
Shine thro' the gloom, and point me to the skies:
Heav'n's morning breaks, and earth's vain
shadows flee:
In life, in death, O Lord, abide with me!

H. F. Lyte hymn

Though memory fails me as to the name of the ancient Anglo-Saxon poet, the sentiment of his lines was that life is like a bird flying from darkness through an open window into a lighted room and out an opposite window into the darkness again. It is a graphic simile in that there is mystery connected with both our birth and our death. And because the unknown gives us all pause, it is easy to understand why men are reluctant to fly "out of a lighted room into darkness."

But the Bible gives help with life's three ultimate questions: Where did I come from? Why am I here? Where am I going? The Book of Books tells us that we were created by God and in His image, that we are here to love and serve Him and our fellow man, and that all who believe on His Son Jesus are received into His kingdom everlasting. But *belief* is the key word, and unless we can cross the abyss of doubt that separates spiritual from material it is difficult to face death without resistance and fear. The triumph over doubt is expressed incomparably by St. Paul when he writes: "O death, where is thy sting? O grave, where is thy victory?" (I Corinthians 15:55)

*You are the Light onto our path, Lord, and we depend upon
You to forever illuminate our way.*

 16 "Train up a child in the way he should go:
and when he is old, he will not depart from
it."

Proverbs 22:6

When I was a boy, I can remember watching my mother dye clothes in a steaming washtub. It was a fascinating transformation. Anyone who has ever worked with dyes at home knows how difficult it is to get a fast color. After a few washings, a solid red can easily fade to tender rose.

One Quaker father, making an analogy between dyeing materials and "dyeing" children with character that lasts, prayed at his daughter's birth, "Fit her for her long journey, O Lord, with virtues that will wash."

What is character? Someone once said, "It's what you are in the dark." Character is also what gets a student up at six a.m. to do some extra reading or what prompts a mother to resew a slightly crooked seam or what directs a person to tell the truth when a half truth would make him or her look better.

"Who shall ascend into the hill of the Lord? Or who shall stand in his holy place?" the Psalmist asks (24:3). He answers, "He that hath clean hands, and a pure heart; who hath not lifted up his soul unto vanity, nor sworn deceitfully." (24:4)

Those are high standards, but of such cloth is good character made.

Raise our expectations, Lord, to goals that are beyond ourselves.

17 "When we are faithful to keep ourselves in His holy presence, and set Him always before us, . . . it begets in us a holy freedom and a familiarity with God."

Brother Lawrence

At age 88, Artur Rubinstein, pianist *par excellence*, played a concert at New York City's Carnegie Hall that won him more rave reviews. That was not new—he's been receiving acclaim all over the world for decades. But a little footnote to the evening's performance captured my interest. It was that Mr. Rubinstein's eyesight had dimmed to the point that he could no longer see the keyboard.

How did he play so flawlessly? By touch, of course. Anyone who has spent as much time at the keyboard as Mr. Rubinstein knows his instrument intimately and needs no more than to place his hands on the keys to feel at home.

So it is with long-time believers, ones who have practiced the presence of God daily for many years. They have a vision that transcends eyesight; they have an inner hearing capable of receiving inaudible guidance; they are in touch with the One who makes music out of life's discord.

If you're in tune with the Master, you've already found the melody.

Remind us that faith takes practice, Lord, and that practice makes perfect.

 "Blessed is he that considereth the poor: the Lord will deliver him in time of trouble."
Psalm 41:1

"A growing human tragedy" is how one social worker described the increasing numbers of homeless women who roam our cities' streets looking for food and a place to sleep. Often a park bench or an office doorway or a bus station platform are their beds, and garbage cans become their primary source of food.

Sociologist Dr. Veronica Maz serves such women in a Washington, D.C., shelter known as "The House of Ruth," named I presume after Ruth in the Bible who refused to leave her aging mother-in-law. Of these homeless women, Dr. Maz says, "Most don't have a family or a friend or anyone who cares about them. Homeless men have missions and shelters, but thousands of women in the same circumstances are being neglected."

Of what concern are people in such straits to you and me? If we call ourselves Christians, we cannot ignore them. Christ's instructions are clear: "For I was hungered, and ye gave me meat: I was thirsty, and ye gave me drink: I was a stranger, and ye took me in: naked, and ye clothed me: I was sick, and ye visited me: I was in prison, and ye came unto me . . . Verily I say unto you, Inasmuch as ye have done it unto one of the least of these my brethren, ye have done it unto me." (Matthew 25: 35,36,40)

Give us more than sympathetic hearts, Lord; give us willing hands.

Earth changes, but thy soul and God stands sure:
    What entered into thee,
    That was, is, and shall be:
Time's wheel runs back or stops;
    Potter and clay endure.

Robert Browning

A few weeks ago my front lawn was lush and green, well watered by the rain. Now it looks like the middle of a well-used football field. Dry and brown, it shows the result of too much August sun and too little precipitation.

I'm reminded of the passage from Isaiah, "The grass withereth, the flower fadeth: but the word of our God shall stand for ever." (Isaiah 40:8) It has a parallel in Matthew 24:35 where Christ says, "Heaven and earth shall pass away, but my words shall not pass away."

It is satisfying to recall these promises when autumn comes to the earth as well as when the shadows grow long in our lives. The seasons remind us that we are finite creatures with limited strength, limited stamina and limited life spans. However, we serve an infinite God who has promised life without end to all who believe in His Son. Knowing that, you and I can view the autumns of our lives not as ends but as beginnings.

We believe that death was swallowed up in Christ's victory (I Corinthians 15:54), Lord, and rejoice that dying has lost its sting.

"The function of fear is to warn us of danger, not to make us afraid to face it."
Anonymous

There is a new book on the market on the subject of *agoraphobia*. People who are reluctant to leave the security of their homes, who panic in crowded places or have an inordinate anxiety about travelling alone are said to be *agoraphobic*. I knew *phobia* meant fearful, but I had to go to my dictionary to find the origin of the prefix. There I read that the *agora* in ancient Greece was the marketplace, an area where people gathered and talked. Thus, fear of crowds, fear of strangers, fear of the marketplace.

As with all psychological problems, there are many degrees of illness. People who are immobilized by such an intense fear of crowds that they refuse to leave their homes need professional help. Others who only dislike large crowds or feel uneasy or anxious in large gatherings can hardly be called agoraphobic.

Yet, we all are asked to do things which frighten us. Speaking or praying before a sizable gathering, for example, can be an intimidating experience. How can we draw upon our spiritual resources to gain the confidence to perform such a task? One answer can be found in Philippians 4:13 where it says, "I can do all things through Christ which strengtheneth me." If you have some difficult job to do today, remember you have Someone who is ready to go before you and prepare the way.

When my confidence ebbs, Lord, reaffirm Your unending love.

"To every thing there is a season, and a time to every purpose under the heaven."
Ecclesiastes 3:1

Recently, a large freighter was reported driven aground during a fierce storm. When the gale winds subsided, rescuers went to the stranded vessel's aid and tried to free it. First, they tried to push the ship off the sandbar. When that didn't work, they attempted to pull it off. Finally, they removed some of its cargo, hoping that by lightening the load, the ship would float free. Nothing worked.

"There's only one thing left to do," said one of the shiphands. "Wait for the tide to come in." They did and the natural action of the sea freed the ship from its bondage.

Sometimes we become bound by uncomfortable circumstances such as sickness, financial difficulty or job complications, and we long for quick release, instant release. We try all sorts of freeing maneuvers in hopes of lightening our load. We implore God to intervene, but time is often the healer. His answer—difficult though it may be to accept—seems to be "wait."

When we accept His timetable, however, a natural action takes place. Like the tide which freed the great ship, a life force that has been operating from the beginning goes to work and in due time our problem is resolved. The wise among us accept God's timing as perfect—never too late, never too early, but always on schedule.

Lord, show us how to wait for things to change when waiting is not easy.

 "Take no thought for your life, . . . for your heavenly Father knoweth that ye have need of all these things."
Matthew 6:25,32

An elderly woman from Texas writes that she is worried about her failing health. "If I can't take care of myself, my children will either have to take me in or put me in a nursing home. I don't like the prospect of either."

"We get old so quick, and smart so slow" goes the saying—and it is true. Age is a horse that gallops up on us before we even hear its hoofbeats. And with age often come physical maladies that create all kinds of concerns and worries like the one expressed by the woman above.

What is the answer? The obvious thing for someone who is not involved is to say, "Don't worry." But saying that doesn't help much.

When troubles come we need something to dispell our worries, something to take their place. One invincible thing is an abiding faith in God. He will not allow us to endure anything of which we are not capable. Of that we can be sure. If you don't believe it, go to your Bible. His promises to the afflicted course through the entire Word. Just for starters, read Paul's second letter to the Corinthians (1:3,4) where he writes: "Blessed be God . . . the Father of mercies, and the God of all comfort; who comforteth us in all our tribulation."

Don't borrow trouble, my Texan friend. Live each day assured that God in His mercy knows of your concern. He will help you deal with it. Give Him your concern and concentrate on living each day as fully and as positively and joyfully as possible.

Strengthen our bodies and minds when we grow old, Lord, so we don't lose sight of Your promises.

23

Got any rivers you think are uncrossable?
Got any mountains you can't tunnel through?
God specializes in things thought impossible
He does what others cannot do.

Oscar Eliason hymn

The other evening we were entertaining some guests, and they were having fun with a conversation piece given to us by friends: a wrought-iron vise that cracks walnuts, pecans, almonds and the like. Though no more utilitarian than the old pliers-type of nutcracker, it is more interesting. The procedure is to put a nut under the hammer, then wind the handle down until the vise closes on it and cracks the shell.

While operating it one time, I was struck by the thought that people are put in vises also. Most often, I suppose, the pressures we feel are the result of our own actions (or inactions), but upon occasion we all find ourselves in predicaments that are not of our own making. Whatever the source, each of us is called upon to face daily difficulties. No one is free of trouble. It is a condition of life, and only the grave is capable of sparing people totally from life's problems.

However, those who place their faith in God have Someone to whom they can turn for counsel, direction, relief and solace. If you are feeling pressure today .that is causing you mental and/or physical pain, stop right now and ask Him to help you cope with your problem. God is not a sadist who joys in our afflictions, but a loving Father who wants His children well. I believe what it says in Matthew 21:22, "And all things, whatsoever ye shall ask in prayer, believing, ye shall receive."

Give me peace, O Father, peace that enables me to live life effectively and fully.

24

"Believe on the name of the Son of God; that ye may know that ye have eternal life. . . ."

I John 5:13

One of the people who gave me editorial assistance with this year's edition of DAILY GUIDEPOSTS was Linda Gramatky Smith. She has a seven-year-old daughter named Tina who is bright way beyond her age. One day when a friend of the Smiths died, Tina asked her mother, "Does a body in a coffin mind being buried?" Linda was momentarily stumped as to how she should answer. Then she remembered a nature experience the family had shared a short time before.

They had found a cicada clinging to a tree. Unlike most times when only the transparent shell remains, in this instance the insect was still inside. They took it home, put it in a jar and, to their surprise, the next morning a magnificent creature with wings emerged. Taking the jar outside, they opened it and watched the locust fly free, high overhead, shimmering in the bright sunlight. The only evidence they had of the insect was the empty shell it left behind.

Recalling the incident, Linda asked her little daughter if she thought the shell would mind being buried.

"No," said Tina, "because the insect isn't in it."

"That's the same way it is with the body of someone who has died," Linda said. "Only their shell remains."

Thank You, Lord, for the promise of everlasting life.

Silently now I wait for Thee,
Ready, my God, Thy will to see;
Open my eyes, illumine me,
Spirit divine.

Clara H. Scott hymn

Once I planted several rows of sweet corn in our garden and watched with pleasure as the stalks grew higher and higher. But one thing was wrong: the corn leaned over at a precarious angle, and when a heavy rain came and the wind blew, much of the corn was uprooted.

Later an old-timer put his finger on the problem. "Too much shade around your garden," he said. "The corn was hungry for light and reached in the direction of the sun. As a result, it didn't have good roots."

There is an analogy between this little incident and a good many people's lives. Because they suffer a shortage of light— spiritual light—in their daily activities, they don't mature properly. They reach out blindly trying to locate this missing ingredient, but overlook the one true Source of it; eventually when storms of adversity beset them, they succumb. Their roots simply are not strong enough to battle life's trials and temptations. Are your roots deep enough to sustain you through the problems that come your way today? They are, if you know the Source of Light.

When I lose my way, Lord, send Your guiding light.

"The world will never starve for wonders
but only for the lack of wonder."

G. K. Chesterton

Last year my two sons still at home—Christopher and Daniel—begged me to take them to Kentucky's Mammoth Cave while we were on vacation. Wife Shirley thought it was a good idea, too, so we detoured south and spent a day trekking through that huge cavern—the longest known cave system in the world. I had been through seven miles of its limestone passages before, but I had forgotten just how expansive its water-carved tunnels were. Our guide pointed out that while 150 miles of passages have been probed since the cave was discovered in 1799, the full extent of the cave is still unexplored.

Can you imagine the adventure it must have been for the discoverers of the cave who first explored their find? Plumbing new depths of land or sea or new heights in outer space are fascinating subjects made real by men and women who take risks to learn the universe's secrets. Most of us must experience these adventures vicariously—through the firsthand accounts of others.

But there is one area of exploration open to all. That is spiritual exploration. Some people refuse to probe the inner recesses of their beings, unwilling to seek solutions from this investigation. Others, often people with desperate needs, reach for that unseen force and find faith, something more real than anything in the world. If you are groping and searching for something genuine, meaningful, relevant, vital, solid, deep, lasting—then open your mind and heart to the Power who shaped the heavens, set the tides in motion and carved the caves of the earth. He will take you on a new path, a new adventure unlike anything you've ever known before.

Give me a lifelong spirit of adventure, Lord, and an appreciation for Your endless handiwork.

 "No wind favors him who has no destined port."

Michel de Montaigne

The young man who repaired the leak in my car tire told me he recently had dropped out of college "because it was irrelevant to life."

"What do you plan to do?" I asked.

"I don't know," he answered. "I'm really not interested in anything."

"Do you plan to return to school?"

"No, I doubt it," he replied. Then, with a satirical smile, he added, "I guess I'll just drift. Become a bum."

I doubt that the young man's forecast comes true. The brightness in his eyes contradicted such an outcome. In general, I have much faith in today's young people—faith that our future is in good hands.

Faith, we are told in Hebrews 11:1, is the substance of things hoped for, the evidence of things not seen. If you are waiting for a perfect set of circumstances before you set forth on a journey or an assignment, a business or a life's work, you may never get started. Furthermore, don't expect a burning bush or a parting of the sea as a sign from God that this is the way. He seldom directs with grand gestures, but rather encourages us with gentle nudges and whispers to the heart. When we follow His leading and step out on faith, spiritual growth always results. If we put our trust in Him, He will put His power in us, and though the outcome may not be exactly what we had in mind, the results are always positive.

Vanquish our doubts, Lord, and fill our hearts with faith and trust in You.

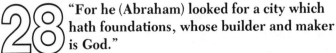

"For he (Abraham) looked for a city which hath foundations, whose builder and maker is God."

Hebrews 11:10

If you recall, after the destruction of Jerusalem (587 B.C.) Nebuchadnezzar took the people back with him to Babylon. There they were held in exile until the Persians defeated the Babylonians. As a result, the captives were allowed to return to Jerusalem and to rebuild the temple. But the job of restoring the walls was left undone. When Nehemiah, who was serving the king in Babylon, heard about the sorry state of things in Jerusalem, he was inspired by God to return and help the Jews put up new walls.

When he arrived, he found the people more than willing. All

they needed was a leader, and Nehemiah proved to be more than up to the task. Despite many obstacles, he united the returned exiles, infused them with enthusiasm and in just 52 days rebuilt the walls from rubble.

In a postscript worth carving in stone, Nehemiah said, "So built we the wall . . . for the people had a mind to work." (Nehemiah 4:6)

When you and I have a mind to work, we can achieve great things. Too often when faced with a difficult job, we dally, counting the many reasons it cannot be done. In truth, there is usually only one reason: because we aren't willing to commit ourselves totally to the task. The secret to building anything is to put our whole selves into it—body, mind and soul. Once we do, our success is assured.

Help us build a strong foundation of faith, Lord, so we can withstand the slings and arrows of life.

Let the lower lights be burning!
Send a gleam across the wave!
Some poor fainting, struggling seaman
You may rescue, you may save.
P. P. Bliss hymn

Dwight L. Moody told the story about a large passenger ship caught in a terrifying storm on Lake Erie. In the darkness, the captain tried desperately to find the harbor channel that would lead them to port. Lower shore lights normally helped him guide the ship, but they were out and he had only the lighthouse beacon to use as a landmark. It was not enough. The ship crashed against rocks; it sank, and many lives were lost.

Philip Bliss, the hymn writer, put the story into a poem and Major D. W. Whittle composed the music to "Let the Lower Lights Be Burning," an evangelical work that has inspired countless Christian workers over the years. The Bible says, "Let your light so shine before men, that they may see your good works, and glorify your Father which is in heaven."

(Matthew 5:16) Remember, it is not the size of your light that is important, but its constancy.

Keep my faith from faltering, Father, even in the darkest storms.

30 "Behold, I stand at the door, and knock: if any man hear my voice and open the door, I will come in to him . . . "

Revelation 3:20

A painting that made a great impression on me as a child was hung behind the pulpit in our church. It showed Jesus standing outside a door, knocking. Obviously, the artist had used the verse above from Revelation as his reference point.

A Sunday school teacher once pointed out that the door had no latchstring or knob on the outside. "The door," he said, "must be opened from the inside." He went on to draw the analogy between Christ and our acceptance of Him. Unless we open the door of our hearts, He cannot come in and be our Saviour.

People have various reasons for resisting His generalship in their lives. The most common is probably the fear that they will be required to give up too much. In truth, when you open yourself to the Lord's leading, you gain access to all the riches of the Kingdom because there isn't anything of lasting value that God denies His children. If you think otherwise, you're in for a great surprise when you open the door fully to Him.

Thank You, Lord, for being willing to enter each and every heart that invites You in.

 "Then said David to the Philistine, Thou comest to me with a sword, and with a spear, and with a shield: but I come to thee in the name of the Lord."

I Samuel 17:45

218

During summer vacation one year, a young man earned college tuition money by working in a coal mine in Kentucky. He figured there was no skill needed to do this job, that anyone could swing a pick. So on his first day he began flailing away with long blows, drawing the pick back over his head and slamming it into the earth. Within half a day, he was so tired he could barely lift his arms.

Then an oldtimer took him aside and showed him that short strokes took less effort and also dislodged more coal. Working at a steady, rhythmic pace, he was soon able to produce as much coal as the veteran miners.

Often we attack an obstacle with a vengeance, mustering all our strength and resources into a mighty onslaught. To our surprise, the foe is implacable, immovable. When we pause to survey the ineffectiveness of our tactics, we conclude there must be a better way.

In such moments of reflection, many have turned to God to seek new direction in their lives. If you have exerted great energy trying to battle a long-standing problem, stop for a while. Take a respite. Turn the difficulty over to the management of God. Pray the prayer of relinquishment, and you like many others may find your burden lifted like fog on a summer morning.

Sometimes our problems loom as large as Goliath did to David, Lord, and we need You to put them into perspective.

SEPTEMBER 1978

S	M	T	W	T	F	S
					1	2
3	4	5	6	7	8	9
10	11	12	13	14	15	16
17	18	19	20	21	22	23
24	25	26	27	28	29	30

Are you troubled about some difficult relationship? The Bible tells us that perfect love casts out
fear. (I John 4:18) This month ask God to help you
focus on the needs of the other party rather than
your own needs. Concentrate on dispensing love,
rather than receiving it. Expect a positive result.

SEPTEMBER 1978

1
   Come, ye thankful people, come,
Raise the song of harvest-home;
All is safely gathered in,
Ere the winter storms begin:
God, our Maker, doth provide
For our wants to be supplied;
Come to God's own temple, come,
Raise the song of harvest-home.

                         Henry Alford hymn

The farmers' market in Trenton, New Jersey, is one of my favorite places this time of year. Filled with the bounty of another harvest, the counters of the market are overflowing with luscious fruits and vegetables—golden pumpkins, tender green beans, juicy apples, squash, cantaloupe, eggplant, tomatoes, potatoes, peppers, carrots, brussels sprouts, peas, onions, swiss chard, asparagus, ad infinitum.

It is a family affair—this bringing the spoils of a summer's work to market. Fathers and sons, mothers and daughters join in the effort, unloading the ripe crop from pickup trucks, then washing, polishing, arranging and selling it. Together, they have planted, watered, hoed, sprayed, weeded and gathered the produce I see before me, and I suspect they are secretly proud of their cooperative effort. Only one contributor is not seen, the God of the harvest who blows life into the tiny radish seed and miraculously transforms it into a golf-ball-sized sphere, so tantalizing that my tastebuds water at the thought.

When it is harvest time, it is also thanksgiving time.

Like the seeds of spring, Lord, nurture our faith and help us grow into mature Christians.

2 "He that hath ears to hear, let him hear."
Mark 4:9

It was not surprising to the youngest clerk of the Salem (Massachusetts) Customs House when his boss laid him off work. The year was 1848, and times were hard.

Sorrowfully, he broke the news to his wife that night. They had a family to support, and he told her that he'd have to look for another job quickly. But his wife disagreed. This shouldn't be looked upon as a setback, she reasoned, but as an opportunity. "You've always said you would write your book if you just had the time."

"I can't feed a family on my writing," he responded.

Then his wife revealed that she had been saving money from her household allowance. It would keep them for some time.

Thus it was that an unemployed customs house clerk turned to his first love, writing. And just two years later he published his first book. Its title page read: THE SCARLET LETTER by Nathaniel Hawthorne.

Opportunity knocks many times in all our lives, but we must have ready ears or we won't hear it. Simon Peter and his brother, Andrew, were fishermen busy with their nets when Jesus came by.

"Follow me," He said, "and I will make you fishers of men." (Matthew 4:19) Did they hesitate, ask questions about the pay or working conditions? No, their ears and hearts were attuned to the Master as is evidenced by the next verse, which reads: "and they straightway left their nets, and followed him." That same kind of obedience and trust is required of all who would call themselves Christians.

Give us attentive hearts, Father, so we can hear Your marching orders.

 Take time to be holy, speak oft with thy Lord; Abide in him always, and feed on his word.
W. D. Longstaff hymn

A woman from California wrote recently to say that she has a problem finding time for prayer in her busy life. In addition to being a wife and mother, she said that she is an executive in an import company, a job that "spills over into the evening after dinner. I just can't find the time I feel I should devote to meditation and prayer."

I sympathize with her and other people whose jobs and responsibilities leave them feeling harried and exhausted. We all need time to be alone, for it is at such moments that we get in touch with ourselves and with God. But sometimes it is difficult to find periods of quiet, leisurely breaks to refresh our minds and souls.

Missionary Frank Laubach, a modern-day Brother Lawrence, was an extremely busy person with a worldwide ministry, so he learned to pray wherever life took him and whenever he could find a free moment. Dr. Laubach wrote in his books that prayer didn't require a closet, but that it could be done while one was in motion. His answer to the question of how long a person should pray each day: "all the time." The Bible supports his contention.

In I Thessalonians 5:17, we are told to pray without ceasing. So don't wait until you have 20 minutes free to talk with God. If you're like many folks, you might wait weeks. Instead, when the need arises talk to Him in sentence prayers. They only take a few seconds and are just as effective as long-winded ones.

Nowhere does the Bible say that the efficacy of prayer is increased as a direct result of its length. No, it is the sincerity of the one praying that is the key.

Lord, like Frank Laubach, let our lives be one continual prayer.

4
Life is a mirror for king and for slave,
'Tis just what you are and do,
So give to the world the best you have,
And the best will come back to you.

Anonymous

Have you ever tried to throw a boomerang? I did once with unspectacular results. How Australian aborigines are able to hunt with them is beyond me. However, I've been told that with practice a person can become quite accurate and hit targets many yards away. Furthermore, when tossed by an expert, a boomerang will arc back in the direction of the thrower, saving a walk to retrive it.

The word *boomerang* is often used in another context—when it refers to an act or statement that backfires or returns to hit the person who initiated it. Gossip, for example, has been known to boomerang on the gossiper. People who are careless with their tongues and make false or inaccurate statements about those they dislike or of whom they're jealous, risk the chance of being felled by their own weapon. Like a boomerang their words can circle back and discredit the source. David wrote in Psalm 19:14, "Let the words of my mouth, and the meditation of my heart, be acceptable in thy sight, O Lord, my strength, and my redeemer." Those who use this prayer as a guide won't have to worry about the boomerang of loose talk.

Give me something better to do with my voice, Lord, than repeat harmful gossip.

5

He leadeth me! He leadeth me!
By his own hand he leadeth me;
His faithful follower I would be,
For by his hand he leadeth me.

Joseph F. Gilmore hymn

A high-school senior once dreamed of attending a famous college that had very demanding admission requirements. Her friends thought she was crazy to even try, but she submitted her application.

In a few weeks she received a letter from the dean of admissions. Unbelievably, she had been accepted! Her father, fearing a misunderstanding, phoned the college's admissions office. "Frankly, we are surprised that our daughter has been accepted," the father said. "Are you sure there is no mistake?"

"No, sir," the college official replied. Then he explained that though the girl was average in most every respect, there was one thing that stood out on her application. "Where we asked, 'Are you a leader or a follower?'—of the thousands of applications we received, she was the only one who said she was a follower. We need more people like your daughter."

So much is made of strong leadership that we sometimes forget the importance of followers. Most leaders learned how to take charge by observing other leaders. In other words, being a good follower may be a prerequisite to taking charge, taking command, taking responsibility.

If you are looking for someone to emulate, for a person worthy as a model, study the first four books of the New Testament and learn of Jesus. The Good Shepherd is One worthy of following—all your life.

Lead us and guide us. O Lord, we pray.
Not once in a while, but every day.

Give of your best to the Master;
Give Him first place in your heart;
Give Him first place in your service,
Consecrate every part.

Howard B. Grose hymn.

One day a dairy herd inspector came around to check on Old Gus' family cow. Though he was accustomed to inspecting farms where 30 to 40 cows were common, he gave Gus' operation the same thorough inspection he did larger herds. In addition to noting cleanliness, his job also required that he record the amount of milk given by each cow and the percentage of butterfat.

"How much milk do you get from her?" the inspector asked, pointing to Gus' single bovine. Gus—who didn't keep records—scratched his head. "I don't rightly know," he said. "All I can tell ya is Old Peg is an honest cow, and she gives all she's got."

Some people who are getting up in years and don't have much in material goods have told me they are a little embarrassed with their offerings. But they needn't be. In I Corinthians 10:13, we read that the Lord will never require more of us than we can give. So you don't have to worry about not being able to meet the demand. The widow's mite was as good as a king's ransom, because it was all she had. When you and I serve God with our whole hearts, He will honor such offerings and bless each giver richly.

Inspire me, Lord, to give my best to You each day.

 "Be ye doers of the word, and not hearers only, deceiving your own selves."

James 1:22

A U.S. Office of Education survey taken in 1975 found that 23 million Americans aged 16 and up were functionally illiterate. That's one fifth of our adult population.

Can you imagine what a handicap it would be if you couldn't

228

read? I shudder to think about it. Somehow, though, you were taught to read. Someone—parents, relatives, teachers—helped you develop a skill that has lasted a lifetime. Such a blessing is reading. Through it you can transport yourself to the far corners of the world, into the laboratories of scientists, into fascinating periods of history, and by being able to read you can learn of God through the pages of the Bible.

Is there something you can do to help others learn to read? Many schools have programs through which citizens can tutor pupils with reading problems. Libraries need volunteers. Other service agencies are getting involved in this area. Give the problem some thought, some prayer. Maybe God wants you involved in   the solution to this problem.   Or is there some other concern He's laid upon your heart? If so, take a step in that direction today. He may have a wonderful surprise in store for you.

Embolden me, Lord, to act upon the marching orders I hear You whisper in my ears.

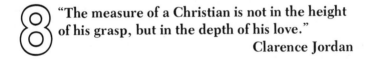

"The measure of a Christian is not in the height of his grasp, but in the depth of his love."
Clarence Jordan

For nearly four hundred years Rugby School in England has operated under this motto—*Orando Laborando*, which is Latin for "by prayer and by work." Were you and I to adopt a personal motto for our lives we would be hard pressed to find a better one.

Brother Lawrence in his classic PRACTICING THE PRESENCE OF GOD urged "offering Him your heart in the midst of your business, even every moment if you can." The French monk's point was that worshipping God is not so much a time or a place, as it is an attitude. How you perform your work, how you raise your children, how you treat people at work, how you use leisure time, the manner in which you drive a car, the courtesy you show in a crowd, all witness to the spiritual condition of your heart.

The Christian faith is not something to be put on or taken off as one would a coat. Rather it is a minute-by-minute, hour-by-hour, day-by-day lifestyle. Kindness, generosity, courteousness, honesty, justice, friendliness and gentleness are the fruits of the faithful whose motto is "by prayer and by work."

Lord, help us see that among our needs
Are not more creeds, but loving deeds.

 All things are Thine; no gift have we,
Lord of all gifts, to offer Thee,
And hence with grateful hearts today
Thine own before Thy feet we lay.
                    John G. Whittier hymn

As a physician, Albert Schweitzer had a little different perspective than most when he read the story of Christ healing the ten lepers. (Luke 17:12-19) The reason only one came back to thank Christ for cleansing him, Schweitzer suggested, was that the other nine were so overjoyed they ran to tell their families. They may have intended to come back later to thank the Lord.

Schweitzer himself no doubt had many patients who returned later to express belated gratitude. That may be why he advised against joining those who are bitter about the world's ingratitude. Said Schweitzer on the subject: "Remember, a great deal of water is flowing underground which never comes up as a spring."

If you have gone unthanked for some act, it could be that your recipient is grateful in his heart but has not yet found the words to express his feelings. On the other hand, don't let even the smallest offering done in your behalf go unthanked. The world needs more giving people and the givers need recognition. So acknowledge every gift that comes your way. That includes daily thanks to your Maker, the One who created you and sustains you every day of your life.

Lord, we thank You for everything we have, including life itself.

10

"Love vaunteth not itself, is not puffed up."
I Corinthians 13:4

Publishers apparently are making fortunes turning out various versions of "Who's Who" books. On the assumption that everyone wants to be included in such a book and that everyone is somebody, the compilers of such volumes have been printing them in record numbers. There are books on who's who in show business, in politics, in cooking, in gardening, in sports, in high society, in dog breeding and even in writing.

On the latter score, I received a form to complete recently that would place my name among a group of what the editor described as "distinguished authors of our time." I was somewhat flattered until I read that buying a copy of the book for $49.50 was a condition of my inclusion. Such is the price of fame (about $49 too much I decided!).

There was a hymn I sang as young man in church called "Is My Name Written There?" . . .

> In the book of Thy kingdom
> With its pages so fair,
> Tell me, Jesus, my Savior,
> Is my name written there?

The New Testament talks about the Book of Life (Revelation 20:12) that records the names of those redeemed. If you know the Lord, believe on Him and live your faith, then you're already included in the most important "who's who" of all. Your job now is to manifest His love so completely that others find their way into the Kingdom, too.

Inspire me, Lord, to live a life that will glorify You.

"For me to live is Christ, and to die is gain."
Philippians 1:21

Not long ago while in Washington, D.C., my children challenged me to walk the steps to the top of the Washington Monument. I agreed to a compromise: walking down after an elevator ride up! That proved to be more than enough exercise.

But while waiting at the base of that 555-foot obelisk, I got to thinking about monuments in general. Over the course of history, humankind has built an unbelievable number of them, hoping to memorialize something or someone with a lasting tribute. It is worth noting that most of these monuments were made of the most lasting material known—stone.

When it comes to personal memorials, there is only one thing more lasting: the quality of a person's life. Christ's life did not need to be recorded in stone to make Him immortal, and neither does yours.

Your place in the Kingdom is predicated upon only one thing: faith. So concentrate on being a pillar of faith, and you'll be a living monument to the love of God.

Help us to so live for You, Father, that there is no question whom we serve.

"So teach us to number our days, that we may apply our hearts unto wisdom."
Psalm 90:12

Writing in my study today, I noticed something different. The house has taken on a new character—it is ethereally quiet. Summer vacation is over, and our children are back in school.

Sometime back a reader from Ravenswood, West Virginia, sent us a back-to-school prayer by Howard Brownlee, an environmental engineer who teaches a church school class at the

First United Methodist Church there. It is full of insights about learning that we all need to remember:

> "Almighty God, as we think of our children and young people returning to school, we are reminded that you gave us the greatest teacher of all time, our Lord, Jesus Christ. The Holy Bible, your Word, is the universal textbook of our Christian civilization and it contains the best course in human relations that was ever written. We are all students of Yours and we never cease learning of the wonders of Your creation and the mathematical exactness of the universe. It is when we try to find the answer to our problems, without raising our hand to ask You the question first, that we fail in the course of Life. Teach us, O God, that the best education we can receive is through a correspondence course with You. May we always seek and find Truth in Your word. In Jesus' name we pray. Amen."

Keep Thou my feet; I do not ask to see
The distant scene—one step enough for me.

John Newman hymn

Trying to find something for her young son Tommy to do one rainy day, his mother took a Sunday school journal and removed from it a colored picture of the world. Then she cut it into irregular pieces and told him, "Here's a puzzle. See if you can put it together."

In no time at all, the boy had completed the task. "How did you do it so quickly?" his mother asked. "I thought it would take at least an hour."

"It was easy," he answered. "There was a picture of Jesus on the back. I used it for a guide and then turned the puzzle over."

When you and I use Christ as a guide, the puzzles of our lives and this world become solvable. He can help us find meaning and peace in situations that seem confusing and hopeless. That's because He really does have the whole world in His hands and we are part of that world He created and loves.

If you have spiritual consciousness, you know that today and every day you are safe and secure in the very hollow of His hand. If you don't have that assurance, you can find it by asking God to take over your life.

Lord, every day, in every situation, keep me close to You.

14 There is a place of quiet rest,
Near to the heart of God,
A place where sin cannot molest,
Near to the heart of God.
Cleland B. McAfee hymn

Some people I know just bought a second home, a lakefront house they plan to use on weekends. "We're going to make it our getaway place," the wife of the family said. "By the time Friday comes, Harold is so tired of seeing people on his job that he needs a retreat spot for unwinding."

Second homes have become quite common in the last few years with several factors contributing to their growth — mobility, increased discretionary income and urban sprawl among them. And many people involved in pressure-packed jobs feel a need to withdraw to a quiet place where they can think and rest.

It is not a new phenomenon. Christ, when hard pressed by the crowds, retreated into the mountains (Matthew 5:1) in order to get some time to Himself. There in that tranquil setting He drew His disciples around Him and delivered His so-called Sermon on the Mount. In point of fact, it was not a sermon, but a dialogue with friends in which He outlined the rewards that are in store for the faithful.

Find some time to be alone during the next few days, at least a few minutes each day, and meditate on Christ's Beatitudes which we are going to discuss. An understanding of them is essential if we are to be serious about our faith.

Give us moments each day, Lord, when we can close out the world and close in on spiritual concerns.

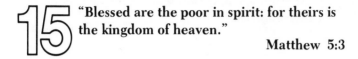

15 "Blessed are the poor in spirit: for theirs is the kingdom of heaven."

Matthew 5:3

Gladys was what they once called "a pillar of society." She came from one of the best families in town and married into an equally prominent family. Together she and her husband appeared to have an idyllic life—plenty of money, a big home, fine cars, beautiful clothes, exotic vacations, membership in the most exclusive clubs. They also belonged to a church, but other than baptisms and weddings for their children, their faith was a perfunctory one. Then, Gladys' husband dropped dead one day while playing golf, and at the early age of 51 she became a widow.

The wheels that had spun so merrily stopped, and her life closed in on her. She began drinking heavily and probably would have found an early grave herself had not a friend invited her to a church where she found Christ. Suddenly, life was restored. It had meaning, purpose and vitality again. In her joy, she exclaimed, "I never knew how poor I was until I accepted Christ."

Gladys had discovered the truth of the first beatitude—blessed are the poor in spirit. She once thought she had everything, but when trouble came she learned how little it all meant. Her spirit was humbled.

We can be enormously rich in worldly goods, and yet be spiritually bankrupt. The word "blessed" as used in the Bible means much more than happy. It also means spiritually complete, at one with God, at peace with God. And the phrase "poor in spirit" means receptive, open, humble-minded. When you and I open ourselves to God's leading in our lives, and willingly let Him have first place, we are able to enter His kingdom full of joy, full of happiness, full of peace.

In You are all the riches we need, Lord. Remind us of this when we forget.

"Blessed are they that mourn: for they shall be comforted."

Matthew 5:4

One night a couple of years ago, my son Chris met me at the front door with tears in his eyes.

"My bike's been stolen," he said. Then, sobbing on my shoulder, he related the whole story of where he'd left it and when he'd discovered it gone. I told him I was sorry and suggested that "maybe the police would find it." But the bicycle wasn't recovered, and for the next several weeks Chris was reduced to walking.

Every time he mentioned the stolen bike his face clouded with hurt. "Why did they have to take my bike?" he complained. Then one day I told him to get in the car, that we were going to buy him a new bicycle, which we did. A short time later I watched as he rode off to show the new bike to his friends. He was full of unrestrained happiness. What a contrast between that moment and the one when I learned of his loss.

Multiply the euphoria Chris must have felt a few thousand times and we may have an approximation of the good news Christ says is in store for those who mourn. Some people believe His second beatitude applies only to the bereaved, but Biblical scholars say that the Lord was including all who are sad or depressed by problems of this life. Jesus' promise to believers is "eschatological" (that means to be fulfilled at the end of this life).

So if you suffer some physical affliction or if you're lonely or poor or broken in spirit or feel rejected or alienated, Christ said that all this will give way in the kingdom to come. Not only will you be comforted; you'll be blessed. That means you can expect wholeness and happiness and healing as well. That's good news indeed.

Lord, thank You for sending the Holy Spirit to comfort us.

236

17

"Blessed are the meek: for they shall inherit the earth."

Matthew 5:5

"If the meek are going to inherit the earth," I heard a man say once, "then it must be the earth on some other planet, because all they ever get here is the part of the chicken that goes over the fence last."

That man's definition of meekness was tenuousness, timidity, hesitancy, uncertainty, but the meekness Christ was talking about meant to be gentle, to be malleable, to be willing, to be disciplined. Moses was called the meekest of men (Numbers 12:3) but it didn't mean that he was spineless or without strength or character. To the contrary, Moses was a leader, but he knew that he was nothing without God. So he deferred to God, acknowledging his total dependence upon Him, and it was this posture that made Moses great in the sight of men and God.

When you and I subordinate our wishes to God's and make Him our Supreme Commander, we become inheritors of a Kingdom that is without end, one that will survive all the man-made governments that ever were or ever will be. That's how the meek will inherit the earth.

We acknowledge Your power in our lives, Lord, and ask You to direct us in all that we say and do.

18

"Blessed are they which do hunger and thirst after righteousness: for they shall be filled." Matthew 5:6

Once I interviewed a woman who, with the pilot of a small plane, had crashed in a desolate section of Alaska. For 49 days they were stranded until another light plane spotted them and they were rescued.

"We were so hungry," she told me, "that we ate toothpaste and chewed on shoe leather, and we used snow to satisfy our thirst." Only their strong faith kept the couple from losing hope.

Few of us know what it is like to go without food or drink for an extended period of time. All we can do is imagine the intense hunger and thirst. However, there are many walking around with unfulfilled spiritual appetites, a deficiency that may last a lifetime. Why? Some people are, of course, without light, without awareness that God could satisfy their longings. Others have rejected Him as a source of help.

What will it take to change the attitude of the second group? The answer is an intense need, and that often results from some traumatic experience in a person's life. It is when we are helpless and in great need that Christ is most real, and in this beatitude He promises to provide sustenance to those who come to Him in want. If you feel spiritually empty or if you are trying to help another who is, note that Christ's condition for filling is a hunger and thirst for righteousness. In other words, we must want Him intensely with our whole selves—bodies, minds and souls.

We confess our thirst for You, Lord. Fill us with Your Spirit.

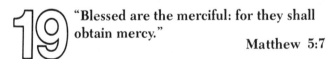

"Blessed are the merciful: for they shall obtain mercy."

Matthew 5:7

A young boy who once had been caught stealing stood before a juvenile judge, awaiting sentence.

"I know this is the first time you have been in trouble," the judge said, "and I have heard all the reports testifying to your good character. Do you have anything to say in your own behalf before I pass sentence?"

"Only," the boy said, choking back tears, "that I wish it had never happened. And I know it won't happen again."

The judge nodded. "I believe you, but the court has a criterion for such crimes and I must sentence you to one year at the state reformatory. However," the judge continued, "I am going to suspend the sentence and put you on two years' probation instead. If you're on good behavior during this period and make restitution for what you stole, you'll get your wish. I'll expunge this offense from the record, and it will be as if it never happened." The boy had no further problems and his indiscretion eventually was wiped off the books.

God is a merciful judge, too. In I John 1:9 we are told that "If we confess our sins, He is faithful and just to forgive us our sins, and cleanse us from all unrighteousness." In other words, He will suspend sentence upon our admission of guilt and upon hearing our plea for forgiveness. Christ's words in the verse above advise us to be merciful to others too, because at judgment God will show compassion to those who have been gentle and tolerant and forgiving and merciful themselves.

When you catch another in some action that is less than virtuous, pause before passing judgment on the offense. Search for words that are moderate and temperate, so as to help the person regain self-respect. Try to be understanding and forgiving. It is mercy of this quality that we appreciate when the shoe is on the other foot, and it is the kind of mercy God will remember when we seek His pardon.

When we fall short of Your high calling, Lord, grant us Your mercy.

"Blessed are the pure in heart: for they shall see God."
Matthew 5:8

When I was a boy I attended vacation Bible school every summer for a least two weeks. Because it followed on the heels of public school and took time away from baseball, I was not the most excited student to attend, but my mother saw to it that I was there.

One time, I remember two dedicated women evangelists named Eva Clausen and Celeste Richardson (I just had a letter from them recently; they are retired in Galion, Ohio) giving a talk on the subject of a pure heart. They must have been very effective teachers because I remember their object lesson well.

They had several different colored hearts—each representing a spiritual condition. The black heart, they told us, represented the sinful heart, unredeemed by Christ. Then they covered it with a red heart which represented Christ's blood shed at Calvary as a sacrifice for us. That for believers resulted in a white heart or a pure heart, one committed to God and His righteousness.

Christ says in the sixth beatitude that we should strive for a pure heart because it is a condition for seeing God. How does anyone achieve a pure heart, one free of conniving thoughts and manipulative self-serving actions? Not by one's own will, that is for sure.

By nature, we follow a road that benefits ourselves first. And according to the Bible only one thing can induce us to change courses. That is an overriding love of God. When we accept Him as Lord of our life, He makes us new creatures, capable of serving and loving others beyond our own human capacities. Does that mean that we are forever free of ulterior motives? Does a leopard have spots? Purity of heart does not come any easier than other spiritual disciplines. But once we see the goal clearly and invite Christ to walk by our side, we are sure to make progress.

Fill our hearts so full of love for You, Lord, that it crowds out selfishness.

 "Blessed are the peacemakers: for they shall be called the children of God."
Matthew 5:9

Once a group of young people were having a comparative-religions discussion, and a girl of 16 or 17 observed, "I believe we are all God's children." To which came the rejoinder: "But don't you think that God sometimes longs for a few adults?"

In the famous love chapter of the Bible (I Corinthians 13) there is an often slighted passage that comes after Paul's definition of charity. It appears in the 11th verse and says, "When I was a child I spoke as a child, I understood as a child, I thought

as a child: but when I became a man I put away childish things."
It has a good application to the seventh beatitude in which
Christ admonishes us to be peacemakers. To be contentious,
quarrelsome or argumentative are childish things—traits that
cause misunderstanding, ill will, and long-standing resentment. The truth is that people fight over the silliest minutiae
imaginable. Even Christians who should know better are
sometimes guilty of actions that parallel a spoiled child's foot
stomping, pouting and breathholding.

If you would grow in spiritual maturity, start today by inven-
torying your responses to people who say and do things with
which you take exception. It is possible to disagree without
being disagreeable. The Lord will show you how because He
loves peacemakers, and if you love Him you can demonstrate it
with words and deeds that heal rather than cut, that encourage
rather than discourage and that build up rather than tear down.

Lord, let me be childlike in my faith but mature in my actions.

22

"Blessed are they which are persecuted for
righteousness' sake: for theirs is the
kingdom of heaven."
Matthew 5:10

When I was in Rome several years ago, I visited the catacombs,
those dark subterranean cemeteries where early Christians
met to worship together out of sight and sound of their perse-
cutors. One of the catacombs I toured is named for St. Sebas-
tian, a Roman centurion, who was ordered to be slain by
archers' arrows because of his defection to Christianity. Hearing our guide tell about this early martyr's courage made me
realize how little comprehension I have of what it would be like
to be persecuted for my faith.

Yet Christ knew that the cost of standing firm in the face of
political opposition could be death, and He no doubt wanted
His disciples to be aware of that harsh reality. That's probably
why He spelled it out in His ninth beatitude. Few of those
reading this page are in danger of physical harm because of
their religious persuasion. However, there is a more subtle

persecution, a verbal one that ridicules and derides the stances of people who take unpopular positions because of their faith.

Were He speaking today, I think Christ might tell us to "hang in there even when it isn't the 'in' thing to do. Follow your convictions even if people criticize and threaten and try to intimidate you, because if you do, you will discover something much more valuable than the approval of men, you'll discover the Kingdom of Heaven."

Lord, give me a kind of faith that doesn't flag in the face of a threat or a challenge.

 "Blessed are ye, when men shall revile you, and persecute you, and shall say all manner of evil against you falsely, for my sake. Rejoice, and be exceeding glad: for great is your reward in heaven . . . "

Matthew 5:11-12

Abraham Lincoln came under heavy political attack while he was president. He was, at various times, characterized as stupid, naive, misguided, unqualified. Yet he faced all the charges with a steady magnanimity and forbearance. Once he answered his detractors with these words:

"If I were to try to read, much less answer all the attacks made on me, this shop might as well be closed for any other business. I do the very best I know how—the very best I can; and I mean to keep doing it to the end. If the end brings me out all right, what is said against me won't amount to anything. If the end brings me out wrong, ten angels swearing I was right won't make any difference."

If you are ridiculed for your faith, made fun of because you try to live by the light God has given you, criticized for taking a stand, lied about by people who would like to discredit you, it is good to have on record Christ's words in the final catch-all beatitude.

It states unequivocally that God will honor such dedication.

Furthermore, He will reward all who witness and serve Him faithfully. Take heart. Rejoice. In the end, you'll come out on top.

In Your words, Lord, we find inspiration and hope that our faith is not in vain.

"Happiness held is the seed; happiness shared is the flower."
Anonymous

Talking recently with Dr. James Dobson, professor of pediatrics of the University of Southern California School of Medicine, I asked him about a survey he mentioned in his best-selling book **WHAT WIVES WISH THEIR HUSBANDS KNEW ABOUT WOMEN** (Tyndale). Dr. Dobson's research led him to the conclusion that low self-esteem is the No. 1 problem of married women today.

"What can husbands do to help their wives deal with inferiority feelings?" I asked.

"Without question," he answered, "his single most important contribution to this problem can be made by keeping romantic love alive." Dr. Dobson went on to say that many men need to work much harder at communicating their love to their wives, keeping in mind the admonition in I Peter 3:7 (L. B.) that says, "You husbands must be careful of your wives, being thoughtful of their needs and honoring them. Remember that you and your wife are partners in receiving God's blessings, and if you don't treat her as you should, your prayers will not get ready answers."

Everyone wants to feel important, essential, needed, and a husband has the responsibility for showing appreciation and affection for his wife and family. The same is true in reverse. Unexpressed love is like a dammed-up river; nothing beyond the barrier receives life-giving water.

You and I both need someone to love, and we need to be loved in return. It is tangible evidence that we are worthwhile as human beings. So don't withhold love from people around you another moment, but make yourself an open channel of God's unfathomable love.

Just as we need You, Father, so we need human love. Today, help us to let our loved ones know they are needed.

 "Delight thyself also in the Lord; and He shall give thee the desires of thine heart."
Psalm 37:4

In March of 1977, the works of Beatrix Potter, creator of THE TALE OF PETER RABBIT, were exhibited in New York City in celebration of the book's 75th anniversary. Actually, the book was printed privately in 1901—76 years earlier, because no publisher was interested in four talking bunnies named Flopsy, Mopsy, Cottontail and Peter. But after seeing the book in print and hearing good comments about it, British publisher Frederick Warne reconsidered and decided to distribute it. He wasn't sorry. Soon any number of publishers wanted it, and to date an estimated 20 million copies of "the rabbit book" have been sold in 13 languages, including Braille.

Beatrix Potter believed she had written and illustrated a children's book that deserved publishing, so she persevered, and time proved her judgment correct and then some. Her example should give hope to others who have dreams that they can't get the world to share.

When you feel God has given you a talent or calling, don't give up just because someone else disagrees. Glenn Clark, founder of Camps Farthest Out and author of many great spiritual books, once wrote one called THE SOUL'S SINCERE DESIRE, which counseled readers to nurture and pursue the dreams and visions God places deep inside each of us. The results for you could be as fantastic as Beatrix Potter's. But even if they're less, you won't be a loser for having persevered in them. God understands your "soul's sincere desire" and nothing would please Him more than to see it come to fruition.

Lord, thank You for giving me dreams. Give me also the perseverance to make them come true.

26   "Oh wad some power the giftie gie us
To see oursels as others see us!"
                               Robert Burns

"Will you please sit down," a coarse woman's voice boomed out of the theater's darkness. The target of her vitriol was a late-arriving man who only had momentarily blocked her view while the usher was hurrying the customer to his seat.

I always cringe when I hear such adolescent behavior, and—make no mistake about it—impatience of this kind is childishly rude, on a par with foot-stomping temper tantrums. Being sensitive and understanding when others delay or impede or inconvenience us is a mark of maturity, certainly a posture appropriate for Christians.

If you give others a "wide berth" when it comes to mistakes or *faux pas*, chances are you'll receive equally tender treatment when positions are reversed. Practice patience today when someone tests you. Every time we resist the temptation to chastise another for some minor indiscretion, we grow as human beings. Look for the Christ in others.

Lord, help me see each person I meet today through Your eyes, and to love them as You do.

27   "For what is a man profited if he shall gain the whole world, and lose his own soul?"
                               Matthew 16:26

When I visited an acquaintance in his city apartment not long ago, I pushed the buzzer and waited for him to answer. Soon he came to the door and began unlocking it. Click, click, click. One by one I heard him release three different locks. Finally, I was invited inside.

"You don't believe in taking chances," I joked.

"Even three locks aren't enough," he answered. "I've been robbed twice in the last year."

Does he live in fear of more break-ins? "No," he told me,

"they can only steal things, and things aren't really that important to me."

He is a very wise man. Sometimes people forget what is really important in life. Christians, too. Some think idolatry is limited to the worship of golden calves and that all anyone need do to eliminate such things is to destroy them, burn them to ashes as Moses did. (Exodus 32:20) But the idols we are apt to worship are more subtle. We don't set some actual statue on a pedestal and bow down before it. No, but more than a few of us pay homage to such idols as money, position, prestige, possessions. Doting over transient things while giving short shrift to lasting, eternal, spiritual matters is folly. Where your treasure is, we are told, there is your heart. (Luke 12:34) The most valuable possession you can have is the knowledge of and belief in Jesus Christ. And that is a possession that doesn't require locks and keys for protection.

Lord, if there be any, reveal the false idols in our lives.

 "Blessed is he that readeth, and they that hear the words of his prophecy, and keep those things which are written therein."
Revelation 1:3

While I was going to college at what was then little Bowling Green (Ohio) State University, I took a couple of courses in economics. Or maybe they took me. Most of the mysteries of that social science have over the years remained just that, a mystery. I do remember something a visiting professor once told our class, however.

"A parrot could be an economist," he said, "if you could teach him to say two words—supply and demand." I suppose there is some truth to that statement because much of the world's production, distribution and consumption of goods pivots on those two factors.

I wonder what two-word formula could be given a new Christian that would capsule the spiritual life. Which two would you choose? There are several which come to mind. How about *belief* and *power,* or *sacrifice* and *gain,* or *die* and *live,* or *faith* and *works*? All have Scriptural support, but if I were asked to distill or synthesize the Gospel of Christ into two words, I believe I'd choose *love* and *service* because I think that is what the New Covenant is all about. I'd support my contention with two key passages. First, the Great Commandment in Matthew (22:37-39): "Love the Lord thy God with all thy heart, and with all thy soul, and with all thy mind . . . and thy neighbor as thyself." Second, Christ's answer to the question, "When did we see thee hungry and feed thee, or thirsty and give thee drink, or naked and clothe thee, or sick or in prison and visit thee?": "As you did it to one of the least of these my brethren, you did it to me." (Matthew 25:40, RSV)

Remind us each day, Lord, that when we love and serve our neighbors, we love and serve you.

"For the artist life is always a discipline, and no discipline can be without pain."
Havelock Ellis

An admirer of Marian Anderson, the famous opera singer, once remarked to her: "I'd give my right arm if I could sing like you."

Miss Anderson smiled and replied thoughtfully, "Would you give eight hours practice a day?"

Sometimes we think success is the result of an intrinsic gift that a person was born with, and in fact some aptitude does seem to be God-given. Yet more often than not, people who have achieved top recognition in their fields have devoted untold years to developing their talents.

Singlemindedness of purpose and sacrifice are integral parts of most success stories. They don't happen overnight as some would have us believe. If you have a talent that you think God wants you to develop, you must decide how much time, energy and dedication you are willing to give to that end. The quantity of your commitment will determine to a large extent the quality that results.

Give my life focus and purpose, Lord, so that I make the most of Your gifts.

30

Breathe, O breathe Thy loving Spirit
Into ev'ry troubled breast!
Let us all in Thee inherit,
Let us find the promised rest.

Charles Wesley

As a kid, I had more than my share of broken bones. In fact, by the time I was 15, I had had casts on two fractured wrists, a broken elbow and a fractured ankle. So it was with great trepidation that I went to the doctor following a football game in which I'd injured the little finger on my right hand. To my happy surprise, he told me that it was not broken, just dislocated. Then, following some deft manipulation, he put the separated bones back in place.

Sometimes our lives get out of joint. We find ourselves at odds with most everyone in our circle of activity. A businessman once told me, "I seem to be at loggerheads with everybody."

When you find yourself in such a position (and from time to time we all have the feeling that no one appreciates us or understands or cares), it is good to remember that we have an advocate, an appeals judge, an ombudsman (that's a person whose job it is to listen to citizen complaints and problems) in Jesus Christ. Christians have a Friend in the Holy Spirit. He will give personal attention to your problems at any hour, day or night; and if you listen closely, He will guide you into a course of action that will mend your bent and broken relationships. God is the healer you and I need when our lives get out of joint and we become separated from His love.

When we are at odds with others, Lord, send Your healing spirit.

OCTOBER 1978

S	M	T	W	T	F	S
1	2	3	4	5	6	7
8	9	10	11	12	13	14
15	16	17	18	19	20	21
22	23	24	25	26	27	28
29	30	31				

If you are sick in body or mind, ask your Heavenly Father to help you deal with your problem. Even if you have sought relief for a long time without improvement, remember that prayer can work miracles. "Things which are impossible with men are possible with God." (Luke 18:27)

OCTOBER 1978

1 "A man of meditation is happy, not for an hour or a day, but quite round the circle of all his years."
Isaac Taylor

"I'm always behind in my work," a young mother lamented. When she listed the duties she had as wife, mother of three children, Sunday school teacher, PTA officer and hospital aide, I understood why she had trouble getting all her chores finished.

Millions of Americans are so harried by duties and responsibilities that they have little or no time for quiet moments that regain their strength, restore their minds, calm their souls. We need these moments not only to keep in touch with our true inner selves, but also to keep in touch with God, who speaks to us when we are still enough and relaxed enough to hear His wisdom.

If your nerves are frazzled, if you are too tired and exhausted to think straight, find some time today (and each day) to withdraw into the serene recesses of your own being. "The Kingdom of God is within," Christ said (Luke 17:21) and you will discover the full dimension of that Kingdom only if you look quietly inward.

In the din of life, Lord, help us to hear Your guiding voice.

251

2

"We should give God the same place in our
hearts that he holds in the universe."
Marcus Tullius Cicero

Recently someone sent me a copy of "An Indian Prayer," which
is distributed by the Red Cloud Indian School, a mission to
Sioux Indian children in Pine Ridge, South Dakota. The prayer
is worth posting some place where it can be reread from
time to time:

> O' Great Spirit, whose voice I hear in the winds and
> whose breath gives life to all the world, hear
> me! I am small and weak, I need your
> strength and wisdom.
> Let me walk in beauty, and make my eyes ever be-
> hold the red and purple sunset.
> Make my hands respect the things you have made
> and my ears sharp to hear your voice.
> Make me wise so that I may understand the things
> you have taught my people.
> Let me learn the lesson you have hidden in every leaf
> and rock.
> I seek strength, not to be greater than my brother, but
> to fight my greatest enemy—myself.
> Make me always ready to come to you with clean
> hands and straight eyes.
> So when life fades, as the fading sunset, my spirit may
> come to you without shame.

3

"Cast thy burden upon the Lord, and he
shall sustain thee: he shall never suffer the
righteous to be moved." **Psalm 55:22**

Asked about the low point in his long and distinguished
baseball career, Los Angeles Dodger pitcher Don Sutton
points to a period in 1974. For better than eight weeks he did

not win a game and his team was suffering a severe slump because of it. Both the fans and press were highly critical of him. So he was not surprised when his manager, the since-retired Walter Alston, called him aside for a word. Sutton thought Alston was going to take him out of the starting lineup and replace him with another pitcher. Instead, Alston said, "If we win, it'll be with you. Come what will, you're my man."

It was the turning point in the season. Sutton soon found himself. With him leading the way, the Dodgers went on to win the pennant. Sutton recalls, "Knowing I had people behind me made all the difference. When we are sustained by our friends and God, we can endure a lot of pain and disappointment."

That last sentence is worth putting on a wall sampler to be read and reread. When we have people who believe in us, we can hold on no matter how tough the going. And if you know Christ you have such a friend. He believes in us and will sustain us no matter what. The bogeymen of life lose their efficacy in the face of His omnipotence. They are cut down to size and we can come out the winner in any endeavor. You can do any and all things through Christ who strengthens you. (Philippians 4:13)

Thank You, Heavenly Father, for giving us supportive friends.

 "Time will not be ours forever."

Ben Johnson

Not long ago Arthur Gordon, *Guideposts'* Editorial Director, and I visited with Billy and Ruth Graham in their North Carolina home and we got to talking about some of the reasons people resist accepting Christ. Dr. Graham mentioned several reasons: intellectual reservations, unwillingness to make a commitment to the high moral demands of Christianity, various idolatries. Then, Ruth Graham suggested procrastination, recalling a recent incident she'd heard about.

According to her source, a certain woman had tried for many years to get her husband to become a Christian, but the man kept putting off the decision. "Later," he said, much in the manner of a saint who prayed in his youth, "Make me chaste, Lord, but not just yet." Then, one night the woman was awakened from a sound sleep. "Wake your husband and ask Him to accept Me now," a silent voice told her. She resisted. It was the middle of the night, but the voice persisted. Finally, she roused her husband and told him what she'd been instructed to do. Surprisingly, her husband responded positively. He got down on his knees beside the bed and accepted Christ as his Lord and Saviour. The long-postponed decision could not have been made any later because in the morning the man was dead.

Life is too short for procrastination when it comes to spiritual matters. If you have some business to talk over with God or if you have some accounts to straighten with others, it is best to do it today. Don't assume there will always be time later; perhaps there won't be.

When I'm tempted to put off things, Lord, prod me into action.

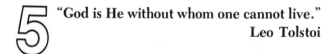

"God is He without whom one cannot live."
Leo Tolstoi

Much has been written of late about the *ozone*, a layer of air in the stratosphere which prevents ultraviolet rays from reaching the earth. It is believed these rays may cause skin cancer and endanger life. Some scientists worry that fluorocarbons such as come from spray-can propellants and exhaust gases from high-flying airplanes may break down the ozone barrier and expose our earth to irreparable damage.

On a recent cloudy day while I was in the car, the sun suddenly burst through with eye-blinding brilliance, and this whole business of ozones came to mind. In a spiritual sense many of us are guilty of setting up barriers between ourselves and God. In this case, we block the good light of His saving grace from our lives. We do it in many ways—by closing our minds (a form of ignorance), by worrying, by doubting, by apathy, by selfishness, by cynicism. When we employ these negating forces we limit God's power and thus our ability to deal with our problems.

If you want to be a dynamic, creative, vital Christian, then you need to rid yourself of the barriers which stand between you and God. Once you do, His light—pure, life-giving, powerful—will shine all the way to and through you, warming not only yourself, but also everyone your life touches.

Wrap us in Your protective light, Lord, and keep us safe.

"Life is real! Life is earnest!
And the grave is not its goal;
Dust thou art, to dust returnest,
Was not spoken of the soul."

Henry Wadsworth Longfellow

In her best-selling book, PASSAGES, author Gail Sheehy discusses the various crises that people face as they go through life. A reader of her book, a man passing through a mid-life stage, told me: "I have just come to the realization that I am not going to live forever, and that I've wasted a lot of precious time."

His comment brought to mind something I once included in a book of poems I wrote:

I visited one sideshow then another
hoping to see everything on the midway
the rubber lady
the cobra charmer
the sword swallower
the five-legged calf
the biggest
the smallest
the longest
the tallest

Time meant nothing until I reached the big tent
too late
the three rings were bare
empty of clowns
acrobats
trick horses
only the heavy hoofbeat in my chest
broke the silence
foolishly I had traded the main attraction
for sideshows
and the circus would be gone in the morning

Point me to the center of life, Lord, and keep me from being distracted by sideshows.

7

**"Honor and truth and manhood—
These are the things that stand."
Ted Olson**

A few years ago, I climbed the steps to the top of the Leaning Tower of Pisa in Italy, and like millions of others marveled at this architectural mystery. "How does it stand?" is a question asked again and again.

One man next to me said, "Maybe it's straight and the rest of the world is cockeyed."

His comment reminds me of the attitude some people have about Christianity. Though their lives have been bent and twisted by the ravages of loose and undisciplined living, they look upon Christians as the ones who are warped and out of step. "Eat, drink and be merry for tomorrow we die," they say. The Christian answer is, "Because He lives, I live."

While the world lists like the Leaning Tower of Pisa, bent by the weight of life's burdens, Christians are able to stand straight and true, sustained by a powerful faith. They can echo the Psalmist (27:1), "The Lord is my light and my salvation; whom shall I fear? The Lord is the strength of my life; of whom shall I be afraid?"

When you are sustained by the God of Abraham, Moses and David, you are lacking in nothing.

Lord, thank You for being the same yesterday, today and forever.

**Fair is the sunshine, fairer still the moonlight
And all the twinkling starry host;
Jesus shines brighter, Jesus shines purer
Than all the angels heaven can boast.**

German hymn

It is not surprising that a trained ornithologist sees more species of birds when he goes to the woods than an amateur birdwatcher, just as a botanist sees more plants and an entomologist more insects. That may also help explain why someone who believes in God sees evidence of Him everywhere and an atheist sees Him nowhere.

Some people see crosses everywhere they look—not just on church steeples but on wooden doors and on Christmas packages. They look at telephone poles and see crosses. Where highways intersect, they see crosses. Others hear God's voice in the wind, in the song of the sea. An elderly woman with an ever-green faith and an imagination to match once told me that the wheels of a train say "God is love," that a clock doesn't say "tick tock" but "Jesus saves," and that a quail doesn't whistle "Bob White" but "He lives."

Crazy? No, just caught up by the spirit of life. Take note of the signs of God around you today. They are reminders that we serve an omnipresent Lord, who is closer than our hands or feet or breath.

There are signs of Your love for us everywhere, Lord. Help us see them when our faith is low.

(Columbus Day)
All things are Thine; no gift have we,
Lord of all gifts, to offer Thee,
And hence with grateful hearts today
Thine own before Thy feet we lay.

John G. Whittier

Recently, my son called me from college to say that he had overdrawn his checking account. In other words he had taken out more money than he had deposited, so I sent him a check to cover the deficit and soon he was solvent again.

Reflecting on the convenience of a monthly bank statement showing deposits, withdrawals, charges and balance, I got to thinking how nice it would be to have a monthly spiritual accounting. That way we'd always know our balance. Any overdrafts would show up immediately and we could correct the shortages.

Then it dawned on me that I would be in arrears all the time because God continues to bless me with more of His gifts than I can repay. What must we do to remain in good standing with the Lord? His great commandment says it all: "Love the Lord thy God with all thy heart, and with all thy soul and with all thy mind." (Matthew 22:37) That would be a big order by ourselves, but He supplies the grace, another deposit He puts in our account.

Thank You, Lord, for the many benefits we enjoy in our life accounts.

 "This is the day which the Lord hath made;
we will rejoice and be glad in it."

Psalm 118:24

One bright, sunny day on an auto trip recently, I was riding along in silence when a cheerful voice came booming over my citizen's band radio.

"Is there anybody out there?" the man asked. "If you're

258

happy, say Amen." Picking up my microphone, I quickly answered, "Amen." Suddenly, Channel 19 was filled with other voices, male and female. "Amen, amen, amen, amen," they responded. What followed was a wave of well wishing and pleasant conversation. It was a heart-lifting moment—a group of unrelated travelers affirming their mutual joy at being alive.

Whether you have a CB radio or not, you can broadcast what's on your heart and mind today to everyone you meet. You can do it with words, of course. But you can also communicate your optimism and faith through your eyes, with your smile, through the way you walk (head high and shoulders back) and through touch—a hug or squeezed hand is a great way to express affection or appreciation. Whatever way you choose to say "Amen" to life, do it enthusiastically, wholeheartedly—and often.

Because we know You and Your goodness, Lord, it's easy to say be positive about life.

 "A room without books is like a man without a soul."
Cicero

RELIGIOUS BOOK SALES UP 24 PER CENT, the headline read. The figures reflected the great recent upsurge in printed materials bearing a spiritual message. Why do you suppose this is so?

The wise Daniel Webster said a mouthful in 1823 when he wrote: "If religious books are not widely circulated among the masses in this country, I do not know what is going to become of us as a nation. If truth be not diffused, error will be; if God and His Word are not known and received, the devil and his works will gain the ascendancy."

If you are having some trial or test today, take time to read something from your bookshelf, something which raises your spiritual sights, something which informs or guides or inspires. If possible discuss what you read with someone else. The Bible is an obvious choice, but there are other books that will feed your soul, too. Words are vehicles capable of transporting our minds higher into the realm of the heavenly or lower into the gutter. Choose the former and your life will take on a new dimension.

Thank You, Lord, for books which nourish our hearts and minds.

12

"By suffering comes wisdom."
Heraclitus

Television star Sandy Duncan once recalled for *Guideposts* a "devastating" loss she suffered in high school. Her heartbreaking setback came when she tried out for cheerleader, and lost.

Forty girls auditioned and six were picked. Sandy finished seventh. When she told her Grandpa Jeff the results, she burst into tears.

"I'm sorry," he consoled. "I know it hurts. The awful thing is it's probably going to hurt for a long time to come. But I remember an old proverb that you need to know. It's just four words long: 'No pains, no gains.'"

Sandy Duncan says that her grandfather's advice has stood the test of time in her life, and it has helped her over some other rough spots.

Grandpa Jeff's proverb is a good one for us all because it distills so much truth. Unless we are willing to risk failure all of our lives, we will not grow. Some people become Christians—accept Christ, say the words "I believe"—but don't mature; they remain spiritual babes. They stay on a milk diet and never get to the meat of their faith. One mark of maturity is a willingness to attempt jobs and skills beyond ourselves. When we do, we often find God's hidden hand reaching out to help us climb heights that were once hard to imagine. But even when we fail and the result is momentary hurt, we

need to remember Grandpa Jeff's words—"no pains, no gains."
Then we need to get up and try again.

Keep me from being stymied by small hurts, Lord. Instead, let
me seek You and then move forward.

13

" . . . He shall give you another Comforter,
that he may abide with you for ever."
John 14:16

The other day I flew over New York City in a helicopter and
looked down upon the streets, rivers, bridges and buildings
which appeared in miniature. One skyscraper in particular
caught my attention. A few days before, I had visited that
building on business, stood outside it and stared at its top,
stretching dramatically into the sky. It seemed immense. Then
I'd gone inside and ridden an elevator to the top where I had a
panoramic view of the city around me. It was a breathtaking
sight.

But now looking down on that building, having an overview
of it and seeing it from a different perspective that allowed me
to compare and contrast it with other buildings around it, it
seemed quite ordinary, quite average.

It's the same when we put time and distance between ourselves and a problem. At the moment when something is causing us heartache and headache and "soul-ache," we have trouble
imagining the difficulty gone. But it is amazing the difference a
few days can make. From the perspective of a week or a month,
a nagging problem often vanishes entirely from our minds.

When trials test us and troubles overwhelm us, we need an
unwavering faith and an invincible trust in our Maker that He
will get us through our ordeal. Thank God, you and I don't have
to bear our crosses alone. Today, if your circumstance is weary-
ing, ask the help of the One who went to the cross. He will help
you carry yours.

Lord, show us how to put our problems into perspective when
they get the best of us.

14

When peace, like a river, attendeth my
    way,
When sorrows like sea billows roll—
Whatever my lot, Thou hast taught me to
    say,
It is well, it is well with my soul.
                    Horatio G. Spafford hymn

Face this simple fact: many people call themselves Christian who do not know Christ or what it means to live a life of faith. John Wesley discovered this early in his ministry.

On his way from England to America in 1735 to preach the Gospel to Indians, Wesley's ship encountered heavy seas and the evangelist was filled with fear, which he expressed to a fellow passenger. The shipmate seemed oblivious to the storm.

"Aren't you afraid?" Wesley asked him.

"No, I know Jesus Christ. Do you?"

For the first time, Wesley realized he did not really know Christ as his personal Savior.

Many people have posed as an intimate friend of the Lord's and nothing refuted their claim until trouble came. That's when our true relationship with God is verified or denied—when dark clouds and uncertainty come close.

The Israelites faced such clouds when they stood on the plain of Moab on the southern edge of the Promised Land. Moses had just the word they needed when he told them: "Behold, the Lord thy God hath set the land before thee: go up and possess it, as the Lord God of thy fathers hath said unto thee; fear not, neither be discouraged." (Deuteronomy 1:21) When you feel overwhelmed by circumstances, call on the God of your faith. He will always respond—of that you can be sure.

The peace You give does pass understanding, Lord. Don't let us forget that You are the Source of such peace when trouble assails us.

"Do not pray for easy lives. Pray to be stronger men! Do not pray for tasks equal to your powers. Pray for powers equal to your tasks."

Phillips Brooks

Several years ago I visited my paternal grandfather's birthplace in the Black Forest region of Germany. One of the souvenirs I brought back from the trip was a handcarved cuckoo clock. It ran well for some time, then one of the two weights that are part of the winding mechanism mysteriously disappeared, and the clock quit running. It wasn't until I got a replacement that the clock ran again, and it has continued to keep time to this date.

In life, weights are considered undesirable handicaps by most of us—burdens to be rid of at the earliest opportunity. But like my clock, some of us need the discipline of weights to develop character. For instance, many a youngster has looked upon early work experiences—farm chores, newspaper routes and around-the-house assignments—as infringements on his or her time and freedom. But these weights have helped develop a sense of confidence and responsibility, valuable assets in adulthood. Others among us have learned valuable lessons from the tests and trials of life. Among them, sensitivity and more understanding for problems not our own.

Though we can be sure our Heavenly Father does not wish any hardship or difficulty on any of us, it must be true that as free agents we often dig deep holes for ourselves. These can be painful experiences, but the good news is that God never turns His back on His children. If you are laboring under a heavy load today, ask your Heavenly Father for relief. It's just a prayer away.

When trials and the problems come to us, Lord, help us deal with them and learn from them.

**Oh Jesus, I have promised
To serve Thee to the end;
Be Thou forever near me,
My Master and My Friend.**
John E. Bode hymn

On the closet door in my eight-year-old son Daniel's room are several marks with heights and dates written beside them. Two or three times a year, and on every birthday, I measure Daniel to see how tall he is. As do all children, he takes great interest in how much he has grown from one period to another.

How good it would be if we could devise some way of measuring our spiritual growth on a regular schedule, I thought the last time I sized up Daniel. Then I rejected the idea. Too many people engage in a form of the practice already. Once we have accepted Christ as our Lord and Savior, our job is not to engage in self-righteous pulse feeling, but rather to live our faith as fully as possible. That means loving and serving God and our neighbors with 100 per cent of our bodies, minds and souls. We don't need a yardstick. We already have one, and His name is Jesus Christ. He's our standard, and He asks only that we do our best.

Keep us from getting discouraged, Father, when we fall short of Your commandments.

**"They never sought in vain that sought the
Lord aright!"**
Robert Burns

Not long ago, I had a conversation with a woman who said that God had caused her son to become seriously ill in order to save her deteriorating marriage. She explained that she and her husband were considering a divorce until their son was hospitalized with a near-fatal disease. Their mutual concern over the boy had reunited them.

Though I'm sure that God wanted this woman and her husband to salvage their marriage, and I'm pleased to learn that it was accomplished, I have trouble with her theology. I resist the thought that God infects small children in order to bring about a result that He no doubt could have accomplished in other ways. The fact that there was a correlation between events does not prove that A + B = C.

The way I read my Bible, God wants His children well; He is a healer, a Heavenly Father who loves us so much that He died on a cross for us. Be careful about blaming Him for illness and disease. It is written, "There shall no evil befall thee, neither shall any plague come nigh thy dwelling place. For He shall give His angels charge over thee, to keep thee in all thy ways. They shall bear thee up in their hands, lest thou dash thy foot against a stone." (Psalm 91:10-12) That's the kind of God we serve.

Help me to remember that all good things come from You, O Lord

To God be the glory—great things He hath
    done!
So loved He the world that He gave us His
    Son,
Who yielded His life an atonement for sin,
And opened the lifegate that all may go in.
                  Fanny Crosby hymn

A wobbly man with alcohol on his breath once stopped evangelist Billy Sunday on a street corner to pay him a dubious compliment.

"Billy," he said with thick tongue, "I want you to know that I heard you preach once, and you saved me."

"I'm sure it was me," said the evangelist. "I know it wasn't the Lord."

Billy Sunday knew his part well. He may have introduced many to Christ with his preaching, but he didn't win any souls. That's the job of the Holy Spirit. Christians with evangelical zeal are to be commended for spreading the Gospel, for living in such a manner that their lives testify to His transforming power. However, "scalp counters" need to be careful. Anyone who keeps score of his or her converts is taking undue credit. Be careful of statement such as "I led so and so to Christ" because the leading is God's role and the following is ours.

Lord, give us humble hearts and willing hands.

**Hear ye the Master's call,
"Give me thy best!"
For, be it great or small,
that is his test.**
S.C. Kirk

The top salesman in one of the country's leading companies was once asked the secret of his success. He said it was putting into practice some advice given him by his first sales manager:

"The key to success is doing a common thing uncommonly."

That is one of the best pieces of advice a young person going out on his or her first job could receive, because often first assignments are of the plain vanilla variety. But how people perform routine work usually determines how quickly they advance.

In Matthew 25 (14-30) Christ tells a parable about three men who were given different talents by their master. A talent was equal to about $1,000. One was given five talents, one, two talents, and the last, one talent. The first two doubled their original talents, while the third man buried his, afraid he would lose it. The latter made the master unhappy and he was required to forfeit his talent, but to the other two men, the master said, "Because thou hast been faithful over a few things, I will make you ruler over many."

Whatever you are called upon to do today, give it your best shot. Don't complain that a job is beneath you or that it isn't challenging. Make the most of it. By approaching a task with enthusiasm you will not only get more accomplished, but your attitude will raise you in the sight of others, because anyone who does a common job uncommonly is anything but common.

Lord, help us do our jobs well, so someday we may hear You say, "Well done, thou good and faithful servant."

"Study nature as the countenance of God."
Charles Kingsley

The maple just outside my study window is throwing off its leaves again. I've observed it now for many years. When struggling for the right words, the right phrase, some spark of inspiration—as all writers are wont to do—I rest my eyes on its leaves or bare branches.

Humans would do well to emulate leaf-shedding trees. From time to time, we need to shake off things in our lives that have lost their vitality—habits that are out of date, commitments that are non-productive, efforts that are ineffective and time consuming. When we rid our lives of dead branches and dead leaves, we make way for new growth spiritually, physically, mentally. And as surely as green leaves will appear on my study maple next spring, you will experience a renewing of your body, mind and soul when you step out in faith and are willing to grow.

Lord, give us the ability to see and accept change as part of Your plan.

Take my life, and let it be
Consecrated, Lord, to Thee . . .
Take my hands, and let them move
At the impulse of Thy love.
Frances Ridley Havergal hymn

Speaking to an audience of several thousand college students last year, Elizabeth Elliot Leitch, former missionary to Ecuador and author of THROUGH GATES OF SPLENDOR, a book about her martyred husband, told them:

"Doing God's will involves body, mind and spirit, not just spirit alone. Bringing the body under obedience means going to bed at a sensible hour, grooming yourself carefully, watching your weight, cutting out the junk food . . . It means when the alarm goes off, your feet hit the floor. You have to *move*."

How well disciplined are you? Your answer will depend on your motivation. If we are dedicated, committed, enthusiastic about an endeavor, we have no problem finding time or energy for it. However, if our interest in a project, job or undertaking is lukewarm, we often find ourselves dawdling, daydreaming, falling behind and making excuses for not following through. Christians who take their faith seriously develop an intestinal fortitude that makes them different. They are stronger, tougher and more willing to give of themselves. When a need presents itself, they find the inner resources to respond no matter how tired or how limited their reserves. And you can have that indefatigable quality if you know Christ, through whose strength you can do anything. (Phillippians 4:13)

Let our lives demonstrate how much You really mean to us, Lord.

 "I am the way, the truth, and the life: no man cometh unto the Father but by me."
John 14:6

There have been many individuals—Christian and non-Christian—who have lived what have been called "saintly lives." Mahatma (which means "great souled") Gandhi was one of them, a man who was full of love and compassion for the oppressed of India and the world.

Sometimes I hear people compare men like Gandhi to Jesus, presuming Jesus to be only one of many saints. Their mistake is confusing God with God-likeness.

A new book, MAHATMA GANDHI AND HIS APOSTLES by Ved Mehta (Viking Press) reveals some interesting things, among them that the Gandhi influence 30 years after his death has waned considerably; this despite the fact that his followers recorded every word he said and despite the fact that 400 books were written about him. According to the author, Gandhi's disciples have scattered. They have found inspiration in new masters and in new causes.

The point is: Gandhi was a great man; Jesus was God. The

fact that men still follow Christ with the same fervor they did nearly 2,000 years ago should be enough to convince skeptics of His divinity. However, the real proof of His heavenly power is in the lives He continues to change.

Yes, the Good News is still good.

You have changed us, Father. Now show us how to lead others to Your life-changing love.

(Veterans' Day)
"For as he thinketh in his heart, so is he."
Proverbs 23:7

"I was lucky," an athlete who had overcome a physical defect once told me. "My parents never told me I couldn't play because I was handicapped." It is a good quotation for us all to remember when we are tempted to say "I can't" to some challenge.

We have two dogs at our house—Heidi, a schnauzer, age 14, and her son, Scampy, age 4. The latter has three legs because of a run-in with a car that resulted in a broken leg. The veterinarian put the damaged leg in a splint and thought the dog would regain full use of it. However, gangrene developed and that led to an amputation. We talked of putting the dog to sleep (that's an interesting euphemism for kill), but my children argued that Scampy was a small dog and would be able to adjust. I was dubious, but Scampy was a lovable six-month-old bundle of fuzz and I had no heart for ending his life. Finally I agreed to the operation. I'm glad I did.

Today, four years later, we have the fastest three-legged dog in the East, make that in the east end of town. Whatever, Scampy doesn't seem to know he has a handicap. He accompanies the kids enthusiastically on bike trips, chases squirrels with verve and out-runs me by blocks when I jog.

Like my athlete friend, Scampy apparently has not entertained the thought that he is handicapped; therefore he isn't. When we minimize our weaknesses and maximize our strengths, we can't help but reach our potential. The secret is in the verse above. More often than not, the mind is the prinicipal limiting factor in life. On the other hand, if you think you can, chances are you can.

Lord, remove the word "can't" from my vocabulary.

24

"If your day is hemmed with prayer, it is less likely to unravel."
Anonymous

I receive a fine magazine called *Prevention* which is dedicated to better health. My service station sends me literature which recommends *preventive maintenance* for my car. When I watch a professional football game on television, the announcer invariably tells me that on third down and long yardage the team without the ball has gone into *prevent-pass defense*. The conclusion I draw is that it is wise to take precautionary steps if one wants to ward off negative contingencies.

I believe that goes double in one's spiritual life. The difficulty with foxhole prayers (other than the fact that we feel like a fox in a hole) is that we go to the Lord like a hat-in-hand stranger instead of son or daughter. Of course, one doesn't need to feel that way because our Heavenly Father has been with us, by our sides from Day One, whether we know it or not. But how much easier it is when problems or difficulties arise to have an open line with the One who can deal with emergencies that knock us off the track and leave us weak and exhausted.

Take some preventive spiritual medicine today. Have a conversation with the Lord about something you fear may loom ahead. Ask Him to guide you toward an early action which will lead to a solution before the problem balloons into one of unmanageable proportions. Even in these inflated times, an ounce of prevention still buys a pound of cure!

I don't know what the future holds, but thanks to God, I know Who holds the future.

25 "For my God shall supply all your needs according to his riches in glory by Christ Jesus." **Philippians 4:19**

"God won't ever, ever, ever let you down," a woman wrote recently. She went on to tell how many times in her life God had met her needs, including a recent incident that caused her much concern.

"I had to have major surgery, but didn't know how I was going to pay for it. I had no insurance. No savings. One day in the hospital, while I was recovering, I broke into tears. 'What am I going to do, Lord?' I cried. 'You promised to supply my needs before I ask.' (Matthew 6:8) Moments later a Christian whom I hadn't seen in years walked into my room. She was now living in another city. 'This morning while I was praying, the Lord brought you to mind,' she said, 'and I knew you were in need. Here I am.' When I told the woman my problem, she dried my eyes and said not to worry, that she would take care of everything, including my hospital bill, and she did."

If you have a mind-boggling problem, one that has you upset and worried, ask God to help you solve it. Then wait for His answer. Chances are it's already on its way.

Lord, thank You for being the answer to all of my needs.

26 "Greater love hath no man than this, that a man lay down his life for his friends." **John 15:13**

Much has been written about commercial fishermen who in their pursuit of yellowfin tuna also trap porpoises in their seine nets. Because porpoises are mammals and must surface to breathe, they often drown before the nets are emptied. But their numbers are further decimated, conservationists say, because of a family loyalty that causes those outside the net to stay below and try to help another in distress. If, for example, a single baby is caught in the net, the whole family may stay and try to release it—and as a result all die.

There is a science called ethology which studies similarities between human and animal behavior, and it's not difficult to see the parallel between a mother breastfeeding a newborn and a bird feeding a young one in the nest. Ethologists contend with good evidence that animals have many instinctual things to teach humans. In the case of the porpoises rallying to a family member in trouble, we might draw many lessons, one of which is stated above in the verse from John. Short of laying down our lives, we might at least show more concern for people sick or hungry or naked or in jail. As Christ told His disciples: "Inasmuch as ye have done it unto one of the least of these my brethen, ye have done it unto me." (Matthew 25:40)

Following You, Lord, demands commitment. Help us support our words with action.

27 "The closer we get to Christ the closer we get to one another. Our differences as Protestants and Catholics are lovers' quarrels."

Fulton J. Sheen

"Another woman driver," an acquaintance of mine remarked derogatorily as a motorist cut in front of him. At the next light, he learned differently. The offending driver turned out to be a young man with blond shoulder-length hair.

The incident reminded me of how often we all are guilty of making generalizations. To assume something is so because someone is male or female, black or white, rich or poor, young or old, Protestant or Catholic is sloppy thinking at best, ignorance at worst. The Bible is full of examples which reveal consequences of prejudicial thinking. Jonah didn't want to go to Nineveh because he looked down on its citizens. In John 1:46, Philip's friend Nathanael engages in some ironic condescension when he remarks of Jesus, "Can there any good thing come out of Nazareth?" Philip's answer is to the point: "Come and see."

It is Christlike for you and me to look for the good in others, not the bad. Guard against making generalizations that cannot be supported. Love is kind, understanding, tolerant, forgiving, accepting. Dispense love today—and that's what you'll receive in return.

Lord, teach us to look on the hearts of people we have trouble loving.

28

"Study to shew thyself approved unto God. . . ."
II Timothy 2:15

Tim Gallwey, author of THE INNER GAME OF TENNIS, not long ago had a good tip for TV's David Hartman, host of the ABC television program "Good Morning, America," who said that one of his biggest problems on the court was returning an opponent's lob, adding that he always feared he was going to mis-hit it and that his fears were usually realized.

Gallwey advised Hartman to forget about everything else and concentrate on the ball. "Study the color, the seams, the rotation as it comes down, then swing at it." Hartman took the pro's advice, forgot his fears and improved this phase of his tennis game dramatically.

When you and I let negative thoughts dominate our minds the result is predictable. But if we can learn to shift our focus away from our fears to the mechanics of the task at hand, we can relax and do our best.

Spiritually, we grow when we learn to remove ourselves from the spotlight and shine it on others. By putting the need of others in the forefront of our thinking, we become less self-conscious and more Christ-conscious. When this happens we become open channels of His love and, as a result, effective Christians servants.

Lord, help us to look away from ourselves to concentrate on the ways we can help others.

> "Grant us the serenity to accept the things
> we cannot change,
> The courage to change the things we can
> change,
> And the wisdom to know the difference."
> **Reinhold Niebuhr**

When we grow frustrated and discouraged by the little daily problems that come our way, it is helpful to remember that we have not been singled out for torment by some vengeful god, but rather that problems are a condition of life. All people have problems—the difference is that some individuals cope with them more successfully than others.

Recently, I was reading about Louis Braille, who lost his sight in a childhood accident. He was a voracious reader, so blindness denied him one of his main pleasures in life. But Louis did more than lament his loss. He set out to develop a system of communication for the blind, and though he was frustrated for many years, he finally succeeded. As a result, countless numbers of blind people have been able to "read" through the Braille raised-dot method.

When a problem blocks your path and you can't get over it, survey it from other angles. Maybe you can go around it or under it or through it. Ask God to help you solve dilemmas that keep you from joy and fulfillment and the abundant life Christ promised. Resourcefulness is something else God gives to the seekers in life. "Ask and it shall be given you; seek, and ye shall find; knock and it shall be opened unto you." (Matthew 7:7)

Lord, remind us that sometimes the way out is the way through.

> "If God be for us who can be against us?"
> **Romans 8:31**

A few weeks ago I went with some friends to Madison Square Garden in New York to see an ice show featuring Dorothy

Hamill, the Olympic figure-skating champion. What a skater! With smooth, graceful, almost effortless motions, she gave a flawless performance. "She makes it look easy," I heard some-one say. And that she did.

But then I recalled reading that she has been skating for eight hours a day most every day since she was a small child; that she has been tutored by some of the best coaches in the world; that her family had made great financial and personal sacrifices to enable her to develop her talent. The ease and perfection with which she skates is the result of a singular goal: to be the best skater in the world. She has a gold medal that testifies to her success.

If you have some lofty goal in your life, be prepared to pay the costs required, otherwise you'll never reach it. What are the costs? Self-discipline is one. Hard work, sacrifice and commitment are others. But probably the most important is faith—faith along the way when the going gets tough that all your efforts aren't in vain. That's why it's essential to include God in your hopes and dreams. With Him on your side, it's impossible to lose.

Lord, help us to remember that with Your strength I can reach any goal.

(Halloween)
**For all the saints who from their labors
    rest,
Who Thee by faith before the world
    confessed,
Thy name, O Jesus, be forever blest.
            William Walsham How hymn**

Like many other holidays, the celebration of Halloween has two sides to it—the secular and the religious.

Where did Halloween originate? Historians tell us that the Druids, Celts who lived in Gaul, were the first to observe a festival on this date, the last day of the year for them. The

Druids believed that upon death a good person's soul entered the body of another human being while the soul of an evil person entered the body of an animal. On the final night of their year, they thought that the lord of death gathered together all the souls which had been dwelling in animals and decided their assignments for the coming year. The cat was a sacred animal in the Druids' culture, incidentally, and it was believed to have mystic qualities, an interesting footnote considering the prominence of black cat decorations at Halloween.

Following the Druids, the Romans were next to make this a red-letter day. They adopted some Druid traditions and added to them their own year-end celebration, the festival of Pomona, which was dedicated to fall harvest. Some 800 years after Christ's birth, Christians began observing a holiday at this time of the year, too. They designated November 1 as All Saints' Day or All Hallow's Day, observing it both the first day of November and the evening before. Because the early church had so many followers martyred, this date was set aside to pay tribute to all who died for their faith.

Though for the secular world Halloween may be nothing more than a time for make-believe and partying, Christians should make note of its religious roots. For those early martyrs, there was nothing sportive or festive or make-believe about the persecution that they suffered. It was practiced by real flesh and blood ogres, monsters who inflicted ghoulish punishment upon those who would not renounce Christ. That's the spiritual significance of this date—the other side of Halloween.

Lord, on this day when we think of ghosts and spirits, let us remember Your Holy Spirit.

NOVEMBER 1978

S	M	T	W	T	F	S
			1	2	3	4
5	6	⑦	8	9	10	11
12	13	14	15	16	17	18
19	20	21	22	㉓	24	25
26	27	28	29	30		

Do you feel God has been ignoring your prayers of late? Continue to seek His counsel and trust His timetable. This month hold tight to this promise: "My God shall supply all your needs according to his riches in glory by Christ Jesus." (Philippians 4:19)

NOVEMBER 1978

1 "Call unto me, and I will answer thee, and show thee great and mighty things, which thou knowest not."

Jeremiah 33:3

"A few years ago," a Kentucky woman writes, "I suddenly lost my husband when he had a heart attack. As a result, I had to take a job. But I hadn't worked for almost 30 years, and I looked in vain for months. Then one day while having devotions, I came upon a Bible verse that gave me the assurance that all was going to turn out okay. The verse was Jeremiah 33:3.

"The next day," she continues, "I applied for a job and got it. Since then, I've had several promotions. Praise the Lord." Would this woman have gotten the job even if she hadn't prayed? Possibly, but the longer I live the more I am convinced that prayer changes things—and people. It frees them from all sorts of bondage and gives them confidence to stand tall.

Too many times, I'm afraid, we stew in our own juices. The prophet Jeremiah knew how senseless this is because we have a merciful God who will not only lend us an ear but also will lend us a hand and get us back on our feet. If you are in a wobbly position today, staggered by worries and problems, ask the Lord to steady you. He will show you great and mighty things.

Lord, I trust You to show me Your great and mighty works.

2 "After years of living with the coldest realities, I still believe that one reaps what one sows and that to sow kindness is the best of all investments."
Joseph W. Martin, Jr.

For any married or newly-engaged women reading this passage who have longed for a larger diamond ring than the one they wear, I submit this report from the *New York Times*:

> "In recent years, fluctuating economic conditions and fear of robberies have made many wealthy people wary of buying large gems. As a result, they prefer and buy more modest ones." Edmund H. Schram, diamond salesman.

I also understand that insurance premiums on expensive gems are so high that some people keep them in safes and wear fake jewelry. All of which brings me to a long-held but reinforced opinion that many material things exact a great price from us and give little in return. A wise man once said, "Anything that can be lost is of no value." Christ told the woman at the well about a priceless water, so priceless that "whosoever drinketh of the water that I shall give him shall never thirst." (John 4:14) Once people drink this life-changing potion their appetites for the superficials of life lessen.

If you are looking for a grade-A investment, one that is sure to increase in value, look beyond diamonds, gold, real estate and the like. Instead create a trust—a trust in the Lord. He guarantees an excellent return on whatever you invest in Him.

Give us clear eyes, Father, so we can recognize the everyday riches of life.

3 "This I do believe above all, especially in times of greater discouragement, that I must believe—that I must believe in my fellow men, that I must believe in myself, that I must believe in God—if life is to have any meaning."

Margaret Chase Smith

Dwight Stones of Long Beach, California, who once high jumped 7' 7¼", a world record at the time, practices a psychic projection or imagining that has been successful for many others in various endeavors. It is the mental technique of picturing oneself accomplishing a goal before it is a fact. When Stones high jumps, he says he can sometimes "see" himself clearing the bar before he leaves the ground.

"The last time I broke the record," he told a reporter , "I could see two steps before I jumped that I had made it."

There is a faith principle involved in this procedure that you can use to achieve goals in your life, too. Say you have a lingering health problem. Of course it goes without saying that you should get the best medical advice possible and follow it. And of course you want to use prayer power. But there is one other thing you can do: that is, *believe* you are going to get better.

Believe it is God's will (because it is) and thank Him in advance for helping you. Act as if your dream is a *fait accompli*, done, realized. Picture yourself as you hope to be—whole, sound, recovered. If faith can move mountains, as Christ said (Matthew 17:20), then it can help you achieve smaller miracles.

Give me a mountain-moving kind of faith, Lord.

4 "So let him give; not grudgingly, or of necessity: for God loveth a cheerful giver."

(II Corinthians 9:7)

The concept of tithing was impressed upon me early in my life. When I was nine, I acquired my first job, delivering newspapers—for the *Montpelier* (Ohio) *Leader Enterprise*, the same paper that gave me my first writing opportunity when I was 15. At the end of the first week, I collected from my customers, paid my bill and had a small profit. My mother and father, who began tithing soon after they became Christians, suggested I do the same.

"But ten per cent is a lot," I protested.

"Try it," Mother replied, "I believe you'll find the 90 per cent left will go further if you do." So I put my first tithe in the collection plate on Sunday—no more than 15 or 20 cents I'm sure. But a habit was begun, one I've never regretted.

When I told this story to a friend one day, he said that he considered tithing a form of Old Testament legalism. "I believe in proportionate giving. Some people with larger incomes would not be hard-pressed to give 15 per cent to the church; while others might find five per cent as much as they could handle."

Without arguing the point, I subscribe to the principle of *regular*, systematic giving as an important one because it recognizes God's gift to us and offers a tangible expression of our appreciation in return. When giving becomes a habit—the earlier in life the better—it conditions us to open our hearts to others. And though it may defy logic and economics, Mother was right: the amount left goes much further.

As Your children, Lord, we've received so much. Now teach us the joy of giving.

 "I am come that they might have life, and that they might have it more abundantly."
John 10:10

A couple of years ago the Washington Redskins football team won its way into the play-offs with a ragtag group of castoffs, players that other teams had turned loose. Most of them were considered beyond their prime, but George Allen, the dynamic Washington coach who is a never-say-die guy if ever there was one, pulled them together and told them differently. He said they weren't old, but *smart*—now that's wisdom that transcends the gridiron: minimize the minuses and maximize the pluses. Well, the long and the short of it is that this group of graybearded athletes (labeled the "Over-the-Hill Gang" by the press) had a great season because they believed in themselves and in each other.

We have a crazy notion in this country that when a man or woman becomes 65, they should retire. Not 64 or not 66, but 65 on the button. One would think that on your 65th birthday you are suddenly struck by the wand of a fairy (a gray, wrinkled one, no doubt), and you become old!

The truth is that no one is old until his mind tells him he is. Deciding to slow down in order to enjoy some of the fruits of your working life is one thing, but being forced to take a seat on the bench is another. The Bible talks about threescore and ten as being a full life (Psalm 90:10), but today many people live productive lives well beyond it. Take what the Lord gives, be grateful for it and use all your days for His glory.

Keep us young in mind and spirit, Lord, even when our bodies testify differently.

"The Lord seeth not as man seeth, for man looketh on outward appearances, but the Lord looketh on the heart."
I Samuel 16:7

A famous radio announcer once committed the cardinal sin of broadcasting: he forgot that all microphones are to be considered alive, that is, ready to transmit anything said in their immediate vicinity. When the announcer finished his program one day he made his usual sign-off, then when he thought he was off the air, he added a profane postscript. Unfortunately for him, his microphone had not been turned off and the man's tasteless remark was heard by millions. It cost him his job.

Sometimes we forget that God is tuned in to all our conversations and that He sees all our actions. We may fool each other by taking pious poses in public or in places where we are known, but the Lord sees us when we are "out of town" and He sees what we are in private. Most of us spend a good deal of time trying to impress people when, in fact, God should be the principal One we are trying to please. He knows the real us. He looks beyond our words, beyond our role-playing and sees our hearts.

What does He find when He takes a spiritual electrocardiogram of your heart?

Cleanse our hearts and minds, Lord, of thoughts and deeds which are unworthy of those who call themselves Yours.

7 **(Election Day)**
"We on this continent should never forget that men first crossed the Atlantic not to find soil for their ploughs but to secure liberty for their souls." **Robert McCracken**

"Vote Yes or No—But Vote!" read the advertisement sponsored by a local League of Women Voters chapter in the Midwest not long ago. And the voters who went to the polls heeded the advice to the letter. When the count was made to determine the result on the local school referendum, election officials were amazed to find several ballots marked "Yes or No."

When you vote today—and I hope that you do because your franchise was a hard-won legacy—do so thoughtfully and conscientiously. Study the issues. Familiarize yourself with the candidates. If you're unsure, question friends whose intellectual and spiritual wisdom you respect. People who don't vote because "politicians are all the same" or "it doesn't matter one way or the other" are wrong. It does matter. Mark your ballot decisively yes or no (but not both!). Today, vote as you feel the Lord would have you. Do it carefully and prayerfully.

We are free two ways, Lord, politically and spiritually, and for both we are grateful.

" . . . I judge no man."

John 8:15

One night my wife, Shirley, was reading CHARLOTTE'S WEB, the E. B. White classic, to two of our children. You will recall that after Charlotte, the spider, helps save the life of Wilbur, the pig, she comes to the point of death herself. It is a moving moment for both the characters in the book and the people who read it.

"Do animals go to heaven?" one of our sons wanted to know when the story was finished. Shirley turned to me. "What's the answer to that question, Daddy?"

"Well," I hesitated as I observed my son's eyes study my face for reassurance. "The Bible doesn't say specifically that animals go to heaven, but Christ talked a lot about birds and donkeys and sheep, and I'm sure He loved them. So I believe He probably made some provision for animals, especially our pets; so, yes, I think they'll be in heaven."

My son smiled, happy with my answer and with that he went off to bed.

The same question about a certain person's eternal fate came to me the other day. This man who died suddenly was from all outward signs an unbeliever. But to pass judgment on him or anyone, I told my inquisitor, is chancy business. We read in the Bible that God's ways are not our ways. He alone has the ability to look on the heart of anyone. I imagine that if you and I get to heaven ourselves, we will be surprised to see some people there and just as surprised to learn that others aren't.

Christ's admonition to take the mote from our own eyes before we try to remove the beam from our brother's eyes (Matthew 7:4,5) is still wise advice. If you and I follow it, we won't have time to spend pondering other people's standing with the Lord.

Lord, instead of passing judgment, help me to pass around Your love.

"With God all things are possible."

Matthew 19:26

There is a memorable exchange between conspirators Cassius and Brutus in William Shakespeare's tragedy "Julius Caesar." They are lamenting the fact that though Caesar is their superior, he is no less a mortal than they. Cassius says: "Men at some times are masters of their fates. The fault, dear Brutus, is not in our stars, but in ourselves, that we are underlings."

Common men talking about their common stations has been an occupation of every generation. The Bible is for the most part about common people who became uncommon when God entered their lives. When God asked Moses what he had in his hand, he replied, "A rod." (Exodus 4:2) It was *only* a stick, a club that shepherds use, but God turned it into a serpent as a sign that He was with Moses. When David went to meet Goliath, he took *only* a slingshot (I Samuel 17:40), but with God's help it became a potent weapon. When it came time to feed the multitude, the disciples could find *only* five barley loaves and two fish in the hands of a young man (John 6:9), but Christ fed 5,000 people with the boy's offering.

Don't limit your life to *only* what you see. Don't settle for things as they are if they need changing. You are the child of a God who works miracles through the hands and feet of those who believe in miracles.

Lord, help us root negative words such as "can't" and "impossible" from our vocabularies.

"Sacrifice alone, bare and unrelieved, is ghastly, unnatural and dead; but self-sacrifice, illuminated by love, is warmth and life."

F.W. Robertson

The other day while I was leafing through a book, my eyes fell upon the picture of an ancient hair shirt, the garment worn by ascetics to mortify the flesh or to do penance for some sin. The shirt, made of rough animal hair, must have been irritating indeed; and if any garment could have served as a reminder of one's low estate, this article was made to order.

Fortunately, we have come away from such times when it was thought that self-flagellation brought one closer to the Kingdom. Christ doesn't ask such behavior as proof of one's commitment. Rather, He admonishes us to become His sons and daughters, heirs of His inestimable riches. As such, our assignment is not to suffer needlessly, but to comfort the sufferers. Any form of pain—whether of the self-inflicted hair shirt variety or from a natural infirmity—is not your loving Heavenly Father's will. Like human mothers and fathers, He wants His children whole, healthy, happy. That's why you can pray in confidence that He will answer your prayers. When you ask for a loaf, He will not give you a stone (Matthew 7:9).

Lord, teach us how to give of ourselves, not so that we will feel more holy but that we may further Your Kingdom.

**I will sing of my Redeemer
And His wondrous love to me;
On the cruel cross He suffered
From the curse to set me free.**
Philip P. Bliss

The hymn quoted above recently became 100 years old. Over that period it has inspired millions of Christians. But save a miracle, it never would have been sung at all.

According to church music historians, 38-year old Philip Bliss, a soloist and songleader for evangelist D. W. Whittle, was on his way to Chicago for an engagement at Dwight L. Moody's tabernacle. But on the night of December 20, 1876, the train on which he was riding was in a wreck near Ashtabula, Ohio. A bridge collapsed and the train derailed, bursting into flame. Bliss survived the crash and escaped to safety, but when he could not locate his wife, he returned to the train and tried to save her. They died together in the flames.

Though the tragedy seemingly ended a brilliant career (Bliss already had composed several popular hymns, such as " 'Man of Sorrows,' What a Name!", "Almost Persuaded" and "The Light of the World is Jesus") he had one more contribution: "I Will Sing of My Redeemer," which was found in his luggage saved from the fiery train wreck.

The story of Philip Bliss' untimely death is a reminder to all that the length of our lives is of an unkown duration. But the measure of it is not in quantity but in quality. Its success depends on how much we help others and how well we serve the Redeemer of whom Philip Bliss wrote so movingly.

Give us the wisdom to concentrate on the day at hand, Lord, and to leave the future in Your hands.

 "He that believeth on me . . . out of his belly shall flow rivers of living water."
John 7:38

This past year much newspaper space was devoted to problems caused by water shortages around the country. People were advised to take baths instead of showers, to flush their toilets less often, to refrain from watering their lawns or washing their cars. Somehow, citizens of the affected areas coped with the inconveniences. Farmers, however, had a problem of greater magnitude. In some states, drought threatened crops; in others, the land's yield was severely reduced. The value of water was never more dramatically proven.

It was also a precious commodity in the arid land in which Christ preached, and He compared it to spiritual matters. In the verse above, He painted a graphic picture for His listeners when He told them that from believers would "flow rivers of living water." Not just a few drops of water, not a trickle, not a rivulet or a stream, but rivers, plural.

Jesus Christ is the answer for a thirsty world. He is the one Person who can satisfy—eternally—the longing spirit of humanity. If you hunger or thirst for something more than what you have found thus far in your pilgrimage, something that goes beyond new homes, new cars, new clothes, look no further. He's the solution.

You have refreshed us, Lord; now inspire us to help others find Your life-giving water.

13

Full many a gem of purest ray serene
The dark unfathom'd caves of ocean bear:
Full many a flower is born to blush unseen,
And waste its sweetness on the desert air.
Thomas Gray,
"Elegy in a Country Churchyard"

Michelangelo never read Thomas Gray's famous lines above because they were written some 200 years after his death, but he would no doubt have agreed with the sentiment. Early in his career no one would give his paintings or sculpture much attention. The critics were admirers of the old masters only, but finally—frustrated and annoyed—Michelangelo resorted to a ruse. Taking one of his works, he put a sepia tint over it to give the impression of age. Then, he buried it near the site where some excavation was taking place. The work was found, hailed as the work of a genius and added to the collection of a famous art patron. Only then did Michelangelo confess, but the critics had spoken and were too embarrassed to reverse themselves. Michelangelo's talent had been recognized and from that time forward his fame spread.

Sometimes we worry about being recognized, about receiving just credit for our labors—and appreciation is something we all want and need. But as a Christian you always are assured of one fan, one supporter, one appreciator. That is the Lord. Don't stop the good works you are doing today just because no one has bothered to express his or her thanks. You may not be able to paint a masterpiece, but your life can be one if you give unstintingly of whatever talent the Lord has given you. And He will reward those who serve Him faithfully. Of that you can be sure.

Take my life and let it be
Consecrated, Lord, to Thee.

14

O word of God incarnate,
O wisdom from on high,
O truth unchanged, unchanging
O light of our dark sky.

William W. How hymn

Today I am writing this entry in a Kansas City hotel room, and on the dresser is a copy of the Bible, placed there by Gideons International (2900 Lebanon Road, Nashville, Tennessee 37214). It's fascinating for me to think that in a place a thousand miles from home some fellow Christians—people who believe the Bible to be the Book of Life as I do—have gone to the trouble and expense to provide me with a copy. I don't know my benefactors . . . yet in a way I do.

They are a lot like John H. Nicholson, one of the founders of the Gideon movement. He made a promise to his dying mother in 1870 that he would read his Bible and pray each day. He kept his promise. Twenty-eight years later, Nicholson was in a Wisconsin hotel and told a fellow traveller, Samuel E. Hill, about his habit of daily devotions. Together they shared their faith in Christ and hit upon the idea of an organization for traveling men. They invited 100 businessmen to a meeting, but only one—Will J. Knights—showed up. Not much of a response, I'd say, but the three were full of enthusiasm, and after prayer, Knights was given an inspiration. "We should be called Gideons"—after the servant of God mentioned in Judges (chapters 6, 7 and 8). From these three men the movement grew until in 1977 thousands of workers in 107 countries distributed over 13,000,000 Bibles and New Testaments. All because John Nicholson promised his mother over a hundred years ago that he'd read his Bible every day.

Make such a promise to yourself. Read at least a few verses from God's Word daily and talk to Him in prayer. If you seek more power in your life, more strength to face your trials, a deeper faith, a more vital role in His service, don't bypass the Source of it all.

Remind me, Father, that in Your word are the answers to my questions.

15

"[It is He] who remembered us in our low estate: for His mercy endureth for ever.
Psalm 136:23

Is there any sure cure for the blues, that depressing feeling that grips us all from time to time? A woman correspondent told me about "a dark morning of the soul" she experienced recently. This is how she described it:

"I spent an hour trying to motivate myself to take out the garbage without success. 'Is this all there is to life, God?' I asked. 'Take out the garbage,' He seemed to answer. So I did. Slowly, I dragged myself to the can and placed the sack inside. But as I closed the lid I saw something through the fence that stirred my soul. It was a single red rose, as fragrant and as beautiful as any I'd ever seen. It was enough to fill my eyes with tears and my heart with sudden joy. 'Thank You, God, for reassuring me of Your love,' I said, and the rest of the day my spirit blossomed as a result of this small touch of beauty."

When your spirits sag and your mood is low, it is important not to languish in your own company. Try to "get outside yourself." Go for a walk, begin some task that needs doing, visit a neighbor, make a phone call to a friend. God can speak to us in many ways, so open yourself to His diversity.

Open our eyes, Father, to our plenty and to others who suffer physical and spiritual poverty, and fill us with a giving spirit.

16

"I can do all things through Christ which strengtheneth me."
Philippians 4:13

Philip Zimbardo, a social psychologist at Stanford University, has made a study of shyness and has written a book about SHYNESS: WHAT IT IS, WHAT TO DO ABOUT IT (Addison-Wesley, publishers). Among his findings are that in some cultures shyness is less prevalent than in others, and that it is a learned rather than an inherited trait. Children from Israel, for example, seem less shy than youngsters in many other lands. One reason, Zimbardo submits, may be that in

Israel children are lavishly praised for "even the most modest performance." Failure is minimized.

Can shy people learn to overcome their handicap? Zimbardo thinks so and has evidence to prove it. He has taught people how to initiate conversations, how to accept and pay compliments, how to stop harmful self-criticism and how to build their self-esteem by emphasizing positives rather than negatives.

Sometimes we fail to love ourselves enough, and the Bible makes it clear that self-love is related to loving others ("Love your neighbor as yourself", Mark 12:31). If you are among the estimated 40 per cent of Americans who consider themselves shy, perhaps you would like to try some of these ideas today: strive to be more outgoing, speak first to strangers, give compliments, smile, be kind, helpful and as positive about everything as possible. You not only will be a good witness for your faith when you practice the art of friendship, but you also will avail yourself of some of life's richest blessings.

Lord, help me forget myself and thereby overcome any shyness.

 "The true way to worship the saints is to imitate their virtues."
Desiderius Erasmus

"Who are saints?" a young catechism student was asked.

Thinking of the figures memorialized in the stained-glass windows of the church, he answered, "The people that light shines through."

That's a good definition of a saint. In nearly 2,000 years, the Christian Church has had many saintlike members who have served as worthy models. And each generation has had people whose Christlike behavior has inspired and guided their contemporaries. I can think of several men and women whose examples helped me as a young man to understand the meaning of Christian service . . . Sunday school teachers, youth directors, ministers, teachers, coaches. They let their light shine among men and their good works were seen. If you would glorify your Father in Heaven, you must try to do His will. When you do, His revealing light will shine through you just as it does through the saints.

You are the light of the world, Lord. Make us conduits of that life-changing light.

18 "For God is not the author of confusion but of peace."
I Corinthians 14:33

One day an acquaintance showed me a piece of jade he'd brought back from the Orient. It was rounded egg-like on one side and flat on the other. The flat side of the green stone was grooved.

"This is a worry stone," he explained. "The groove is for your thumb. When you are worried, you're supposed to rub your thumb here."

"And what will happen?" I asked. He shrugged. "Maybe the activity will take your mind off your problem."

Worry is universal, and no person is totally free of it. But some people cope with cares and concerns better than others. The best practical advice I know is not to dwell on problems. Most of the things we worry about are in the past or in the future, and it is counterproductive to give time to things beyond your control.

What you can do is act now. You have it within your power to use today—this hour, this minute—for something positive. Rather than waste it rubbing a stone or wringing your hands, put the time to good use, for yourself or for someone else. Ask God to deal with the problems that are causing you concern. He's willing to take them if you're willing to give them.

God, we relinquish to You the things that would rob today of its joy.

"After the verb 'to love,' 'to help' is the most beautiful verb in the world!"
Baroness Bertha von Suttner

Although the girl had shown early evidence of an extremely high I.Q., she was unable to complete the easiest of classroom assignments. She couldn't add two figures together or spell correctly or read a simple story. And she was messy.

Particularly annoying to her teachers was the scribbling and doodling she did on all her work. One maze of letters always appeared in the upper left-hand corner of her papers. It wasn't until the 11th grade that psychiatrists were able to pinpoint her learning disability and unblock her learning difficulty. At that time they discovered the meaning of the crazy doodle in the left-hand corner of her papers. The girl had been writing a note, placing letters on top of each other. The letters were "H-e-l-p M-e."

All around us are people crying for help. But not all the cries are easily understood. Some people hide their signals behind criticism; others do disgusting things to get attention; still others camouflage their inferiority feelings behind the shadow of boasting.

How can we be more sensitive to the hurts of people around us and more responsive to their needs? One way is to be a better listener, a more caring friend. Discernment is a gift of God we are told in I Corinthians 12:10, and we need His help if we are to hear the silent cries of the hurting, those whose hearts are breaking and whose souls are empty. Ask God to improve your spiritual hearing and at the same time make yourself a ready instrument of healing when He shows you an unmet need. You'll not only be a blessing, but you'll receive one, too.

Open my ears to the needs of others, Lord, and show me how to minister to them.

Some see the bush the rose adorns,
Others see nothing but prickly thorns.
F.B.

How grateful are you for life, its wonders and its beauty? To whom do you give thanks? Your mother and father? Such expressed appreciation is certainly appropriate if they are living. If not, you have Someone else deserving of your thanksgiving, as the author of the following poem realized:

> One midnight deep in starlight still
>   I dreamed that I received this bill:
> " . . . In account with life:
> Five thousand breathless dawns all new;
> Five thousand flowers fresh in dew;
> Five thousand sunsets wrapped in gold;
> One million snowflakes served ice cold;
> Five quiet friends; one baby's love;
> One white mad sea with clouds above;
> One hundred music-haunted dreams
>   Of moon-drenched roads and hurrying streams,
>   Of prophesying winds and trees,
>   Of silent stars and drowsing bees;
> One June night in a fragrant wood;
> One heart that loved and understood."
>   I wondered when I waked at day
>   How—in God's name—I could pay.
>   Courtland W. Sayres

We recognize Your generous hand, Lord, in the beauty about us.

"In all these things we are more than conquerers through him that loved us."
Romans 8:37

Lillian Carter, the President's mother who at age 68 joined the Peace Corps and served as a nurse in India, tells an interesting story about her first encounter with leprosy. An 11-year-old girl suffering from the disease was brought into the hospital for an injection. At first, Mrs. Carter was repulsed by the sores on the girl's body and did not think she could touch her, but she prayed that God would give her strength and finally she was able to overcome her fears and give the girl the prescribed injection.

"Then, I washed and washed and washed my hands," she recalls, "all the time ashamed for washing them." The next day, however, she says she only washed her hands once after the injection, and in the weeks that followed, treating the girl became almost routine and she washed casually after touching her. "What happened," Mrs. Carter says, "is that I learned to love her. But it took a lot of prayer."

Six months later, the little girl, who was now much improved, returned to the medical center and brought flowers to her nurse. When she saw Mrs. Carter she ran to her, threw her arms around the woman's neck and kissed her. "And do you know," Mrs. Carter says, "I didn't wash my face or hands at all."

The anatomy of such a story can be told in five words: involvement, prayer, strength, love, victory. When you face a task beyond yourself, learn to say with St. Paul, "I can do all things through Christ which strengtheneth me," (Philippians 4:13) and you'll receive the power to accomplish anything.

Lord, make us willing and obedient servants.

 "Be not conformed to this world: but be ye transformed by the renewing of your mind, that ye may prove what is that good, and acceptable, and perfect, will of God."
Romans 12:2

When I was a boy I heard people talking about a man in town who once held the world's record for flagpole sitting. He set the mark, since broken, in the early 30's. The Guinness Book of World Records reports 273 days is the current record.

The Church also has had some famous pole sitters. One was to gain sainthood—St. Simeon the Stylite, who grew up near Antioch. He decided that the spiritual life could best be lived away from others so he became a hermit. But word of his piety spread throughout the Roman Empire and soon vast numbers came to seek his counsel. To get away from the hordes, he erected a 60-foot pole with a platform on top (stylite is from the Greek word which means pillar.) There Simeon lived in relative peace. People still gathered in great numbers at the base of his abode, and occasionally he would preach to them. When he did, his words were reportedly full of power and wisdom, and many received Christ as a result.

Though the Lord apparently was able to use Simeon the Stylite and his pole, this is not what the Bible means when it advises us to "come out from among them (unbelievers) and be ye separate" from the world. (II Corinthians 6:17)

Rather, it means that we should live in such a way that our acts witness to the difference between us and nonbelievers. "Let your light so shine before men," states Jesus, "that they may see your good works and glorify your Father in Heaven." (Matthew 5:16)

Lord, show us how to be part of the world and apart from it, too.

 (Thanksgiving Day)
" Every good gift and every perfect gift is from above."
James 1:17

In the fall of the Pilgrims' first year in America, Miles Standish led an expedition of men from Plymouth north to Boston Harbor for the purpose of engaging and making peace with the Massachusetts Indians. Governor William Bradford had heard rumors that the Massachusetts Indians were a warlike people and he wanted to dispel any fears that they might have about the colonists.Though the Indians first ran from the white men, Captain Standish was able to show them he meant no harm. After eating with them and doing some trading for beaver skins, Captain Standish returned to Plymouth with a positive report.

In addition, he waxed poetic about Boston Harbor, suggesting that possibly it was a better site than Plymouth. But Governor Bradford was not receptive to the idea of moving, reminding him of the blessings they had where they were. Not the least of which was 20 acres of corn nearly ready to harvest.

"The Lord assigns all men the bounds of their habitation," the young governor said, and he was thankful for the place he believed God had assigned them. Thus, the thought of moving north was put aside and a short time later the colonists celebrated their first Thanksgiving not at Boston Harbor, but at Plymouth.

Today, like William Bradford acknowledge what you have. There may be other inviting harbors calling, and there may be merit in them, but on this day pause to give thanks for the blessings God has sent you where you are.

Thank You, Lord, for Your endless blessings and boundless love.

24

"Oh well," said Mr. Hennessy, "we are as th' Lord made us."
"No," said Mr. Dooley, "lave (leave) us be fair. Lave us take some iv the blame oursilves."
Finley Peter Dunne ("Mr. Dooley")

The other day I overheard a conversation between two commuters. The younger of the two was discussing an office problem. Apparently, an order had been mis-shipped, through simple human error, and the man's boss was raising cain. (That's not exactly what the man said his boss was raising, but anyway . . .)

"It's not fair," the man complained. His companion agreed but had some advice. "Because it happened in your department and you're in charge, your boss is saying you're responsible. Accept the responsibility; you don't have to discuss blame. Just tell him that you're sorry and let the whole matter drop." Whether the advice was taken or not, it is about as good as the young man will receive.

Wise managers in business are quick to take responsibility for a mix-up, especially when it is a result of simple human error. At the same time they distribute credit for success freely,

298

knowing it is a positive contribution to the morale of their employees. You can improve your relationship with others and gain both their friendship and cooperation if you do likewise.

The next time you're involved in a discussion about who's to blame for something (if you share any part of the error whatsoever) volunteer, "Maybe it was my fault." It is amazing how others usually will come to your defense.

Forgiveness is easy if we keep our thoughts on Your forgiving Spirit, Father. Help us forgive.

25 "All things work together for good to them that love God." Romans 8:28

Recently, I met a tremendous young woman Laurel Lee of Seattle. She gained recognition by writing a heart-tugging book entitled WALKING THROUGH THE FIRE (E. P. Dutton). It is about her fight against Hodgkin's disease, discovered while she was pregnant with her third child. Doctors advised her to abort the baby, but she refused, just as she refused to give up when pain racked her body and death seemed imminent.

Few stories of faith are more moving than this one, or more filled with insights about suffering. "My agony with Hodgkin's disease," she wrote, "turned into a great joy that was beyond understanding, and joy is one with peace."

Suffering is never easy for any of us, but some Christians have come to grips with pain in such a way they not only bear it with magnanimity, but they turn it into spiritual triumph. What is their secret? I believe it is contained in the wisdom-filled eighth chapter of Romans.

If you have a lingering health problem that fills you with doubts and discouragement, read those inspiring 39 verses. They contain the key that Laurel Lee used to find victory in her affliction, and taken to heart they will help you.

Lord, when things look bleak, let us turn our lives over to You.

**Jesus, Savior, pilot me
Over life's tempestuous sea.**

Edward Hopper

After more than 100 years of service, the Coast Guard is discontinuing use of red flags (or Maggie's Drawers as sailors often called them) to warn ships of approaching storms. Small craft advisory (one red pennant), gale warning (two red pennants), storm warning (red flag with black square), and hurricane warning (two red flags with black squares) will be replaced by a series of regular radio broadcasts transmitted over fixed shortwave frequencies (162.40 and 162.55 megahertz).

The thought strikes me that people could use some warning system for the approaching storms of life, too. And sometimes there *are* signals that advise of imminent distress. They come in the form of warnings from others, physical signs, inner nudges. The problem is that many people heading for heavy seas or dangerous shoals don't have their radio tuned to the proper frequency. In the vernacular of C.B. radio buffs, "They don't have their ears on."

Committed Christians are supersensitive receiving stations. When they get off course, they are able to hear God's voice directing and correcting their courses. When they are caught in rough storms, they ride them out assured that He will bring them through. You have God's promise that He will look after you in Hebrews 13:5, where it says, "I will never leave thee, nor forsake thee."

You commanded the waves "Peace, be still," and they obeyed. Remind me, Father, that You can also calm the storms in my life.

"He healeth the broken in heart, and bindeth up their wounds."

Psalm 147:3

A worried mother wrote a few months ago asking us to pray for her daughter and son-in-law who had separated after seven years of marriage. They had two young children. What a joy it was to open the mail today and read that the problem had been resolved.

"It is with much thanksgiving that I write to tell you that my daughter, son-in-law and grandchildren are now a happy, reunited family. God has answered our prayers! All through this period of anguish, I prayed with supplication, asking Him to reunite this family and at the same time thanking Him in advance for what I knew He was going to accomplish. Praise God! Faith still moves mountains!"

If you have been plagued with some serious problem that hasn't yielded to human pushing or pulling, turn to the One whose wisdom and power transcend all. Ask Him in faith believing that He will give you a positive resolution. He can mend cloth no others can join. He can heal the unhealable. He can make the broken whole.

We place our hopes in You, Lord, knowing full well You will hear and respond.

"Fire is the test of gold; adversity, of strong men."
Seneca

An old violin maker was once seen struggling up a mountainside.

"Where are you going?" a friend asked.

"To the timberline," he answered. "I need some wood for a violin."

"But you have fine trees all around you. Why must you go so far to get wood?"

"Ah," said the violin maker, "because the wood up there is the most resonant of all. The trees on the timberline have struggled all their lives, fighting a never-ending battle with the winds. As a result of their struggling, they are of rare quality, strong and full of character. Violins made of their wood produce the most beautiful music in the world."

Struggle is something none of us covets. We all long for smooth sailing, for level walking, for steady, tensionless work. But growth always comes from new experiences, new undertakings, new adventures.

When you face some difficult task—a new responsibility or a personal struggle you wish you could bypass, but can't—ask God for strength to meet the test. Out of illness can come wholeness, out of defeat, victory, and out of wind-whipped souls some of the most beautiful music in the world.

Lord, remind us that to struggle and then achieve a goal is always more gratifying than having an unearned gift.

 "The state of faith allows no mention of impossibility."
                                                        Tertullian

"How can I get rid of these warts, Doctor Akers," a young man asked, pointing to several brown spots on his hand.

"I have something that will help," the physician answered. He went out of the room for a few minutes and came back with a small vial of red liquid.

"Apply Dr. Akers' magic wart remover three times a day," he said, "and in a month your warts will be gone." The man did as he was told and the warts disappeared. What was Dr. Akers' formula? Three ounces of water and two drops of red food coloring.

Was this a single isolated experience? you may ask. Not according to my source. The doctor used the same "curative" for years and with spectacular results. Why did it work? Because his patients believed it would.

Claude Bristol once wrote a classic called, THE MAGIC OF BELIEVING. In his book, he gave scores of examples of how people believed their way to success. Faith requires commitment and conviction, otherwise it will be inoperative, powerless. Unlike Dr. Akers' mythical medicine, however, your belief in Jesus Christ is based on fact. But to activate your faith, you must believe it can produce miraculous changes. Christ wasn't exaggerating when He said, "If thou canst believe, all things are possible." (Mark 9:23)

Father, give us the kind of faith strong enough to move mountains.

30

**I love to tell the story
Of unseen things above,
Of Jesus and His glory,
Of Jesus and His love.
Catherine Hankey hymn**

Every day I am reminded of things I depend upon but take for granted. For example, the Bible that lies open on my desk before me and the pad on which I'm writing are both made of paper—a material that wasn't available when early Christians were recording God's word.

Clay, stone, metal, wood, papyrus, leather and parchment were some of the substances for record-keeping then. Of these, the dried, stretched and treated skins of animals were the most expensive; and because of the cost, a piece of parchment or vellum (calfskin) was often scraped and reused. Biblical scholars refer to such a document as a *palimpsest*, that is parchment on which previous writing can be seen faintly, but which is subordinate to the last text.

All Christians, it seems to me, qualify as a form of palimpsest. Before they came into the saving knowledge of Christ, their lives had another central focus and their stories had a different emphasis. But then they discovered the power of God, and they became new creatures in Him. The parchment upon which their stories were being recorded was wiped clean. Every sordid thing was erased, every sin scraped away. The old writing may still be slightly visible, as a poignant reminder of where they've come from, but it has been superceded by new writing—bold, positive, emphatic, powerful, permanent.

If you know the One who can forgive all sin and can turn you into a new creature, you can repeat with the prophet Isaiah (53:5), "he was wounded for our transgressions, he was bruised for our iniquities; the chastisement of our peace was upon him; and with his stripes we are healed."

Your grace is amazing, Lord, and Your love without equal.

DECEMBER 1978

S	M	T	W	T	F	S
					1	2
3	4	5	6	7	8	9
10	11	12	13	14	15	16
17	18	19	20	21	22	23
24	25	26	27	28	29	30
31						

If you are worried or afraid of something that you must soon face confess your anxieties before the Lord. Then hear His reassuring words, "Fear thou not; for I am with thee: be not dismayed; for I am thy God: I will strengthen thee; yea I will help thee; yea, I will uphold thee with the right hand of my righteousness." (Isaiah 41:10)

DECEMBER 1978

 "It is much easier to be critical than to be correct."
Benjamin Disraeli

Arthur Gordon, who recently wrote the inspiring book A TOUCH OF WONDER, once told me a story about two groups of fledging writers that formed on a Midwest campus many years ago. One group of male students called themselves the Stranglers, and when they assessed papers written by other members of their group, they were merciless in their criticism. The other group composed of female students named themselves the Wranglers. They took a different tack. Instead of tearing apart the work of their fellow writers, they tried to offer each other praise and encouragement and constructive comments.

Long after the students had graduated, someone made a discovery. Not one of the ultra-critical group ever wrote anything of significance while several women in the more positive fellowship went on to literary accomplishment.

If you want to achieve some distant goal or if you want to help someone else climb a difficult pinnacle, remember that encouragement and praise are the bricks to build on, not brickbats. Critics and cynics belong to a demolition company bent on destruction, while positive, enthusiastic people are in the construction business, dedicated to the advancement and building up of others.

Today, choose words that inspire others to make the most of themselves. Help them reach their God-given potential.

Intervene, Lord, when we're about to criticize unwisely, and give us softer words.

 "In all thy ways acknowledge him, and he shall direct thy paths."

Proverbs 3:6

Landmarks are fascinating to me, not only for the boundaries they delineate but also for the history that they tell. I remember once in Oklahoma walking over the indented ground that had been shaped by millions of cattle hooves, horses' hooves and wagon wheels. The route was known as the Santa Fe Trail.

We leave a history in the ground that we traverse, too. Sometimes our footprints tell of visits to places we should have avoided. Other times our tracks testify to our courage and commitment. The work you do today is part of the pattern, a thread in the tapestry, a piece of the mosaic, that will someday tell the whole story of your life. Others who follow will be looking for landmarks to guide them on their pilgrimage. Your example of faith could point the way.

Guide me, O Holy Spirit, in every path I take, in everything I do.

 "Fear not that your life will come to an end, but rather that it shall not have a beginning."
Cardinal John Henry Newman

An inquiring reporter for a newspaper once posed this question: "What do you fear most?" Dozens of people responded.

Many of their answers were related to growing old, becoming an invalid and dying.

All are understandable concerns because they have to do with circumstances that are beyond our control. Barring unforeseen events, most of the people reading this page will grow old. If their health fails, they may have to depend on someone else's help, and every last person reading these words will die. That is for certain.

What is the proper spiritual attitude about these matters? Each has the same answer: Trust the Lord. "Growing old," one octogenarian told me, "is a case of mind over matter. It doesn't matter if you don't mind."

Growing old is a condition of life—as natural as water running down instead of uphill. As far as needing the care of someone else, don't fret about such a contingency. It may never come to pass. If you already require the aid of another to get along, consider the possibility that God may be using you as a "spiritual bundle" for someone else's spiritual growth. He may have something to teach them about Christian compassion, and you're His vehicle. As far as death is concerned, the Bible tells us that nothing can separate us from the love of God. If you know the Lord, you have no cause to fear the end of this phase of existence because you know a new beginning is just around the corner.

Drain us of fear, Lord, and fill us with a strong faith.

 "He that findeth his life shall lose it: and he that loseth his life for my sake shall find it."
Matthew 10:39

"To be a Christian," I once heard Billy Graham say, "one must have the total commitment of a Cortez." It's a good analogy.

You'll recall that Cortez was so consumed by his dreams of conquest that, upon landing in Mexico, he instructed his sailors to destroy all their ships. Though there is some debate as to whether he ordered the vessels burned, or run aground, or just dismantled, the result was the same: they had no means of retreating.

When we burn our bridges behind us and accept Christ as our sole commander in chief, we make an amazing discovery. We learn a lesson that is kept from those who bring only half-hearted commitment. That truth is that suddenly we are set free. Once we submit to His sovereignty, we are no longer in bondage, but instead heirs of His Kingdom, enlightened sons and daughters who can go forward confident that their course is right and that the end will bring victory.

Give us the courage, Lord, to follow You—and to do it without reservation.

5 "Behold, I stand at the door, and knock: if any man hear my voice, and open the door, I will come in to him, and will sup with him, and he with me." Revelation 3:20

Not long ago while driving down the highway, I saw a huge billboard which read: *God still makes house calls. All you need to do is answer the door.* For my money, that's a great advertisement.

Though doctors are not mentioned in the ad, there is a not-too-subtle reference to them and their once-common practice of coming to the homes of the sick. In most cases, I suppose, it is easier today for patients to get to doctors than the reverse. Also, a doctor has modern equipment and instruments in his office, things that won't fit into a little black bag.

Whatever, for anyone who has a sick spirit, the sign spells it out loud and clear: the Lord is only a prayer away.

If you have a concern today that has you perplexed (buffaloed, my dad would have said) your Heavenly Father is in the neighborhood. Invite Him in for a chat.

Lord, Your word is the best prescription for maladies of the soul. Remind us to take this medicine daily.

"He that dwelleth in the secret place of the most High shall abide under the shadow of the Almighty."

Psalm 91:1

An enormously rich businessman once told me that he had arranged hundreds of loans for his company which totaled millions of dollars.

"And," he noted, "I can tell you the exact amount of each, the interest rate, the payment schedule and the balance due on each one without going to the books. I have that information all in my head."

I expressed amazement to him, but to myself I also thought, how sad. There are many things worth committing to memory—many things I wish I could write indelibly on my mind—but columns of figures are not among them. A Scottish minister once impressed me by quoting the entire 91st Psalm. Now that's something worth memorizing. In Luke 12:34 we read that "where your treasure is, there will your heart be also." If you put great store in money, your heart is likely to be there. The same goes for fame, power or prestige.

Anything that separates you from God or anything that subordinates Him is a barrier to faith. Put nothing before your love of God, and you won't have to worry about the love of things.

Your love for us dwarfs all others, Lord. Make us mindful of that when we are ordering our priorities.

 "Incline your ears to the words of my mouth."

Psalm 78:1 ____

The other day I was talking with Norma Zimmer, the charming and talented singing star of the "Lawrence Welk Show," about the person who first recognized her vocal potential. It was her high school music teacher in Seattle, Carl Pitzer.

"Do you sing in a church choir?" he asked her one day after class.

"No," Norma answered, because her family never attended church.

"How about singing in my church choir then?" the school-teacher said. Norma accepted, and as a result her whole life was turned around. Reared in a dismally poor family, she grew up thinking she was an ugly duckling, stupid and without a single thing she could do well.

"But then God sent Carl Pitzer into my life," she recalls with gratefulness, "and everything changed."

Not only did Norma find her calling in church, she also found the Lord and ever since she has been using her talent to glorify Him.

I have a theory—no, it's more than a theory, it is an observation—that God often sends people into our lives at crucial points to nudge us in certain directions. Carl Pitzer was that person in Norma Zimmer's life. If you are faced with some problem or some difficult decision, be alert to the possibility of God sending someone to help guide you. Listen for His voice in theirs. It could be a turning point in your life.

Lord, thank You for sending just the right people into our lives at just the right time.

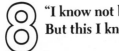

**"I know not by what methods rare,
But this I know, God answers prayer."
Eliza M. Hickok**

A DAILY GUIDEPOSTS reader from the Southeast writes to ask if I think prayer was responsible for a recent occurrence in her life.

"My car broke down one evening over fifty miles from home. I tried to flag down several cars, but no one stopped. It was getting dark and I was getting scared. A woman in similar circumstances was raped and killed near here just a few weeks before. Suddenly, a car came over the rise, but upon seeing me the driver only seemed to speed up. Then, I telegraphed a prayer at him: 'Lord, please tell him to stop.' I had no more than sent the thought than the driver applied his brakes. He then backed up and helped me get my car started. At first, I thought it was an answered prayer, but upon reflection I wonder if it was just coincidence."

The word coincidence contains the prefix "co" which means two factors coming into play at the same time or place—cooperation, correlation, co-exist. Often, I believe, what the world calls coincidence or fate is really God bringing His power to bear on a situation.

To answer the specific question raised in the woman's letter, I could only respond: keep praying and judge the results for yourself. The proof of the pudding is in the eating.

Thank You, Lord, for using many methods to answer our prayers.

 "I shall pass through this world but once. If, therefore, there be any kindness I can show, or any good thing I can do, let me do it now; let me not defer it or neglect it, for I shall not pass this way again."
attributed to Etienne De Grellet

Gordie Howe, ageless star of National Hockey League, recalled for *Guideposts* how during the Depression his mother once helped a neighbor who was having financial difficulty.

"I'm trying to sell these things," the woman told Mrs. Howe. She opened a laundry bag that contained an everything-but-the-kitchen-sink assortment of odds and ends. Gordie knew that his parents were hard-pressed, too, and he knew his mother was not really interested. But Mrs. Howe apparently sensed the neighbor's desperation because she sorted through the grab bag of things, feigning interest in several articles.

"How much do you want for these items?" she finally asked.

"$1.50 for the lot."

Mrs. Howe went to her purse and returned with a handful of change. The woman handed her the bag, thanked her profusely and left. Mrs. Howe set the collection aside unopened. Then one day Gordie looked inside. What he found was a pair of used ice skates just his size, something his family could not afford to buy him. It was these skates that put Gordie on the road to fame as one of the best hockey players in the world.

When we give from the heart, we set in motion goodwill that spreads like ripples in a pond. It is never the size of the gift, but the gesture itself that changes the complexion of life—for recipient and giver alike. God loves a cheerful giver (II Corinthians 9:7) the Bible tells us and He blesses every act of kindness.

Lord, make me be a cheerful giver–every day.

 "Faith, if it hath not works, is dead."
James 2:17

Once I got a bleak assessment of the helpfulness of church members from a fellow who had spent a good share of his life riding freight trains.

"If you're in need and in a strange place, go to a bar. There'll be people there and they'll usually give you a hand. Forget knocking on church doors. Unless it's Sunday morning there probably won't be anybody there. Even if you locate someone, though, you'll find they're only inclined to help guys in white shirts and ties."

I didn't argue then with a man who had so much firsthand experience, but recently I read a Gallup poll that, in part, challenges his statement. In this survey, people were asked if they were involved in charitable or social work such as helping the poor, sick or elderly.

The figures show that 30 per cent of the church members responding said yes, versus 19 per cent of non-church members. Furthermore, evangelicals—who have sometimes been accused of being too concerned with their own salvation and too little concerned about feeding the hungry—were the most active volunteer workers with 42 per cent of them being involved in some charitable or social activity. The over-50 group was more involved than any age group and college-educated were more active than any other group in that category.

Someone might argue that the figures for church members should be higher. The question I'm left with is, "Am I doing my part?"

Lord, help me to be on the lookout for ways I can serve You by serving others.

 "Though he slay me, yet will I trust in him."
Job 13:15

In Dr. Margaret Mead's fascinating book BLACKBERRY WINTER (William Morrow and Co.), an autobiographical account of her early years, she tells of visiting a doctor's office when she was 16 and seeing a sampler on the wall which read, "All things work together for good to them that love God." (Romans 8:28) She says for her that means "if you set a course, bend your sails to every wind to further the journey, always trusting that course to be right, it will, in fact, be right even though the ship itself may go down at any time during the voyage." Such a philosophy might help explain why she has become the leading anthropologist of our time.

No better definition of faith could be written than Dr. Mead's. Trusting God in fair weather is no test. It is only when trials come that we discover the depth and the mettle of our convictions. What we must do is what the old verse states:

> "Trust Him when dark doubts assail thee
> Trust Him when trust is small
> Trust Him when simply to trust Him
> Is the hardest thing of all."

Into Your hands, dear Lord, we commend our lives.

"Kindness is a language the dumb can speak, and the deaf can hear and understand."

Christian N. Bovee

A friend from Ohio wrote me recently, and in her letter reminisced about the old days. Among the things she recalled was the generous and helpful spirit that somehow seemed to be more prevalent then. "For example," she wrote, "Mother was never too busy to fix a meal for the many hobos who stopped at our door." (I could say the same of my mother.)

"One cold day," she continued, "an unshaven man in raggedy clothes knocked and asked if he might have an old sweater to keep him warm. She tried to find one, but everything she offered was too small. 'I'm sorry,' she said to the man as he shuffled off. 'Maybe Mrs. Thomas up the way will have something. Good luck and God bless you.'

"Years later the man returned to tell my mother that her simple blessing had saved his life. 'I was considering suicide,' he said, 'but your kind words reminded me that God still loved me.' "

"When did we see you naked or hungry or thirsty or in prison?" is the question asked of Christ. (Matthew 25:37-39) His answer still applies: "Inasmuch as ye have done it unto one of the least of these my brethren, ye have done it unto me."

Make us sensitive, Father, to the unuttered cries of those around us.

 "Nobody will know what you mean by saying that 'God is love' unless you act it as well." **Lawrence Jacks**

"That's an extravagance we don't need!" a young wife told her husband last Christmas season. He had suggested buying an artificial tree, one that revolved and played music, and she thought the idea absurd. Although they didn't buy the tree, she later had second thoughts about her victory.

"As happens too often," she told me, "I failed to consider Mike's wishes. His feelings were more important than whether we bought the tree or not."

To paraphrase another axiom, too often we speak in haste and repent in leisure. Like gunfighters we shoot from the hip—and think later. But this kind of action can get us into grievous trouble.

Before you call another's ideas or suggestions worthless, give them a second or third thought. Some people develop little prefaces to their responses that buy time for a more generous or sensitive remark. "That's an interesting concept" or "That's a novel idea" or "That's certainly worth consideration" are some examples that might be appropriate. Outright rejection is something none of us likes.

How then should we treat each other? Peter suggested the following way: " . . . Add to your faith virtue; and to virtue knowledge; and to knowledge temperance; and to temperance patience; and to patience godliness; and to godliness brotherly kindness; and to brotherly kindness charity." (II Peter 1:5-7) It sounds like a big task, but with God's help you and I can grow spiritually if we take it one day at a time.

Lord, help me to be more considerate of others and more sensitive to their feelings.

14 "For if the trumpet give an uncertain sound, who shall prepare himself to the battle?"
I Corinthians 14:8

Several blocks down the street from my home in Princeton, New Jersey, is a cemetery that has served as burial place for many famous people. One of the gravestones there marks the place where Dr. John Witherspoon was laid to rest after his death on November 15, 1794. A Presbyterian minister who came to America from Scotland to head what is now Princeton University, Dr. Witherspoon gained a place in history by being a leader of the rebellious colony and a signer of the Declaration of Independence.

"There is not a single instance in history in which civil liberty was lost and religious liberty preserved entire," he said in a pre-war sermon delivered in Nassau Hall. Thus, Dr. Witherspoon, the only minister to serve in the Continental Congress, helped his followers see the undeniable relationship between religious and political freedom.

When we thank God for our four freedoms (freedom of religion, freedom of speech, freedom to peaceably assemble, and freedom to petition for a redress of grievance guaranteed in the first amendment of the Bill of Rights)—incidentally, tomorrow is Bill of Rights Day—we need to remember men like Witherspoon whose courage was interwoven with his faith. It is when we are filled with such devotion to God and to our fellowman that we find the words and the strength to act in times of trial.

Give us wisdom, Father, to act prudently when faced with conflicting loyalties.

They were hoping for a king
A man of wealth and might
But God sent forth a Babe
A Child to bring us light
                    F.B.

Only seven more shopping days until Christmas your newspaper will remind you today. Once again, like runners in a race, we've entered the homestretch in our annual dash to Christmas.

Yes, it's too commercial; yes, it's too frantic; yes, it's too exhausting; but it's also the most exciting, exhilarating time of the year—especially if you are a child, and at Christmas we all need to become children again if we're to enjoy the season to its fullest.

What can you remember about your Christmases as a child? What is the first gift you can recall receiving? In my case it was some stuffed animals—a cloth-covered horse, a lion, a giraffe, an elephant—gifts on my fourth Christmas, my mother told me recently. She remembers them well because it was still Depression time and finding money for gifts put a great strain on family finances. But to me, a child, all I can remember is the joy of playing with those animals.

The miniature animals are, of course, long gone, but happy memories of them prompt me to let the child inside me come out, come out and wrap my children with the same kind of love I received. It must certainly be related to the feeling God had when He sent His Son to earth. At Christmas, it's easy to understand why He chose to send Jesus in the form of a child.

Lord, let me—childlike—put my faith and trust in You.

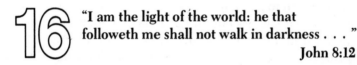

"I am the light of the world: he that followeth me shall not walk in darkness . . . "
John 8:12

Every year since I've come East from Ohio, over 15 years ago, I've taken a bus ride down New York City's Fifth Avenue a few nights before Christmas. It is a fantastic light show, almost breathtaking in its beauty. Each store is a decorated Christmas package, inviting passersby to open it.

The ride from Central Park south to 34th Street is about 25 blocks so it doesn't take long, but in the middle of so much hustle and bustle I find that trip fills me with an indescribable peace. (It's something like the feeling I get when I walk through freshly fallen snow. Though the cold is everywhere, it doesn't penetrate my heavy clothing.) At Christmas time the preparation has reached a fever pitch, but I come away from that ride down Fifth Avenue mentally refreshed.

The busyness of Christmas can sometimes obliterate its meaning. If you find that happening this year, take steps to correct the problem. Perhaps you need a break like my bus ride. Whatever form it takes, find a few minutes to put aside Christmas chores and compose yourself and reflect on God's goodness to you. As ones who have received His all-revealing light, we have much for which to thank Him.

Lord, thank You for lighting our lives with Your good news.

17 "... and when they had opened their treasures, they presented unto him gifts; gold, and frankincense, and myrrh."
Matthew 2:11

Of all the contemporary stories about Christmas, I suppose my favorite is O. Henry's THE GIFT OF THE MAGI. In that tale, you'll recall, the master of surprise endings tells about the dilemma of a penniless couple trying to buy Christmas presents for each other. Finally, the young husband decides to sell his treasured watch to buy combs for his wife's beautiful hair, only to discover that she has cut off her crowning glory in order to buy him a watch fob. It is a love story of rare beauty.

Sacrificial acts have a way of touching and inspiring us as no other. That's the reason we are so moved by God's reconciling gift of His Son, Jesus. At Christmas when much of our spiritual focus is on Luke's account of Christ's birth, we cannot help but leaf over to John who in one verse spells out completely the reason for our Heavenly Father's unprecedented gift: "For God so loved the world, that he gave his only begotten Son, that whosoever believeth in him should not perish, but have everlasting life." (John 3:16) That is God's gift to us at Christmas.

Remind us, Lord, that serving You means sacrifice that brings joy.

 18 "When they saw the star, they rejoiced with exceeding great joy."
Matthew 2:10

When I go into a Christian church or a Christian home this time of year, I am reminded that the celebration of Christmas is made memorable to a large extent by the symbols we use: stars, lights, gifts, mangers, sheep, shepherds, camels are some that come easily to mind.

For centuries, writers and artists have been attracted to the story in Luke and thousands have tried to interpret the Bethlehem happening in contemporary language and illustrations. One of my attempts, made a dozen or so years ago, went like this:

> *It was that ethereal night when*
> *a matchless star stood glowing in the East*
> *trailing a man, a woman, a burdened beast.*
>
> *It was that incredible night when*
> *an innkeeper became the first to say*
> *I have no room for You today.*
>
> *It was that incomparable night when*
> *Gabriel came ecstatic to the earth*
> *proclaiming glad tidings of a royal birth.*
>
> *It was that immortal night when*
> *a caring God reached gently down to lay*
> *His supreme gift, Love, upon the hay.*

"Freely ye have received, freely give."
Matthew 10:8

At last report, the all-time best-selling phonograph record was Bing Crosby's "White Christmas." Written by Irving Berlin, it is the lament of a person in a warm climate at Christmas time, dreaming of the snowy setting many of us have come to associate with the season. But it is important to remember that Christmas has nothing to do with weather, climate or temperature. Some scholars believe Jesus may have been born in the spring, maybe April 19 or 20. Whatever, there was no snow in Bethlehem.

I've spent a few Christmases in warm climates—Florida and Hawaii—and I must admit feeling a certain longing for a snowy Currier and Ives setting. Yet, the spirit is the most crucial element, and that has never been lacking.

Has the spirit of Christmas caught hold of you yet this year? If not, take inventory of your preparations. Remember, it is a time for giving. If you want to experience the blessings of the season, you must give fully of yourself. That's the price of admission.

Lord, I'm grateful for what I've freely received. Let me show it by giving just as freely.

 "And thou shalt bring forth a son and shall call his name Jesus."
Luke 1:31

A good share of the Christian poetry that we recite at Christmas, or sing as a result of its being set to music, has been with us for many years. But back in 1960 a television performer named Aladdin who was a regular on the "Lawrence Welk Show" introduced the public to a new inspirational poet named Helen Steiner Rice. The poem was "The Priceless Gift of Christmas" and it was the beginning of a love story between its author and Christians around the world. Since that Christmas in 1960 I've come to know Mrs. Rice as a personal friend, and her life is every bit as inspiring as her verse. Here then is the last part of Mrs. Rice's "The Priceless Gift of Christmas":

> *The Priceless Gift of Christmas*
> *is meant just for the heart*
> *and we receive it only*
> *when we become a part*
> *of the kingdom and the glory*
> *which is ours to freely take.*

For God sent the Holy Christ Child
at Christmas for our sake,
so man might come to know Him
and feel His Presence near
and see the many miracles
performed while He was here.
And this Priceless Gift of Christmas
is within the reach of all,
the rich, the poor, the young and old
the greatest and the small.
So take His Priceless Gift of Love,
reach out and you receive,
and the only payment that God asks
is just that you believe.

"Fear not, for I am with thee and will bless
thee . . . "

Genesis 26:24

I called it "The C-C-Choir Boy" and it's only a story but requests to reprint it have continued over the years, so I'm
including it today with the hope that it has something to say to
you:

Everyone was surprised—everyone except Mrs. Brown, the
choir director—when Herbie showed up in November to re-
hearse for the church's annual Christmas cantata.

Mrs. Brown wasn't surprised because she had persuaded
Herbie to "at least try." That was an accomplishment, for lately
he had quit trying nearly everything—reciting in class, playing
ball or even asking his brothers or sisters to pass the potatoes.

It was easy to understand: he stuttered. Not just a little,
either, and sometimes when his tongue spun on a word, like a
car on ice, the kids laughed. Not a big ha-ha laugh, but you can
tell when people are laughing at you even if you're only nine.

Mrs. Brown had figured Herbie could sing with the other
tenors—Charley and Billy—and not have any trouble, which

is exactly the way it worked. Billy was given the only boy's solo and the rest of the time the three of them sang in unison, until Charley contracted the measles. Even so, Billy had a strong voice and Herbie knew he could follow him.

At 7:15, the night of the cantata, a scrubbed and combed Herbie arrived at church, wearing a white shirt, a new blue and yellow bow tie and his only suit, a brown one with high-water pant legs. Mrs. Brown was waiting for him at the door.

"Billy is home in bed with the flu," she said. "You'll have to sing the solo." Herbie's thin face grew pale.

"I c-c-can't," he answered.

"We need you," Mrs. Brown insisted.

It was unfair. He wouldn't do it. She couldn't make him. All of these thoughts tumbled through Herbie's mind until Mrs. Brown told him this:

"Herbie, I know you can do this—with God's help. Across from the choir loft is a stained-glass window showing the manger scene. When you sing the solo, I want you to sing it only to the Baby Jesus. Forget that there is anyone else present. Don't even glance at the audience." She looked at her watch. It was time for the program to begin.

"Will you do it?"

Herbie studied his shoes.

"I'll t-t-try," he finally answered in a whisper.

A long 20 minutes later, it came time for Herbie's solo. Intently, he studied the stained-glass window. Mrs. Brown nodded, and he opened his mouth, but at that exact instant someone in the congregation coughed.

"H-H-Hallelujah," he stammered. Mrs. Brown stopped playing and started over. Again, Herbie fixed his eyes on the Christ Child. Again, he sang.

"Hallelujah, the Lord is born," his voice rang out, clear and confident. And the rest of his solo was just as perfect.

After the program, Herbie slipped into his coat and darted out a back door—so fast that Mrs. Brown had to run to catch him. From the top of the steps, she called, "Herbie, you were wonderful. Merry Christmas."

"Merry Christmas to you, Mrs. Brown," he shouted back.

Then, turning, he raced off into the night through ankle-deep snow—without boots. But then he didn't really need them. His feet weren't touching the ground.

When we forget ourselves and look to You, Lord, we know we can overcome any stumbling block.

22 "It is more blessed to give than to receive." Acts 20:35

A couple of Christmases ago I read about a successful businessman who was giving away winter gloves on a New York City street corner to people who had none.

"Why?" he was asked.

"I do this every Christmas," he explained, "because there was a time many years ago when I was very poor and could not afford to buy a pair. I remember how cold my hands got and how much I envied people who had gloves."

Our needs should sensitize us to others who have needs. A person who has known hunger can identify with another who has gone without food. A prisoner knows what it is for another to lose his freedom. A person who has been bedridden understands how lonely and depressing it can be for another to be hospitalized or shut-in with illness.

The problem is that sometimes we forget. That's the inspiring aspect about the story of the man who gives away gloves at Christmas. He remembers.

Whether you can identify with another's problem or not, there is something all of us need to remember at Christmas and all the days of the year. That is that we are our brothers' keepers (Genesis 4:9) and when we minister to others we become ministers of God.

Give us grateful hearts, Lord, so grateful that we are prompted to share our riches with others.

**What you are is God's gift to you.
What you make of yourself is your gift to
God.**

Anonymous

What can you give the Christ Child on His birthday? This fable
that I wrote many years ago suggests an answer:

The most frightened shepherd that night was little Ladius,
just 10. He cowered behind his three older brothers when the
blinding star lit the hillside. When the angel appeared, he hid
behind a huge rock.

Yet after Ladius heard the glad news, fear left him and he
limped back to his brothers who were planning to set out for
Bethlehem.

"Who will tend the sheep?" asked Samuel, the oldest at 16.
Ladius, leaning against his shepherd's crook to support a crip-
pled foot, volunteered:

"I'd only slow you down. Let me stay with the sheep." He bit
his lower lip as he talked. The brothers weakly protested, then
made plans to go.

"We must each take a gift," said Samuel. One brother chose
his flint to start a fire for the Christ Child. Another picked
meadow lilies to make a garland for the King. Samuel decided
on his most precious possession, his golden ring.

"Here, take my blanket to Him," said Ladius. It was badly
worn—a faded blue with patches.

"No, Ladius," said Samuel tenderly. "The blanket is too
tattered to give even a beggar—let alone a King. Besides, you
will need it tonight."

The brothers departed, leaving Ladius alone by the fire. He
laid his head upon the blanket and buried his face in his hands.
Tears forced their way between his fingers, but soon the hush of
night soothed the boy's heartbreak. *The world in silent stillness
lay* . . .

"Are you coming, Ladius?" called a voice. Standing nearby
was the same angel who had brought the news. "You wanted to
see the Child, didn't you?"

"Yes," nodded Ladius, "but I must stay here."

"My name is Gabriel," said the angel. "Your sheep will be watched. Take my hand—and bring your blanket. The Child may need it."

Suddenly, Ladius was outside a stable. Kneeling by a manger were his brothers. Ladius started to call out, but the angel lifted a finger to his lips.

"Give me the blanket," Gabriel whispered. The angel took it and quietly covered the Baby. But the blanket was no longer faded. Now it glistened like dew in the brilliance of a new day.

Returning, Gabriel squeezed Ladius' hand. "Your gift was best because you gave all that you had. . . ."

"Wake up, Ladius, wake up." The boy rubbed his eyes and tried to shield them from the glaring sun. Hovering over him was Samuel.

"Did you find Him?" asked Ladius.

"Yes," smiled Samuel, "but first tell me why you were sleeping without your blanket."

Ladius looked about wonderingly. The faded blue blanket was nowhere to be found—then or thereafter.

Lord, we commit our all to You who gave Your all for us.

24

(Christmas Eve)
"Arise, shine; for thy light is come . . ."
Isaiah 60:1

This was my Grandma Strayer's favorite night of the year—one for which she literally prepared a whole year, from one Christmas to another.

When she was growing up, her family was desperately poor and Christmas gifts were few. (At age seven, she once told me, a lone banana in her Christmas stocking was the only present she received.) But in adulthood she apparently was determined to erase the memory of those austere times and so Christmas eves in her parlor became gala celebrations. Room not taken by an enormous tree, which always seemed to sag under the weight of lights and decorations, was occupied by gaily wrapped presents, which made it hard to find a seat by the time all her children and their mates and her grandchildren crowded into the room. Buffets and tables were covered with aromatic dishes—cakes and pies, fudges and divinity, popcorn balls, things she'd been preparing for days.

When it came time to begin, she gathered her clan in a tight circle for a reading of the Christmas story from St. Luke. This she followed with prayer, thanking God for the year's many blessings. Though Grandma had a hard life and worked at all sorts of jobs to supplement the family income (or was it to finance her annual Christmas party?) she could always see more pluses than minuses. Perhaps because of such things as one-banana Christmases.

Finally it was time to open the gifts—grandchildren first—and Grandma always sat on the very edge of her chair, anxious to see whether or not her loved ones were pleased. She usually went to great lengths to choose just the right gift—the extra long sled, the doll with four changes of clothing, the dress with the special lace—so she watched for reactions with fixed gaze. I can see her now wringing her hands or nervously attending her beautifully coiffed white hair while someone opened one of her gifts. There was never any question that it would be appreciated, but when a child squealed with delight, a sigh would pass from Grandma's lips and her beautiful round face would glow brighter, I think, than her over-decorated tree. And her eyes, those wonderfully animated blue-gray eyes, they would flash like diamonds behind her rimless glasses. Yes, there was something special about Christmas Eve at Grandma's.

But alas she's gone, and so are several others who once made up her happy circle on the night before Christmas. But one thing that remains is my memory of those exciting nights. And whenever I begin to think that all this harried preparation, all the time and money spent on gift giving, is not worth the candle, I think back to Grandma's shining face on her favorite night of the year, and suddenly I remember what Christmas is all about.

Lord, in this wonderful season I'm grateful for wonderful memories.

(Christmas)
"And Joseph also went up from
Galilee, out of the city of Nazareth,
into Judaea, unto the city of David,
which is called Bethlehem . . .
to be taxed with Mary his espoused wife,
being great with child.

And so it was, that, while they were there, the days were accomplished that she should be delivered.

And she brought forth her firstborn Son, and wrapped Him in swaddling clothes, and laid Him in a manger; because there was no room for them in the inn.

And there were in the same country shepherds abiding in the field, keeping watch over their flock by night.

And, lo, the angel of the Lord came upon them, and the glory of the Lord shone round about them: and they were sore afraid.

And the angel said unto them, Fear not: for, behold, I bring you good tidings of great joy, which shall be to all people.

For unto you is born this day in the city of David a Saviour, which is Christ the Lord.

And this shall be a sign unto you; Ye shall find the Babe wrapped in swaddling clothes, lying in a manger.

And suddenly there was with the angel a multitude of the heavenly host praising God, and saying, Glory to God in the highest, and on earth peace, good will toward men." (Luke 2:4-14)

Lord, help us be instruments of Your peace.

Hark! the herald angels sing, "Glory to the
newborn King;
Peace on earth, and mercy mild; God and
sinners reconciled."
Joyful, all ye nations, rise. Join the triumph
of the skies;
With angelic hosts proclaim, "Christ is born
in Bethlehem."

When Charles Wesley wrote "Hark! the Herald Angels Sing" in

1739, the prolific author of 6,500 hymns began it, "Hark how the welkin rings, Glory to the King of Kings." Also, the original version included 10 verses compared to the four that are included in most hymnbooks, and the tune we associate with Wesley's words was not used until 1855—116 years after the lyrics were composed. Dr. William Cummings of Guild Hall School of Music is credited with joining the Felix Mendelssohn music "Festgesang" (which means an anniversary memorial) to Wesley's words.

Changes aside, nothing has diminished the beauty and majesty of this 239-year-old hymn. It proclaims the Good News of Christ's birth with unrestrained joy and states in clearest possible fashion the import of this unprecedented event: "Peace on earth and mercy mild, God and sinners reconciled."

In a season that is full of noise and unrelated celebration, it is good to think on Wesley's words. They are magnificent when sung, true, but their fuller meaning can only be comprehended in quiet contemplation.

Thank You, Lord, for poet's words serene.
They help us hear the silent and see the great unseen.

"The first demand which is made of those who belong to God's Church is that they shall be witnesses of Jesus Christ before the world."

Dietrich Bonhoeffer

Though I never met Henrietta Mears, I wish I had. Billy Graham called her "one of the greatest Christians I have ever known," and Bill Bright, founder of Campus Crusade for Christ, told me she had a profound effect on him and the direction of his life. Thousands of others probably could say "amen" to both tributes.

Dr. Mears was for many years director of Christian education at the First Presbyterian Church in Hollywood. She helped increase a Sunday school program from 400 to 6500 members and was such an effective teacher that a publishing company, Gospel Light, was founded to distribute her lessons. She also founded the famous Forest Home Christian Conference Center.

Hailed for her evangelical zeal, she was a tireless witness for Christ, believing that the one-on-one method of introducing people to the Lord was most effective. "If you want to fill a dozen milk bottles," she once said, "you must not stand back and spray them with a hose. You can get them wet, but you won't fill them. You must take them one by one."

Christ told us to go into the world and preach the Gospel to every living creature. (Mark 16:15) Henrietta Mears took that command seriously. Do you?

Lord, we thank You for the example of great Christians such as Henrietta Mears. Fill us with the same dedication.

**I fear no foe, with Thee at hand to bless;
Ills have no weight, and tears no bitterness.
Where is death's sting? where, grave, thy
   victory?
I triumph still, if Thou abide with me.**
Henry F. Lyte hymn

It was the job of Hermes to guide dead souls to the underworld, we read in Greek mythology, but Zeus, called the mightiest of the Olympian gods, got so angry at Sisyphus, known as the cleverest being who ever lived, that he (Zeus) dispatched Hades himself to "bring him in." According to the legend, Zeus had stolen a daughter of the god of rivers, and Sisyphus had told on him.

"I'm greatly honored that you came for me," said the wily Sisyphus. "But why didn't you send Hermes?"

Hades stammered, trying to fabricate an answer, and while

he did Sisyphus wound a chain about him and locked him to a post. As a result, no one could die as long as the Lord of Death was held captive.

Down through the ages men have sought ways to make time stand still in order to delay death. But eventually it comes to all mortals, and given our threescore and ten (plus or minus a few years) we all meet the same end. Some may die richer than others in material goods, but it will do them little good. For in the last analysis, our success or failure is measured not on length of life, but by contribution to life.

Christ lived only 33 years, but He has been changing the world for 20 centuries. Why? Because He lived, served and died with no thought for Himself. None of us are so selfless. We are asked only to love others as we love ourselves. (Mark 12:31)

If you want to leave a lasting legacy, focus your life on others. They will be living memorials to your Christlikeness for generations to come.

Lord, help us make the most of the time You give us.

 "Holding forth the word of life; that I may rejoice in the day of Christ, that I have not run in vain, neither laboured in vain."
Philippians 2:16

Runners of short races often use "starting blocks" to help them lunge forward quickly when they hear the starter's gun. These devices are anchored into the track, and runners place their feet into them and push off when the race begins.

Getting a good start in any endeavor is important, but it doesn't mean a thing if you don't maintain a steady pace and make a good finish. The story of the tortoise and the hare is a memorable parable that illustrates the point. So sure of himself was the hare that he had a nap during his race, and by the time he woke up it was too late. His overconfidence had cost him the prize.

Fortunately, when it comes to the Christian life, it is never too late for us to make amends, to ask and receive forgiveness, to make up for lost ground. Because we serve a loving and merciful Heavenly Father we know He will never turn a deaf ear to His children. The parable in Matthew 20 of the early and late reporting vineyard workers, all of whom received the same wage, shows that our final reward will be the same, whether we find the Lord when we are young, middle-aged or old. The important thing is that we discover the life that makes us new creatures in Him. And the sooner we find it, the better.

Help us, Lord, to run with patience the race You have set before us.

 "And Jesus spoke unto them saying: All power is given unto Me in heaven and in earth."
Matthew 28:18

Though I was not in New York City when the lights went out in July 1977, it brought to mind the power outage of November 1965. I was on hand for that one.

When that blackout occurred, I was in a New York office building. At first no one knew what to make of the phenomenon. Someone suggested we might be under attack by a foreign power. Another, with a nervous laugh, that it was the end of the world. All I can say is that New York City is an eerie-looking place at night with all its lights off.

Finally, someone located a portable radio, and we learned of the gigantic power failure that affected much of the Northeast seaboard. Fear vanished and people began to move about.

Sometimes I wonder just what *would* happen if we were forced to give up some of our technological advances. There is great fear that we will run out of oil and that our transportation system will be curtailed. Would that mean estranged neighbors would stay at home and speak to each other again? What if television were no more? Would families become closer and more caring? What if we ran out of power and had to heat our homes by wood and light them with candles? Would we be driven back to the Stone Age, as some predict, or just back to some old-fashioned virtues that seem to be in short supply?

Few want to return to another time with a harsher, more austere style of living, and there is no reason we should. But there is a need for all of us to realize there is only one indispensable source of power. It is the power that moves the tides, the power that holds the universe in orbit, and the power that whispers to the hearts of men, "Be still and know that I am God." (Psalm 46:10)

It is not things that most of us lack, Father, but a faith in You. Fill us with loving compassion for each other.

The years race by in furious procession, Making each hour a priceless possession.
F.B.

"Closed December 31," the sign on the door of the hardware store read, "Taking Inventory." Many businessmen will be taking inventory today. By counting the materials on hand and assigning a value to them, companies can determine their profit or loss for the year.

Few are like the corner grocer I knew who, when asked if he made a profit, replied, "Sure, I always have more money in the cash register at night than I do in the morning."

If you were to take inventory of your spiritual profit or loss this year, what would the ledger show? Did you realize some growth? What areas of your life need improvement? What habits do you think God would like to see you eliminate? What disciplines do you need to initiate in order to accomplish what you should?

Whether 1978 was all you had hoped or not, it is behind. But before you lies a brand new year, full of possibilities. What are your goals for 1979? In a couple of sentences write in the blank space below what you hope to accomplish in the next 12 months:

The good news is that you can see any dream to fruition if you include God in it. Go to Him daily. Share your hopes and dreams with your Heavenly Father, and ask Him to bless them. Then believe that they will come to pass and they will, because all things are possible to him that believes. (Mark 9:23)

The Lord bless thee, and keep thee: The Lord make His face shine upon thee, and be gracious unto thee: The Lord lift up His countenance upon thee, and give thee peace.
                                        (Numbers 6:24-26)